THE UNICORN QUEST

Advance Praise for the Book

'*The Unicorn Quest* is an important chronicle of India's startup journey so far. In devoting an entire chapter to Digital Public Infrastructure, the book highlights what has been one of the most consequential features of technology-driven entrepreneurship today and for the future'

Nandan Nilekani, Chairman and Co-founder, Infosys, and Founding Chairman, UIDAI

'Incisive. Reveals the struggles, triumphs and untold stories behind the subcontinent's meteoric rise in the startup world'

Deep Kalra, Founder and Chairman, MakeMyTrip

'A compelling read. Tells it like it happened. Plenty of insights and anecdotes. A must-read'

Sanjeev Bikhchandani, Founder and Executive Vice Chairman, Info Edge

'Archana has not only chronicled the evolution of the Indian startup and entrepreneurial ecosystem but has captured its spirit and its human stories in meticulous detail. This book is in fact a collective biography'

Nithin Kamath, CEO, Zerodha; and
Kailash Nadh, CTO, Zerodha

'India is host to the third-largest startup ecosystem in the world, after the US and China. *The Unicorn Quest* is a fast-paced narrative which takes the reader on a long journey, from the early days of internet-enabled companies, which were being set up by a rising generation of entrepreneurs, to the thrills and spills of a still-maturing industry. It is a must-read for anyone interested in India's amazing rise as a startup nation'

Bodhisatva Ganguli, Editorial Director, *The Economic Times*

'In *The Unicorn Quest* Archana, with her engaging storytelling style, has unveiled the roller-coaster ride of India's startup revolution, spotlighting the people, passions and breakthroughs that have come to define this transformative era. Through this book, you can explore the highs, lows and the promising future of Indian entrepreneurship'

Ranjan Pai, Chairman, Manipal Education and Medical Group

'Archana's book uncorks the special blend of aspiration and defiance that fuels India's startup economy. The tale of this quest takes you far beyond India's borders and reveals how we are lifting each other up to become world-class product builders. History is often best written while it's still happening, and this book places you squarely in the middle of an adventure whose peak moments are still on the horizon'

Girish Mathrubootham, Founder and CEO, Freshworks

'A gripping account of the making of India's startup ecosystem during its most defining years. This book is a must-read'

Vijay Shekhar Sharma, Founder and CEO, Paytm

'This is a super attempt to connect the dots on everything that's got India's internet businesses to where we are today! If you assume the next twenty years will be a force multiplier on the past twenty, there's a lot to look forward to as well! Thanks, Archana, for putting it together'

Subrata Mitra, Partner, Accel

'This book is a really enjoyable and compact version of all the many watershed moments that the Indian startup ecosystem has seen over the last two decades. I hope this creates even more awareness about starting up in India and inspires more founders to create magic'

Sriharsha Majety, Co-founder and CEO, Swiggy

'This book does a great job at penning down the early days of the nascent startups in India—it showcases how two people with a dream can kick-start a thriving ecosystem that we have today and why a nation should provide a fertile ground to its youth. Thanks for bringing the background stories to the everyday dreamers'

Abhishek Goyal, Co-founder, Tracxn

'In two decades as a venture investor, I have seen many twists and turns in infrastructure development, new sectors and business models. But the most seminal has been the emergence of domestic capital to support Indian funds and startups. This is more resilient money and creates a great virtuous cycle. *The Unicorn Quest* has captured this very well'

Kanwaljit Singh, Founder, Fireside Ventures

'Over the last fifteen years, as startups grew from consumer to SaaS and B2B marketplaces, we have seen a significant transformation. Professionals are getting into business and founding companies at an amazing pace. Thanks to Archana for capturing that fundamental change succinctly'

Shekhar Kirani, Partner, Accel

'One of the most engaging books that uncovers startup stories with words that stir up the truest of emotions. There's so much magic in Archana's words and narrative. It's unmissable!'

Avinash Raghava, Founding Volunteer and CEO, SaaSBoomi Foundation

'A well-encapsulated narration of the technology startup evolution in India. A riveting read!'

Suvir Sujan, Co-founder and Managing Director, Nexus Venture Partners

'*The Unicorn Quest* captures the zeitgeist of the tech-driven Indian business landscape of the 21st century—new enterprises built around new needs, new relationships, new ways of working. With her ringside view as a business journalist, Archana knits a kaleidoscope of events into a compelling narrative that takes the reader deep into India's startup journey. It's a journey that is intense in the middle and fascinating from the sidelines'

Kunal Bahl, Co-founder, Titan Capital, and Co-founder, Snapdeal

'In highlighting the momentum provided by the exits delivered by India's earliest internet startups, *The Unicorn Quest* underscores the importance of building robust businesses from the get-go. A must-read for anyone interested in entrepreneurship'

K. Ganesh, Partner, Growthstory.in

'Archana covers a lot of ground on the waves of the digital age for India. It's a must-read for anyone keen on understanding the companies that form the Indian internet along with the personalities behind them'

Yashish Dahiya, CEO and Co-founder, PolicyBazaar

'Archana Rai has meticulously researched and thoughtfully crafted an enormously valuable book on visionary entrepreneurs and investors who have shaped Indian new economy businesses through ground-breaking innovations with unyielding determination. A book worth reading and inspiring many more young entrepreneurs in time to come in India'

Sudhir Sethi, Founder and Chairman, Chiratae Ventures India

'Archana's book is a fascinating deep dive into the evolution of the Indian startup landscape, tracing the rise and fall of technology companies in a new era of business. Filled with stories, insider insights and data, it is a must-read for anyone with an interest in the world of Indian entrepreneurship'

Mukesh Bansal, Founder, Myntra, and CEO, Cult.fit

'This is the story of an ecosystem that made redBus possible. I am grateful to all those who laid this foundation. Archana has done a great job in telling this story, it is a must-read'

Phanindra Sama, Co-founder, redBus

'A sweeping chronicle of the early years of the India startup evolution and the roller-coaster ride of the previous decade, *The Unicorn Quest* brings together some of the most impactful events and people shaping technology entrepreneurship in the country'

Ash Lilani, Managing Partner, Saama

'Reading through these chapters felt like I was reliving the last ten years of my life. Archana's book captures the optimism, energy and even the dilemmas of Indian startup companies as they have grown from scrappy companies to household names'

Sahil Barua, Co-founder and CEO, Delhivery

'*The Unicorn Quest* offers a fast-paced exploration of the tech-savvy visionaries who played a pivotal role in India's remarkable ascent in the global startup landscape during its crucial years. It serves as an invaluable narrative for those seeking insights into the future of entrepreneurship, accompanied by compelling behind-the-scenes accounts of the journeys undertaken by several prominent Indian startups founders'

Anand Daniel, Partner, Accel

'For a fund that was born in 2010–11, each chapter in Archana Rai's *The Unicorn Quest* feels like a burst of nostalgia pops in the head. A lot of this contextual and colourful history is an important foundation to understand what built today's audacious founders and ambition that India's startups have developed'

Karthik Reddy, Co-founder and Managing Partner, Blume Ventures

'Refreshingly original and comprehensive take on the rise of startups in India. The excitement built into the storytelling and narration captures the passion and years of hard work that went into building our startup ecosystem. Surely an inspiration for the next generation of entrepreneurs in India'

Ritesh Arora, CEO and Co-founder, Browserstack

THE UNICORN QUEST

India Learns to Start Up

Archana Rai

BLOOMSBURY
NEW DELHI • LONDON • OXFORD • NEW YORK • SYDNEY

BLOOMSBURY INDIA
Bloomsbury Publishing India Pvt. Ltd
Second Floor, LSC Building No. 4, DDA Complex, Pocket C – 6 & 7,
Vasant Kunj, New Delhi 110070

BLOOMSBURY, BLOOMSBURY INDIA and the Diana logo
are trademarks of Bloomsbury Publishing Plc

First published in India 2023
This edition published 2023

ISBN: PB: 978-93-89449-83-9; e-Book: 978-93-89449-76-1
2 4 6 8 10 9 7 5 3 1

Typeset in Fournier MT Std by Manipal Technologies Limited
Printed and bound in India by Thomson Press India Ltd

MIX
Paper from responsible sources
FSC® C010615

To find out more about our authors and books, visit www.bloomsbury.com and sign up for our newsletters

In gratitude
to the memory of my father,
and to Amma,
Dinesh and our daughter
Ashrutha

CONTENTS

ACKNOWLEDGEMENTS

The explosion of technology-led entrepreneurship during the past two decades across India's metropolises has altered the physical profile and the societal fabric of these cities. To write about some of these people and events through these years has been a privilege beyond compare.

In stitching together this narrative, I have drawn on extensive conversations stretching over four years with a large cast of people, most of whom feature in these pages, as central characters or supporting ones. That was over a hundred hours of conversation, with some of the most inspirational members of the Indian startup ecosystem. Their candour, insights and willingness to discuss issues of importance through the course of their startup journeys has helped light up the story that follows. Several of them also introduced me to another, who would then introduce me to yet another until a chain of connections helped weave this tale of India's incredible journey to becoming a Startup Nation.

Those who made time include, in no particular order, Abhishek Goyal, Alok Mittal, Anand Daniel, Abhinav Asthana, Aadit Palicha, Aprameya Radhakrishna, Arvind Parthiban, Ash Lilani, Ashish Gupta, Bejul Somaia, Deep Kalra, Avinash Raghava, Girish Mathrubootham, Harsh Jain, K. Ganesh, Kanwaljit Singh, Karthik Reddy, Kirti Jangre, Kitty Agarwal, Kris Gopalakrishnan, Kunal Bahl, Rohit Bansal, Meena Ganesh, Mekin Maheshwari, Mukesh Bansal, Nandan Nilekani, Nithin Kamath, Kailash Nadh, Phanindra Sama, Pramod Varma, Prashant Prakash, Rajan Anandan, Ranjan Pai, Ritesh Arora, Sachin Bansal, Sahil Barua, Sajith Pai, Sameer Mehta, Sanjay Anandaram, Sanjay Nath, Sanjeev Bikhchandani, Sanket Parekh, Sharad Sharma, Shailendra Singh, Sridhar Vembu, Subrata

Mitra, Shekhar Kirani, Sudhir Sethi, Suresh Sambandam, Suvir Sujan, Thomas Oriel Binford, Vani Kola, Viral Shah, Yashish Dahiya and so many more who cannot all be named.

I owe each of them a debt of gratitude for making time. Suffice it to say, what's lost in translation is due entirely to me.

Although I would like to think of this as a 'collective chronicle' of the industry over the last fifteen years or so, it is by no means the definitive one. More has been left out than included, and many events, trends and personalities could go into crafting an entirely different chronicle.

I owe thanks also to the Editorial Director of *The Economic Times*, Bodhisatva Ganguli, for granting me permission to pursue this project way back in 2019. *ET* has been the bedrock of my professional career, from the time I entered its portals as a trainee reporter and more so on my return to its newsroom in 2010.

To the wonderful people at Bloomsbury Publishing India who have shown patience and immeasurable support, none more so than Nitin Valecha, I owe thanks. I am equally grateful to the skilled team of editors led by Jaishree Ram Mohan.

Friends and family have seen me through the highs and lows of this, my very first attempt to write a book. Sharmila Bhaktaram, my sounding board and dearest friend since school, as well as those who goaded and pushed me, read through the initial drafts and even helped transcribe hours of recordings—none of this would have been possible without all your help.

To my family, Amma, Dinesh and my brother Arun, words are never sufficient and certainly not for Ashrutha, my daughter, my true north.

Introduction

To start up is to begin one of life's great adventures. And Indians, in ever greater numbers, have been signing up for the adventure of their lives. In doing so they are transforming their own lives, and they are transforming India. The promise that today's technology entrepreneurs offer—to remake a nation and the fortunes of its citizens—is why Indians, young or old, urban or rural, rich or poor, man or woman, are transfixed. Everyone can feel the frisson of change in the air. They can smell it, they can touch it, and many of them have waded in to be a part of the adventure.

India was home to over 90,000 startups by mid-2023, making it the world's third-largest such ecosystem.[1] Over the past decade and a half—beginning in 2005—when venture capital funds began to establish base here in significant numbers, the country has witnessed an outpouring of entrepreneurial energy that has delivered over a hundred companies valued at more than a billion dollars, which are popularly termed unicorns. This has enriched founders and employees and laid the framework for innovation in sectors ranging from digital commerce to financial and technology services, healthcare and biotech, education, shop-floor automation, agriculture and urbanization, mobility, water and energy.

How did this phenomenon come to pass? What triggered this explosion of entrepreneurial energy? Who are the people scripting this riveting drama? After all, dhanda is not new to Indians; half of the country's working population is self-employed,[2] even if with varying degrees of success. But what we are witnessing today is unprecedented. What technology entrepreneurship has irrevocably changed is the outlook of vast swathes of the educated middle classes towards business as a viable proposition, indeed as a vocation.

Previously, the act of starting a business was reserved for those for whom it was already a way of life—traders, shopkeepers, small-scale entrepreneurs and those wealthy enough to fashion corporations. For the bulk of India's professional classes, a solid education and a job at an upscale corporation was the avowed dream. There was good reason for that. Business in the past meant struggling to grow in a state-controlled economy, bending rules and getting by with jugaad. Success was reserved for the few and not for the many, prompting most to give entrepreneurship a miss.

But the economic reforms of the 1990s—when tariffs were slashed, exchange controls scrapped and the 'licence raj' that strangled businesses with red tape largely abolished—put an end to that script book. The reforms opened doors for technology entrepreneurs who catapulted India on to the global stage. Pioneers like N.R. Narayana Murthy and Nandan Nilekani, Azim Premji, Shiv Nadar and others showed that Indians could not only dream big but also turn those dreams into reality. Their enterprise marked the start of a journey for thousands of Indian engineers who flew West, writing software code at rock-bottom prices as the country carved out a profitable franchise as a provider of low-cost information technology (IT) services. This labour arbitrage model put disposable money in the hands of an emergent middle class while providing a kaleidoscopic view of global markets beyond the once walled-in Indian economy. To see and to experience is to want more. And that is exactly what happened to a generation of Indians who realized there was more to be won than just the approbation of overseas clients looking to cut costs.

This new breed of technology professionals were also developing a taste for the global stage, its mores, best practices and culture. And more importantly, they were acquiring cutting-edge skills at work. This fuelled the next wave of aspiration—to start up on one's own—at a time when the world was being irrevocably recast by the reach of the internet.

The introduction of the internet in the mid-1990s had already transformed aspirations in a newly liberalized India. By 1995, Indians would have access to the World Wide Web—courtesy Videsh Sanchar Nigam Limited (VSNL), a state-owned enterprise that was later bought by the Tata Group—kick-starting a desi dotcom era at about the same time that events were unfolding in the US. For perspective, it is good to recall that even the US was taking baby steps in the digital world with the launch of the first internet browser, Netscape, in 1994. A year later, India too would go online.

India's digital agility, through which it would repeatedly leapfrog over legacy technologies to embrace new ones, was first visible in the dotcom era. No sooner was the internet unveiled than Indian entrepreneurs got to work translating concepts available elsewhere into products and services for an emerging cohort of desi netizens. This led to an entrepreneurial upsurge that spawned a gaggle of startups that effectively defined India's early internet profile.

It also marked a shift from the labour arbitrage years of IT outsourcing to the internet-driven concept arbitrage era during which internet commerce would take root in the country. India's online commerce platforms, ride-hailing apps, food-delivery services, etc., would be birthed in this era, spawning billion-dollar ventures and catapulting the country into the world's third-largest startup ecosystem, trailing only the US and China.

Two decades ago, it was precisely this zeitgeist that an overflowing roomful of aspirants was attempting to capture at the Indian Institute of Management (IIM) in Bengaluru. They crowded into a cavernous lecture hall, all agog about listening to an entrepreneur who had just sold his startup for a whopping ₹500 crore. In the year 2000, this was India's first big acquisition of an internet startup. Rajesh Jain, the bespectacled IIT Bombay graduate, had just sold his internet portal IndiaWorld

Communications, launched in 1995, to Satyam Infoway, snagging one of Asia's largest internet deals of the time.

IndiaWorld had a motley collection of India-centric websites: Samachar (news), Khel (cricket), Khoj (search) and Bawarchi (food). In the past, creating such goods and services for locals would have been impossible, and not just for the fact that there was no internet to provide a distribution channel. Business itself was subject to a plethora of rules and regulations. Economic liberalization and the era of software exports and the internet had broken that vicious cycle. A slew of graduates, including some from Jain's alma mater, would go on to reap the benefits in the years ahead. In effect, technology startups were shaping up to be the early harbingers of India's growing aatma nirbharta.

Dil Maange More

Jain's winning turn was one of the catalysing moments for the rise of the concept of arbitrage in the fledgling Indian startup ecosystem. Ideas drawn from overseas would be replicated in India. To wit, a wave of companies like Rediff and hiring portal Naukri had already been launched. More would follow such as travel services provider MakeMyTrip and, finally, the online e-commerce startup Flipkart, in 2007.

That the birth of Flipkart—founded by two twenty-six-year-olds from the northern Indian city of Chandigarh—coincided with the ascension of another small-town star, Mahendra Singh Dhoni, to the pinnacle of Indian cricket is no ordinary coincidence. It marked a growing sense of self-assertion for middle-class Indians, proof that they were shaking off the sense of national diffidence that had hobbled the country for long. Out of this kernel of aspirations was born the great Indian internet startup dream.

Eighteen years after Jain scored his big win, Flipkart sold 77 per cent stake to American retailer Walmart for a whopping $16 billion.

But starting up is not just about business. In the life of a young nation such as India, it means much more. It points to a revolutionary change in norms, culture and aspirations. The 'audacity' of Flipkart's Bansals—Sachin and Binny—who believed they could best their former employer Amazon, the world's largest e-commerce company, at its own game was more than just individual flair.

India as a country had been changing for near on two decades at that time, led by gains delivered by economic reforms and the export of technology services. A generation of young Indians had cast off the shackles and tested new waters, landing well-paid jobs in the service sector and the booming IT industry. Newly emboldened, these professionals would borrow to fund the purchase of homes, cars and even holidays. In the process, they were upturning the received wisdom that debt is the ultimate evil. This helped trigger the longest burst of economic growth since Independence. Those who partook of this dream run would say there was magic in the air.

Between 1990 and 2013, India pulled 168 million people out of extreme poverty.[3] Its technical prowess boosted software exports, creating an industry now worth $225 billion that contributes handsomely to the country's robust foreign exchange reserves. People of Indian origin run some of the world's largest corporations, and are also among the key global policymakers, from the vice president of the United States of America to the prime minister of the United Kingdom. As the world recoups from the ravages of the COVID-19 pandemic that triggered national lockdowns and quelled economic growth, as well as from the geopolitical strife triggered by Russia's invasion of Ukraine in 2022, the World Bank has said that India 'shows resilience amid global uncertainties'.[4]

But global volatility comes at a price. It has put the brakes on an era of easy money that in large part fuelled the deluge of foreign capital into India between 2005 and 2022. Indian startups have been brought face-to-face with what is now termed as a 'funding winter'.

How will companies weather the coming storm? Will ride-hailing apps, food-delivery startups, fintech giants and hotel-room aggregators survive? Companies that offer discretionary services might struggle while those meeting the needs of consumers and businesses will survive. Then, of course, there are other factors. Are they generating profits? Can they rejig pricing without losing paying customers?

It has never been more important for entrepreneurship to thrive. The Economic Survey 2021 estimated that as many as 4,70,000 jobs were created from more than 39,000 startups registered with the government as of December 2020.[5] This book will seek to illustrate how this wave of change—different from earlier ones in the history of Indian business—has come about. And what it means in an era that looks set to be dominated by the uncertainties of climate change and the transition from a fossil-fuel economy to one dominated by electric, solar and wind energy, as much as by the rise and threat of artificial intelligence (AI).

There is little doubt that technological innovation backed by governance and market reforms can boost India's economic competitiveness. A report by the McKinsey Global Institute in 2020 posits that India needs to triple its number of large firms—those with revenues over $500 million—from about 600 to 1,800 in this decade.[6]

If consumer internet was the only game in town at the start of the 2010s, Indian startups are striding ahead in the new decade with ventures in areas ranging from education and healthcare to robotics and agriculture, space technology and AI. Change is slow in India, but when it comes it does so with a bang. There will be pain, and those that survive to emerge on the other side will reap the benefits of the flowering $5 trillion Indian economy.

For Indian startups this is a now-or-never moment.

Part I:

2006–12

1

The Gold Rush

Was it the thrum of the sarangi that drew him back? Or the promise of a new professional beginning in a country he had been entranced by as a thirty-year-old at the Tata Institute of Fundamental Research? Either way, when he retired from his post as a professor of computer science at Stanford University at the turn of the century, Thomas Oriel Binford packed his bags and headed East once more.

In the Bombay of 1965–66, Binford had frequented classical music concerts on Nepean Sea Road, developing a taste for the sarangi—of all stringed instruments the one regarded as closest to the vocal range of humans. So deep was its hold on him that once back in New York, he had hunted for Hindustani music concerts that featured the bowed instrument. Unsurprisingly, such instances were hard to come by.

Drawn as much by the lure of its music as by its engineering prowess, Binford returned to India at the start of a brand new century. And this time, he picked the southern city of Bengaluru, which was by then fast gaining the moniker of the Silicon Valley of India.

Feted for his role as a 'founding father' in areas such as computer vision, Binford was regarded as a guru in the then-rising arena of AI. In Bengaluru, home to giant IT services companies and scores of multinational back offices, he hoped to discuss the hard problems of AI and find solutions. And maybe hear the notes of the sarangi once again.

With Ione, his wife and the company's chief executive officer (CEO), he had set up an online handwriting-recognition software firm—Read Ink—hiring a slew of young engineers.

Sentiment may have played some part in Binford's decision to head back to India but the main driving factor was hard business needs. After five years of an unprecedented bull run, fuelled by investments in internet-based companies during the waning years of the twentieth century, the US's technology index sank like a stone in 2001.[1] It was becoming clear that the much-hyped internet portals would not be delivering profits anytime soon. This spectacular meltdown had led to the shuttering of thousands of internet startups and pushed venture capitalists (VCs), who had wagered plenty in the so-called dotcom boom, into a paralysis of inaction. The US technology industry was in a flux. Capital was scarce and the cost of hiring engineers and developing technology products in places like Silicon Valley was becoming near impossible. This was forcing even smaller technology startups, such as the one Binford was planning, to look overseas—to China, India and even Israel—for affordable talent.

For Tom as well as for Ione—who had put in twenty years at Hewlett Packard—the aftermath of the terrorist attacks in September 2001 at New York's World Trade Center also played a part in hastening the journey eastwards.[2] In their adopted city of Bengaluru, the two Californians turned out to be early harbingers of the coming deluge, when multitudes of people from near and far would turn to the city of 7 million inhabitants in search of the next El Dorado.

By November 2001, the Binfords had set up shop on Brunton Road in the city's central business district. The tony neighbourhood, better known for high-priced dwellings and upscale eateries, was an unlikely setting for a startup, especially one that was looking to break new ground in a technology that was closer to fiction than fact at that time. It would take nearly two decades more for AI to take the world by storm.

In the winter of 2022, on a blustery morning in his adopted hometown, the now-octogenarian Binford posited that AI could solve problems at a scale of the next hundred years, not at a scale of the next year or the next ten years. Just weeks later—on 30

November 2022—Sam Altman, who had dropped out of his computer science course at Binford's former college, Stanford University, announced the public unveiling of his company's AI offering: a chat interface christened ChatGPT. It would go on to clock about a million downloads within the first six days of its launch. It had something for everyone, from teenagers looking for help with a college essay to developers looking to write faster, smarter code. The world would not be the same again.

Binford could hardly have anticipated this tectonic shift. In the go-go years of the early twenty-first century, globalization was the buzzword. And the Stanford professor with a yen for India was moving with the times when he turned to the Asian nation. But while Binford would come looking for prowess in foundational technology, India's nascent startup sector was priming for something different. Indian techies looking to ride the internet bandwagon were looking to aggregate services from retail to transport for India's vast consumer market. It was also what the investors backing these new founders wanted. They had done the same in China, in turn reaping disproportionate rewards.

Two years after Binford struck roots in the software hub of Bengaluru, one of the world's storied lenders to technology founders then would hang its board at the same address. Silicon Valley Bank, better known simply as SVB, was also hunting for the elixir of affordable technology talent as well as for purchase from the vibrant consumer market taking shape in the country.

For years, SVB had been the bank of choice for swathes of Indians making their way as on-site engineers in the US. This had helped it gain a fairly robust understanding of the Indian zeitgeist, which was uncommon know-how in the days before globalization gathered force. Moreover, its international operations at that point were led by a genial banker of Indian origin—Ash Lilani—who had grown up in Bengaluru. Following an MBA from Philadelphia University, Lilani, a quintessential people's person, joined SVB, building and nurturing vast networks of friends, colleagues and associates spanning geographies. Posted in California, he had been hearing of the troubles tech startups were facing both in raising capital and in hiring top engineering talent in the Valley all through 2002. SVB's clients, amongst the bluest of the Valley's blue-chip venture funds, were struggling to keep these portfolio firms afloat in a market that had cratered after the dotcom bubble burst.

This got Lilani thinking. What if he could build a model of cross-border tech startups with development centres in low-cost destinations like India, while sales and marketing remained close to customers in the US? After all, American corporations had been outsourcing technology services to India's top software exporters—TCS, Infosys, Wipro, HCL and several more—for decades. Over a million Indian engineers were delivering services outsourced by some 400 of the Fortune 500 corporations, and what's more, at wages roughly a fifth of what peers in the US were being paid.

Bengaluru-headquartered Infosys and Wipro had registered spectacular debuts on US bourses, the former in 1998 and the latter a year later on the New York Stock Exchange (NYSE). Indian engineering talent was by then a byword in the Western world as it had also famously delivered code to help avert the doomsday predictions of Y2K at scores of US companies. That Indian engineers could code was established, but could they go the whole nine yards and build technology products?

Lilani knew there was a case to be made here for his home country. And he set about doing it in quite remarkable fashion. He began advocating the thesis that it was an inefficient use of capital to build technology products in America, although the country remained the primary market for such products and services. He would soon convince his bosses at SVB to consider organizing exploratory missions to China, India and Israel for its top clients who were on the lookout for alternate development centres.

In December 2003, he gathered a posse of twenty-three of Silicon Valley's heavyweight investment firms, including Sequoia Capital, Bessemer Venture Partners, NEA, Lightspeed and Accel Partners, and brought them to India to experience its sights, sounds, smells and technology fizz.[3] Nothing was held back from the visitors, several of whom were travelling overseas for the first time. The group did a walking tour of traffic-laden Bengaluru, watched an India–Australia cricket match to get a first-hand experience of the Indian consumer, and attended an array of art, music and cultural shows. They hobnobbed with the technology elite, including Infosys founders N.R. Narayana Murthy and Nandan Nilekani on their glitzy office campus, and flew to Mumbai to meet Reliance Industries scion Mukesh Ambani at the new-age facility he was building in Navi Mumbai. The carefully curated week-long visit ended with nineteen of the nearly two dozen funds represented returning to do business in India.

Lilani had pulled off a coup.

In 2004, when SVB opened its India office, it marked the start of a period of unprecedented expansion in venture funding for internet commerce in the country. Scores of investment firms followed in the wake of SVB's clients, and in quickening succession poured hundreds of millions of dollars into emerging ventures that went on to transform the way Indians work, play, learn and live. The likes of the Binfords, in small measure, and that of Lilani, with far greater span, were weaving the early strands of the multi-hued tapestry that is now Startup India. It was a time of infectious optimism.

For long, technology entrepreneurship in India had been dominated by big bets on outsourcing, an industry that was clocking revenues of $17 billion by 2005[4] and accounting for nearly 44 per cent of the global offshoring pie comprising both software and back-office services. It had created a phalanx of coders, researchers, marketers, technology salesmen and consultants who could speak the tongue and decode the world of technology.

Now, under its giant overhang, a new breed of internet natives were casting about for the big ideas that could take wing. In Bengaluru, famed for its salubrious climate, swathes of young engineers were snagging high-paid jobs in development centres being set up by Yahoo, Amazon, Cisco, Google and Microsoft, among others. Even as they built next-generation solutions at these multinationals, the twenty-somethings were also frenetically hunting for ideas that would help them start up on their own. With good reason.

The Indian economy had crossed the crucial milestone of $1 trillion,[5] and its demographic dividend was also an alluring prospect—every second Indian was below the age of twenty-five. An admittedly small but growing base of some 20 million internet users was eager to sample the global lifestyle. In the years since it embraced widespread economic reforms, the country had managed to trim the share of people living below the poverty line from 45 per cent of its population in 1993 to about 37 per cent by 2005.[6]

It was truly an India Shining moment. While the ruling political party which coined the slogan—the Bharatiya Janata Party (BJP), led by Atal Bihari Vajpayee—would come a cropper at the hustings in 2004, the country's technology elite and aspirants catapulted to giddy heights on the back of India's electrifying rise on the global stage in the second half of the noughties.

If the buzz in Bengaluru was all about technology, up north in the national capital region (NCR) of Delhi, Gurugram and Noida, it was all about entrepreneurial hustle. In the decade ahead, the two sprawling metropolises would emerge as the magnets holding together the crucible of India's turbo-charged internet ecosystem. So much so that if asked what it takes for a startup to thrive in India, most Indians will say, 'Bengaluru's tech muscle combined with Delhi's street-side hustle.'

Quite aptly so. In fact, the NCR region had stolen a clean march over Bengaluru in the early days of internet enterprise, buoyed in no small measure by the exploits of two of the country's most consequential internet entrepreneurs: Sanjeev Bikhchandani and Deep Kalra. The two had a lot in common, apart from being Dilliwalas. To start with, neither was an engineer. Educated at Delhi University's elite liberal arts college St Stephen's, they both had a master's degree from IIM Ahmedabad, graduating a few years apart. What's more the two had even attended the same school—St Columba's—in their home town, Delhi. The paths they took to their eventual culmination as internet pioneers, however, would vary.

While Kalra took the classic approach after IIM—a corporate job at GE Capital, later GE Money—before starting up, Bikhchandani, who had graduated in 1989, before economic liberalization, would tool around looking for startup ideas a few years after finishing college.

While working at HMM Ltd, now called GlaxoSmithKline, Bikhchandani had noticed that colleagues spent a lot of time looking at job listings in the business press. They would incessantly discuss new openings and gloat when they were cold-called by recruitment agents. But none of them would make the shift. There just weren't as many great jobs on offer, and few avenues for people to actually compare, contrast and pick from the best openings. There were even fewer ways to match skills and qualifications with the right job. Bikhchandani watched this with interest and filed it away in a cavernous mind buzzing with entrepreneurial possibilities.

Restless with corporate routine, he quit and tried his hand at a variety of tasks: teaching, salary surveys, writing, whatever he could get. In 1996, he got his first view of the internet at an exhibition in Delhi, IT Asia. Amid the mega stalls set up by technology behemoths such as Microsoft were hundreds of tiny ones touting myriad products and services. Drawn to this bustling marketplace, Bikhchandani bumped into a reseller for the state-owned VSNL, which held the monopoly to internet access at that time. Soon he was listening to a sales pitch about how email on the internet was more cost-effective than fax and so on, none of which appealed to his keenly cost-sensitive mind. So what if he subscribed to an email service—who would he communicate with, how many others were using it? He was about to walk away, not interested, when the reseller stopped him, saying, but there's more I can show you, do you want to see the internet?

Intrigued, Bikhchandani returned to the man's computer to be shown a site called Yahoo, where he was introduced to the search function. Up came thousands of web pages by NRIs on topics covering the Taj Mahal and other tourist sites. It appeared meaningless to the curious thirty-two-year-old who wasn't interested in videshis; he wanted to do business with desis. Declining the offer of an email account, he quizzed the sales guy further to find out how one could host such a website that others could access freely, and was told that he had to go via a server hosted in the US. But there were workarounds. At that point, broke and with no real cash in hand, well aware that central bank restrictions didn't allow him to send money abroad, a disconsolate Bikhchandani returned home.

But the internet bug had well and truly bitten him. He dialled his UCLA professor brother to find out more. To his complete astonishment, his brother told him that he had been using the email and the internet for a while now. He volunteered to get Bikhchandani a shared server at $25 a month—which he would pay for in America—that would allow the young entrepreneur to log in from India and start up by offering job openings aggregated from all published job listings to the general public on one website. This was essentially a model he had drawn up some years ago, called Jobs Net.

It took Bikhchandani just a week to rustle up tech support on the ground and have a website up and running. This was still the pre-Google era, and search sites like Excite, Yahoo, Lycos, Rediff, etc., were used to power Naukri.com. Little of the coming revolution would have been visible when he first set it up as a salary surveyor for human resources (HR) managers. But soon enough, HR managers began to pay him ₹350 apiece to list postings they weren't advertising elsewhere, and later ₹6,000 annually for unlimited job listings.

Bikhchandani's business instincts were fired up with these first few paid subscriptions, and from what he had internalized from his advertising days. Keeping David Ogilvy's saying in mind that 2 per cent of direct mail received a response, he went direct. He mailed the 3,000-odd companies in his database, offering his subscription plan, thinking that even if 2 per cent responded he would break even. Even though it meant he couldn't take a salary.

No venture capital, no chasing eyeballs, just a dogged determination to break even is how one of India's first internet ventures took wing. Despite his self-avowed lack of mega ambition, Bikhchandani's efforts would soon draw the attention of overseas internet investors circling the nascent Indian internet ecosystem. One such travelling VC would invite him for coffee to a Delhi hotel and lecture the thirty-six-year-old about his disappointing lack of vision. Fluently berating him for sticking to his mantra of break-even while there was the opportunity to take venture money and grow without the thought of profits, the twenty-three-year-old investor announced he could put ₹8 crore into Info Edge, the parent company of Naukri.com, and take it public on NASDAQ in the following year.

Flummoxed and not a tad annoyed by the young man's effrontery, Bikhchandani would leave in a huff, but the magnitude of the decision to turn down ₹8 crore did give him many sleepless nights. He stuck to his guns primarily because the very idea of a venture-capital-backed business model which put growth above profits was alien and simply unintelligible.

But he would have to realign his stance pretty soon as the dotcom revolution was in full flow, and competitors were muscling in with investor money behind them. India's nascent internet industry had also registered its first mega milestone—marking a phenomenal exit for an entrepreneur—when Rajesh Jain sold his website IndiaWorld to Satyam Infoway for ₹500 crore. India had well and truly boarded the speeding internet express.

Bikhchandani couldn't be the only one left behind. But when he did acquiesce and take venture capital, he would pick a homegrown firm with local partners. After looking at deals from a couple of funds, he picked ICICI Venture for the first funding of ₹7.29 crore even though it wasn't the highest valuation. But it was a 'local' firm and this mattered to him because the money managers across the table were 'people like him'. He knew that listing on NASDAQ in a year was not his goal, neither was getting rich quickly—what he wanted was to 'build a good company and build it right'.[7]

He had bootstrapped for ten years and knew the exact worth of his business. As it turned out, soon after he raised cash, the dotcom crash happened. It was a meltdown, and he knew just what had to be done—conserve cash but invest in sales (not advertising), expand markets and launch new products, and do it frugally. For the first two years of the dotcom meltdown the company made losses, but came out in the third year with revenue that had grown thirty times from the pre-funding era, and ₹1 crore in profit. All this with the solid backing of his venture investors.

Recollecting those early years amid the pandemic-induced lockdown nearly two decades later, he said, 'For ICICI Venture, India was the only gig.'[8] And they were in it for the long haul.

Unbeknown to him, this was exactly the conundrum that his college junior Kalra was wrestling with during the worst of the dotcom meltdown as he fought to salvage his fledgling online travel business after his blue-chip investors walked out.

He had started up in April 2000 after an eight-year stint in corporate India, the final years of which were spent looking for new avenues of distribution for GE Capital's consumer finance businesses. And the biggest new avenue of the time was, quite simply, the internet. Fired up by the challenge, Kalra would soon discover that for a legacy business, a new business opportunity was more of a weekend project and not central to operations. If he wanted to work on the internet, he realized he had to do it on his own time.

His was no casual whim; he had already seen at close quarters the power of disintermediation that the internet was throwing up. Keen to get the best price for an old car his wife wanted to sell, he went online, dissatisfied with the offers being made by offline dealers. Within a day, he found a seller and got ₹20,000 more than his original intended price. Weeks later, the Kalras were planning a final holiday as a young couple ahead of the arrival of their first born. Eager to ensure a safe trip, Kalra badgered his travel agent for the best tickets and best hotels with on-ground support facilities. While the tickets came through, he wasn't happy with the accommodation options and instead decided to find a hotel on his own, online. Embarking on the trip with some trepidation, he discovered that not only did they land a great place to stay, it also came at a much lower cost than what his agent in Delhi was offering.

Back home, it didn't take him too long to decide to take the plunge. He knew the easiest things to take online would be the services that required the minimum person-to-person contact. Travel, one of his biggest joys, was an obvious choice; the other was online stockbroking. It wasn't an easy move to make—he had a young family and some savings, but the road ahead was unknown. On the plus side, offering courage was his blue-chip education that could always get him back into the workforce—an advantage that he has since exhorted countless youngsters to use 'as an insurance policy and not a noose'. But he also knew that as a non-engineer he would have to draw on others for technical heft. He scoured through global sites like Expedia, hoovered up personal savings and took early-stage funding from the newly launched venture fund eVentures to set up MakeMyTrip (MMT) in 2000.

The fund—a joint bet by Masayoshi Son's SoftBank and Rupert Murdoch's News Corp—was being managed by three partners in India, one of whom, Neeraj Bhargav, was Kalra's senior from St Stephen's. The two met at a food court in Crossword Mall in Mumbai and agreed on terms 'drawn up on a napkin'[9] for a $2 million investment in what was then just an idea.

On the strength of that commitment, Kalra quit his job and set out to build a travel site that was ready by April 2000 and open for business in October the same year. The mission statement was to offer the best services for travel to India, from India and around India. But within three months of the launch, Kalra realized that while there were lots of 'lookers, there were no bookers'[10] from within India. In contrast, the inbound travel by NRIs was robust—they were willing to pay online using credit cards right through the dotcom crash and even after the reverberations of the 9/11 attacks.

But by early 2001, things had turned sour for the newly minted venture. Markets the world over were crashing and investors were turning skittish. Kalra's money managers came to him and said that their limited partners (LPs) wanted their money back as they were shutting down eVentures. They told him he had two options: either to return the $2 million or to buy out the eVentures stake in MMT. To say he was pole-axed was an understatement, recalls Kalra with the distance of time. He had had no inkling of these clauses in the contract he signed, much less knowledge of what or who an LP was—a partner who provided capital for a venture fund that was then managed by professional VCs. Bhargava and his then partner at eVentures, Sandeep Singhal, who went on to become pivotal to the fortunes of scores of Indian entrepreneurs in the years ahead, would back the young founder. It would have been the end of MMT, but Kalra managed to rustle up angel money from a swathe of people, including Singhal, to buy back the investor stake in his fledgling venture for ₹50 lakh at a distressed valuation. For the next three years, well into 2003, the company was completely bootstrapped. Kalra would forgo a salary for eighteen months, while his colleagues took pay cuts. The office had to shift to the cheapest part of town. But on the ground, conversion metrics were improving. Shell-shocked as he was, Kalra could see that his team and he were on to something.

Despite advice to the contrary, he stuck to his guns and kept pegging away, watching the data and backing his instincts that told him there was light at the end of the tunnel. He had colleagues who would pack a toothbrush and sleep on chairs overnight, working through weekends in the tiny office where if they stretched their hands they could touch the ceiling.

In 2003, just like that, the sun broke through. One of their NRI customers from Atlanta, Georgia, who had used the site multiple times, walked into their office and told them he loved the portal and wanted to invest in the company. The next thing they knew, he had handed them a cheque for $150,000. He would go on to become one of the angel investors who sold stakes for handsome return to venture capital firm SAIF Partners in 2005, when the Ravi Adusumalli–led firm invested in MMT. By then, both MMT and India were very different.

SAIF's bet on MMT in 2005 was arguably the first strike that would open doors for the coming gold rush of capital for Indian internet ventures. It began tentatively, gathered velocity and hit a crescendo a decade later.

Meanwhile, within techie circles in Bengaluru, all the talk was about Google's acquisition of video-sharing site YouTube and how a price was set for such an asset. The two-year-old site, which was snapped up for $1.65 billion in October 2006, would go on to contribute nearly 11 per cent of parent Alphabet's $182 billion revenue in 2020.

When the famed trio of Steve Chen, Chad Hurley and Jawed Karim—former employees of PayPal—came together in 2005 to set up YouTube, they reportedly had the idea that ordinary people would enjoy sharing home videos. Two years later, a Harvard undergraduate posited that sharing pictures of campus students would encourage millennial users to get to know each other better, leading to the creation of the internet behemoth Facebook, now Meta. India is now one of its largest markets.

Watching from afar, young and restless Indians just waking up to the promise of the internet began to fancy their chances too. The idea that one could build such a product and sell it for an insane amount was an alluring one. If they could rustle up an idea that involved selling on the internet they knew some of the pools of venture capital forming around them would flow their way too.

Technology mavens who had gained handsomely by focusing money and attention on China in the post-dotcom years were looking for fresh landing spots for capital. Exploratory forays such as the SVB-led trips that had forged connections—with blue-chips firms like Sequoia meeting future partner Westbridge Capital in Bengaluru; Accel Partners linking up with their eventual Indian partner Erasmic Venture—were all combining to hasten the pace of globalization. If the big question in technology circles was 'After China, where to?', the answer most often turned out to be 'India'.

Watching all this at close quarters in Bengaluru was Ashish Gupta, who declares, 'It was magical.' The IIT Kanpur graduate was no casual observer. He was an early rock star in global technology circles for having sold Junglee—the comparative shopping site he had cofounded with three others—to Amazon way back in 1998. Since then he had put in stints at the online retail giant, founded a second startup, and was now in Bengaluru to oversee its Indian operations. He had also been closely following the explosion of interest in India across the world's business press, which by the winter of 2005 was centred on comparing and contrasting it to the other Asian giant, China.

Interestingly, Gupta's former startup Junglee would be the entry vehicle for Amazon when the e-commerce major began testing Indian waters in 2012 ahead of a full-fledged launch. Gupta's internet instincts, you could safely say, were very sharply honed indeed. He had also returned to India because his erstwhile partner at Tavant Technologies, Subrata Mitra, was leaving to set up a venture fund—one that would go on to ally with Valley heavyweight Accel Partners and which famously put the first dibs on small online book retailer Flipkart, which till date remains India's most valued startup.

Gupta wasn't resting on his laurels either. In Bengaluru, he had set up base in a sylvan gated community called Palm Meadows on the city's eastern outskirts, the favoured destination for scores of returnees. They would get off the planes and drive straight to the picket-fences-and-palm-tree-adorned enclave, the closest one could get to recreating suburban California. It was strategically situated just a few kilometres north of the city's then international airport. Locals would call them the B2B gang: Bay Area to Bengaluru.

Once there, Gupta began to forge connections with Carlyle's Kanwaljit Singh, with Sanjeev Aggarwal, best known for having earned his entrepreneurial stripes by helming the sale of outsourcing company Daksh to IBM, and with S.K. Jain from Westbridge Capital. They would shoot the breeze and discuss why India needed many more venture funds that would look at investing beyond technology. Soon talk turned into action and they began the process of fundraising. But they discovered that the first few months were a washout; no one heard them out seriously. Until the rash of business reports touting the coming Indian miracle hit global headlines. In November 2005, after *The Economist* cover featured a dragon racing with a tiger, Gupta says that money managers who had refused to answer his calls earlier were all dialling back. India was the flavour of the season.

Among those flocking here were big-ticket names—the bulk of venture funds active in India today were born in that first flush of venture fund creation in 2006. The only one Gupta estimates to have arrived early was SAIF's Adusumalli, 'the one guy who had been holding the flag well before all the rest of the lemmings showed up, he was already tilling the hard soil'.[11]

Until 2005, foreign direct investment (FDI) into India had never exceeded $10 billion. In two consecutive years that trend was broken—with $22 billion flowing in as foreign capital in 2006–07. In the next year, FDI posted a near 50 per cent increase, swelling to $32 billion. This had the country's central bank positing burgeoning domestic demand and high capacity utilization by local companies as causative factors for the gold rush.[12]

For Indians flocking back home, there was also the push factor at play. In the US of 2006, a housing bubble had already built up and to many the situation appeared dire. There was a lot of nervousness in America, in contrast with the enormous amount of optimism in India.

The RBI Economic Review for the year 1 July 2005 to 30 June 2006 points out that India had recorded an average growth of above 8 per cent for three years on the trot.

The centre of startup gravity was moving, and for many it was tilting towards Bengaluru. Talent was available in droves, the weather mild, the people amiable and land available in plenty.

Corporations would strike roots in the city as well, and in some cases buy land and build the massive glass-fronted buildings that have become so much a feature of India's urban landscape in the twenty-first century. This remaking of the physical and the professional spaces across the country's metropolises would only gather momentum as people and capital began to flood into the cities which emerged as entrepreneurial hot spots—Delhi NCR, Bengaluru, Chennai and even Mumbai. A generation of internet entrepreneurs who would catapult Indian technology startups on to the global stage had been created.

Binford may have come to Bengaluru to work on the 'deep problems of AI', but two young Indian engineers who answered to the name of Bansal were looking to do something very different. They wanted to simply sell books online. Their journey began, aptly enough, in a tiny, ramshackle office in an industrial zone of Bengaluru.

2

The Indian E-Commerce Mela

Mahendra Singh Dhoni's triumphant leap when his unheralded cricket team trounced arch rivals Pakistan in the final of the inaugural World Twenty20 championship in September 2007 was more than just a celebration of a sporting triumph. The young man from Ranchi, his long locks flying in the air, presented an image of renewed freedom, of youthful India unshackling itself in the twenty-first century from a tentative, maybe even timid, past. Millions, including those from the country's hinterlands, watching the exuberance of the twenty-six-year-old Indian captain who had risen from provincial beginnings would have seen a glimmer of possibility, showing what could be achieved in the absence of fear.

In the life of a nation, there are these infinitesimal moments when the cycle of change moves, when the old gives way to the new. Dhoni's leap mirrored the start of exactly one such moment in the vast arc of Indian business.

Just two weeks after that Twenty20 triumph, two Bengaluru engineers—both twenty-six years old—Sachin Bansal and Binny Bansal teamed up to launch an internet commerce site called Flipkart. They had more than age in common with Dhoni—like the Indian captain, they too had grown up in a small city, Chandigarh. But unlike the cricketing icon, they had plumbed for the classic Indian middle-class model. They bagged seats at an elite IIT to ride out of town and into the wide world. They started up quietly, with none of the fanfare that surrounded Dhoni's high-decibel triumph. But the ripple effects of the Bansals' gambit, which began by laying out ₹2 lakh apiece to start selling books online, continues to reverberate in what is now the world's third-largest startup ecosystem.

It was not what they set out to do but how they went about their business that renders Flipkart and therefore the moment of its launch—in October 2007—as seminal in the annals of India's internet history. Within two years of starting up, the IIT Delhi graduates raised capital from one of the world's most elite technology investors, Tiger Global, to kick-start rapid expansion at a pace unseen in the country. Embracing the challenge of scale and the fear it comes with, they went for broke. And in doing so, forever altered the prevailing mindset that required a business to first be profitable before aiming for expansion. This was a model inspired by Amazon that touted growth first and profits, if at all, much later. When it was eventually sold to American retail giant Walmart in 2018, Flipkart had soaked up over $6 billion of growth capital and was yet to break even.[1] Still, it was deemed to be worth $22 billion, a valuation that no other Indian internet startup has been able to rack up either before or after. To this day, it remains the country's most valued internet enterprise.

This raw, untested venture delivered several other industry firsts as well along its journey. Placing the Indian customer at the centre of its operations, it provided the option of cash-on-delivery payment for a population leery of paying by electronic mode and launched its own delivery network.

It all began from a two-bedroom apartment in Bengaluru's Koramangala—a neighbourhood that would soon become ground zero in the great Indian startup boom. The Bansals began by taking maybe one, two or a dozen orders per day from customers online.They would pick up the books from distributors and then deliver them. It was a start. In their first workplace—Amazon Web Services (AWS)—all water-cooler conversations centred on launching one's own venture.[2] Thousands of engineers would come to work every morning and hear of chatter ranging from YouTube being bought out for a staggering $1.65 billion by Google[3] without ever having made any money to news closer home of yet another colleague who had left to start up. Others from the Bansals' cohort at AWS had already waded in. E-commerce site Infibeam's co-founder Vishal Gupta was ex-Amazon, while the online commerce venture Let's Buy stayed apace with the Bansals' online bookselling business for quite a while. In the techie world of 2007, one either launched a startup or suffered the fear of missing out. A desi cauldron of enterprise was bubbling up, and every techie and his cousin believed they had a chance.

To wit, the average cost of starting up then would have been about ₹3.5 lakh (or $8,000) for all the equipment required by a typical web-based tech startup. This would include the bare minimum hardware and software requirements such as one Windows Small Business Server for Email, SharePoint, Domain Controller, another server for the front-end web-based app and a second for the back end, a couple of desktop computers with licensed software and a laptop for the business guy. Add to that ₹50,000 for an office generator—which the Bansals got—to weather the regulation power cuts in Indian metros. Voila! A full-time startup setup would be up and running.

The Bansals had tossed around the idea of building a price comparison engine but Amazon and the idea of the 'everything store' was a heady draw. The idea of an online store that sells everything akin to Amazon was even then a shot in the dark despite the looming example of Amazon's scale, and the growing talk of Alibaba from China. There was also America's eBay and other portals in South America. The Indian boys knew their market offered even bigger scale but they had no clue as to how big.

Books, the Bansals decided, would be the starting point. It was a cool category; the items could be classified under documents and shipped through IndiaPost. What's more, in a pre-goods and services tax (GST) era it attracted zero tax, no state border issues, and no value-added tax payments. Not even import duty was applicable, so it was a pretty no-fuss category. But yet, the fledgling venture wasn't named BookKart, because even then the Bansals were sure that one day they would 'sell everything'.

At that point India already had its share of e-commerce websites: Rediff, Indiatimes Shopping and smaller ones like Indiaplaza. To find out what consumers wanted, the Bansals began quizzing friends and family, only to discover that there wasn't a single person in their circles who shopped online. This is where their entrepreneurial spark revealed itself. Instead of finding the glass empty, the duo saw it as half full. India was a trillion-dollar economy with less than 20 million internet users at that time, with an average internet speed of about 128 kbps. To the Bansals, this meant the only way these statistics would grow was higher, faster, stronger. It was also the time when Indian consumer internet pioneers MMT and Cleartrip were advertising aggressively. Elsewhere, a team of graduates from Birla Institute of Technology and Science (BITS), Pilani, was building the bus-ticketing venture redBus. Around them, the first generation of consumer internet companies were fast gaining pace.

From a well-paid engineer at a global tech giant to a 'kitaab bechne wala', as his mother termed it, for Sachin Bansal, these were both heady and testing times. Despite their doubts, his family would be very supportive. They understood business; none of them had ever held a salaried job. For all the talk of India's conservative middle class prizing stable employment in a blue-chip corporate firm or in the government over business or dhanda, there are large pockets of community entrepreneurship that have served to make this a nation of small businesses. The Bansals belonged to the best known of such groupings—banias—or India's dominant mercantile class. Unsurprisingly, the first flush of consumer internet enterprise in India would be powered by the Bansals, Aggarwals and Goyals, who burst on to the startup scene, quite often wielding IIT degrees. Their native chutzpah, sharpened by new-age education, turned out to be a winning combination.

Flipkart's Bansals also had luck on their side. At AWS, one of their colleagues was IIT Kanpur graduate Abhishek Goyal, who would come to play a defining role in their professional destiny.

But at work, they saw little of him although they all had common friends. Goyal had put in a stint at Yahoo before heading to AWS and was that rare animal for mid-2000s India—a fully developed internet professional. A colleague who sat next to him in the office bay left to start up a movie content site—Chakpak, the IMDb of India—by raising seed capital from a small venture fund called Erasmic Venture. He encouraged Goyal to meet the partners there and test out his own startup ideas.

The founders of Erasmic, Subrata Mitra and Prashanth Prakash weren't only VCs. They had built technology startups of their own—Firewhite Inc. for Mitra and Netkraft for Prakash. After successfully exiting the companies, they were starting out yet again. But this time as VC investors, not founders.

Towards the end of 2004, they pooled together their own capital as well as from friends and family to launch a $10 million venture fund. The fund would make a bunch of investments, such as in Mu Sigma, a technology services firm, as well as in a bunch of nascent e-commerce ventures. By 2008, they were seeing more and more ideas from raw founders looking to build businesses on the internet. Given their primarily technology services background, the internet was a new animal for them. They realized they would need specialized know-how to navigate it, despite having backed internet ideas like Chakpak and personalized gifting portal Myntra.

When Goyal with his impressive internet résumé walked into the Erasmic office to test the waters for a startup venture, he was instead offered a job in the venture fund. Goyal freely admits that all he knew about VCs at that time was from the US webzine TechCrunch. In the space of two weeks, he had gone from being a coder at AWS to a principal at a venture firm. Such was the power of the 'internet magic' spilling over into Bengaluru's streets in those years.

The city had scores of groupings and informal events that allowed startup aspirants to connect with others of their ilk, creating a subculture of technology enterprise that played an outsize part in stoking internet entrepreneurship.

Serendipitously, Goyal would meet Sachin and Binny Bansal at one such event hosted organized by a grouping called Open Coffee Club.

Meanwhile, Erasmic would merge with the newly opened Accel India partnership. Soon after, an investor based in Silicon Valley—Sameer Gandhi, who was part of the Lilani-led investor foray to India in 2003—would join Accel in the United States. He was a great supporter from the word go, recalls Mitra.

Erasmic Venture's office in downtown Bengaluru—later the Accel India office—was tucked into a leafy alley. It was a magnet for twenty-somethings, curious journalists, investors and engineers, who would all pass through looking for leads, connections and the latest chatter about the internet world being fashioned in the city. It was a meeting point for the city's first crop of internet entrepreneurs, an adda for those looking to smell out deals, find investors, colleagues and even co-founders. The floor above the venture fund's was occupied by Mu Sigma, led by mercurial founder Dhiraj Rajaram. He had given up a job at Booz Allen Hamilton to build a consultancy services model of outsourcing. It was one of the Erasmic fund's two early bets in addition to Small Devices, which provided a testing platform for games.

The most footfalls, however, were from young engineers. Many of these visitors worked at the AWS office, which at that point had thrown up no less than twenty startup ventures. In-house lore at the Accel office was that if an aspiring entrepreneur could make it to their office without calling for directions, she should be taken seriously. It was an office hiding in plain sight.

The two founding partners each brought with them significant connections in the technology ecosystem. Prakash, a Bengaluru native with deep roots in the city, had met up with Mitra at grad school in the US way back in the 1990s. Mitra had led the Indian operations of Tavant Technologies, a firm founded by Helion's Gupta. The frankly tribal nature of India's early internet era is hard to miss. Multitudes of criss-crossing networks across India's IITs and IIMs, grad schools in the US and early starters at consulting firms such as McKinsey would form the kernel of the industry. They would back each other, pony up initial capital, provide mentoring and handholding and finally take the big bets that would define an entire era of tech enterprise.

This was the secret sauce that the swathes of overseas investors flooding into Bengaluru were in search of. The 'father' of Intel's Pentium chip, Vinod Dham, would forge a partnership with US-based Vani Kola to launch IndoUS Venture Partners. Another one among just a handful of women venture managers, Bharati Jacob teamed up with industry veteran Pravin Gandhi to launch a focused early-stage fund called the Seed Fund, which would famously draw in Google as a limited partner.[4] Elsewhere, Valley blue-chip Sequoia Capital would buy out another local fund, Westbridge Capital. It was a heady period with money managers of all stripes and colours, money bags either modest or overflowing, looking to see if the sparks being lit by Chinese internet entrepreneurs would catch fire in the land of the tiger.

The Bansals, emboldened by the fast clip in their business and the steady click of cash counters, would pitch for funds to nearly all these investors, only to be rejected by all of them. Only the talks at Accel stayed warm, due in large part to Goyal's unswerving belief in them. As a newly minted venture analyst, Goyal began noticing the 'insane reviews'[5] on Twitter being garnered by the tiny bookselling venture. Why would a customer who had just bought a book go online and start raving about it, he wondered. He dug deeper to discover that the near adulation Flipkart was getting was to do with its speed and friction-free delivery process. Correlating it with his own experience of trying to buy books online when he had to endure a month-long wait for an order, he soon understood what the noise was all about. The Bansals had identified a pain point—poor customer service—and were focused on solving that problem.

They were looking to raise a couple of crores to start expanding the warehouse network in Delhi and Bengaluru in order to move away from the initial model of just-in-time procurement. They were basically bagging an order, picking it up from the distributor and then shipping it. While this could work 90 per cent of the time, a 10 per cent failure rate was no business at all. For the Bansals, the goal was a 99.9 per cent fulfilment rate and that was possible only by owning the inventory. And that's why the venture money was so crucial.

Meanwhile, they checked other items off the to-do list. They hired their first employees: Sujeet Kumar and Tapas Rudrapatna. They opened a warehouse in Delhi and prepared to stock inventory. Watching their progress made Goyal increasingly restive. He went up to the Accel partners and declared that he would pool in his savings and invest ₹10 lakh in Flipkart himself if the fund wouldn't do it.[6] It would take another twenty-seven-year-old—an internet native—to intuitively understand that the Bansals were up to far more than just wowing India's early internet shoppers.

So taken aback were Mitra and team by this profession of faith that they turned serious. They decided to invest ₹70 lakh for a 10 per cent stake. By the time the due diligence got done and June 2009 rolled around, the Bansals were on a different trajectory. Their business was growing like a 'rocketship'. They had figured out search engine optimization and were the first port of call for almost all book lovers shopping online. The two decided they could sell 25 per cent equity for about $1 million. The money, which came in tranches, would include a seed investment of about ₹10 lakh from Helion's Gupta, who would go on to become the first angel investor in the company. Accel would put in about $800,000.

Meanwhile, in the US, where the venture capital flowing into markets like India was pooled, a series of events was taking shape that would have long-term ramifications on India's nascent internet industry. As the world battled the aftermath of the global financial crisis triggered by the collapse of investment bank Lehman Brothers in 2008, the US voted in Barack Obama as its forty-fourth President. Faced with a financial crisis, the most dire since the Great Depression, Obama would bail out Wall Street, a moniker derived from the name of the iconic street on which some of the world's largest financial services firms are located. Responding to Obama's lead, the US Federal Reserve reduced interest rates even further than the near zero that prevailed at that time. This quantitative easing, where the central bank buys longer-term securities from the open market in order to increase the money supply and encourage lending and investment, stoked the creation of mega pools of capital.

Sizeable amounts of this money began flowing to India, which was at that time only a partially open economy. But it was deemed to be more stable than its BRICS peers—Brazil, Russia, China and South Africa. The Indian economy was expanding at a steady trot of about 8 per cent. A successful nuclear deal with the US had boosted relations between the two countries to their best-ever phase. The zero-interest-rate environment in the US, at that time, has since come to be regarded as one of the biggest drivers for the boom in startup investment in India.

On the ground, young Indian engineers were casting aside the American dream to pick up high-paying product engineering jobs at home. Salaries were getting meaningful—the cohort, which included the Bansals, had several members who were earning in the region of ₹14 lakh–₹15 lakh per annum by the mid-noughties. This army of young professionals, tech savvy and armed with disposable income, began to crave a 'better life—better restaurants, better houses, better internet services'.[7] It was the millennial vibe manifesting itself. If people even two or three years older went the extra mile to save money in keeping with middle India's propensity for prudence, this emerging cohort was able and willing to 'pay ten rupees extra for slightly better service'.

As the first decade of the twenty-first century drew to a close, this bunch of young Indians were not just a world-class pool of talent but also an aspirational generation that would kick-start a consumption culture in the country. This would play no mean part in stoking the second era in Indian technology enterprise.

One that marked a shift from the initial wave of labour arbitrage that delivered the giant IT services companies to a new era led by concept arbitrage. Here, creating what could be slotted as the x of y (the Amazon of India or the Asos of India, etc.) would become the reigning model.

It helped also that India's early internet entrepreneurs were coasting along. Kalra's MMT was inching closer to a Nasdaq listing, while Bikhchandani's Info Edge, which housed job portal Naukri.com, was already a listed entity, having debuted on Indian bourses in 2006.

Into this cauldron of enterprise would wade in a money manager who went on to single-handedly alter the trajectory of Indian internet entrepreneurship: Lee Fixel. A year older than Sachin Bansal, Fixel had trained as a chartered financial analyst before joining the storied East Coast investment firm Tiger Global in 2006. The firm was one of the so-called Tiger Cubs that were born at the start of the century when hedge fund pioneer Julian Robertson dissolved his firm and ploughed capital into nearly two dozen or more new firms set up by his associates. It had already backed internet stars such as Facebook in the US and taken a splendid bet on China's rising internet star of the time, JD.com, which would go on to list in a blaze of glory on Nasdaq. Soon the New York firm turned its attention to India. Starting slowly, it took a small bet on local search firm Just Dial, and led an investment round in Kalra's MMT in 2008. Its biggest Indian investment of the time—$110 million in the National Stock Exchange—would happen in 2009. Its biggest and best, though, was still to come.

Fixel, who had seen and experienced the explosion of internet enterprise in China first-hand, was watching the signals emanate from India. Trawling for information on the country's startup sector he had come to know of Flipkart. Intrigued, he dialled a contact number provided on the Bengaluru company's website. This was the call centre number that the Bansals would sometimes keep off the hook to cancel the din outside their one-room office. In September 2009, Fixel's call was answered by one of Flipkart's newest recruits—Mekin Maheshwari, a tech wizard who had put in a stint at Yahoo's Indian operations and had recently joined Flipkart. The Bansals, who had had their eye on him for over a year, managed to get him on board once they raised a first round of funding from Accel Partners.

In his first days on the job, Maheshwari was manning the customer care line to get a feel of the business. That was when Fixel came on. Introducing himself as an investor from New York, he asked to speak to the founders and said he was interested in investing in the firm. Maheshwari, who turned to Sachin for a suitable reply, was told to shoo him off and tell him that the startup had just raised cash, it didn't need money.

When cold-calling yielded no results, Fixel turned to consultancy firm McKinsey to get him on a call with the Bansals. On D-day, five minutes before they were to dial in for the conference call—organized by McKinsey—the Bansals realized the one telephone in their office did not have international subscriber dialling (ISD). And that would have been it, if not for Fixel's dogged pursuit of the twenty-seven-year-olds, from whom he wasn't that much older himself—just a year more, in fact.

Even more determined to get through to the stubborn Bansals, Fixel tried another tack. He got in touch with MMT's Kalra, the suave founder whose firm by then was already on the Tiger Global portfolio. Kalra would be more than persuasive when he got in touch with Sachin Bansal. It also helped that for the normally combative Flipkart founder, the MMT CEO was a hero of sorts. Bansal was well aware that, 'At a small startup, if Deep Kalra calls, you just pick up the phone.'[8] Abashed by the near-historic talking-to that he received, Sachin finally acceded to have a conversation with Fixel. But not before thinking, 'Yeh kaun hai . . . baar, baar har jagah . . .' Who was this person who kept popping up?

Still, the Bansals would not get an ISD connection. So Fixel dialled them from New York.

But beneath the banter, something was clearly changing. Kalra had minced no words in making plain to the Bansals that they needed to have Fixel on their side. Sure, they had a million dollars in the bank, but it was about what lay ahead. Onlookers believe this talking-to changed the world view of the Bansals. They became serious.

As for Fixel, he had no time to waste. Within a week of the successful telephone call with the Bansals, Fixel landed in Bengaluru. Kalra was in the city too, and met the American investor for dinner. They dined at Karavali, a charming restaurant serving south Indian coastal cuisine. Located downtown, it would go on to become the American's favoured dining spot in the coming years as he launched an investment blitzkrieg.

Meanwhile, the Bansals, bolstered by Accel's funding, had found new digs in a far more respectable part of town. They rented two new buildings in the industrial zone of Koramangala. On the day that Fixel arrived, the local municipality was digging the roads in front of the new office. His car got stuck in the mess.

After some adroit moves, the Bansals finally ushered him into their still bare office where a small circle of chairs awaited. The negotiations began with the Bansals demanding a $100 million valuation for their two-year-old startup. They would be hammered down to $50 million, but not without a fight.

In just two months after it first raised $1 million from Accel Partners, the small e-commerce company with outsize ambition received fresh funding of about $10 million from Tiger Global at a $50 million valuation.

To peers, Sachin Bansal was now slowly revealing what would become his best-known trait: audaciousness. It would often be pointed out in the years ahead as the online bookstore was propelled to internet stardom as India's version of the 'everything online store'.

Bansal was demonstrating the same ability—of embracing a challenge without fear—that Dhoni had displayed on the cricket pitch. A quality that has grown to be the anthem of new India, a country of millennials and Gen Z-ers, people born in a country with a liberalized economy, limitless talent, aspiration and hope.

To more sedate onlookers, the Flipkart–Tiger Global deal evoked jaw-dropping awe. 'Kya aisa bhi hota hai?' was the most common refrain. It signalled a leap in imagination—an understanding of the high stakes possible—that would rapidly become the defining trait of e-commerce in India.

Fixel was not valuing Flipkart's existing business when he ascribed a value of $50 million to it in 2009. Rather, he was betting on what it could grow into. Even more importantly, he was putting his money where his mouth was. It was Fixel's outsize capital that allowed the Bansals to gun for growth at all costs, to set aside conservative business requirements of breaking even and turning profits in the hunt for scale. In the world of internet commerce, big was beautiful and speed was de rigueur.

Raw code-writing engineers watching this spectacle unfold began scrambling to acquire such know-how. To imagine and conceptualize a business model where burning capital of up to $100 million yearly for the next ten years in search of exponential growth would become the norm rather than the exception. All this in a country where, until liberalization, businesses had been driven by scarcity. Where lock-in investments were made only by the government, and private enterprises were all cash-flow driven.

The tectonic changes underway were similar to what Newton's Law proclaims, where every object remains in rest until an external force acts upon it. In India's emerging online commerce industry, Lee Fixel would be that force.

In the months to follow, the optimism about India in general and Flipkart in particular among venture investors would be driven in large part by the successful initial public offering (IPO) floated by MMT, India's largest travel portal, in July 2010.

Before that, there was still work to be done on the ground. The Bansals were packed off to China, to see first-hand what the scale Fixel was envisaging actually looked like. Also making that journey in those years were Accel's partner Mitra as well as another Bansal—Mukesh—who was readying his own dizzying climb to stardom. An IIT Kanpur graduate, he had work experience from a number of startups in Silicon Valley.

To some investors, he was the real deal with his overseas work experience that set him apart from the raw gaggle of IIT graduates pitching the next big idea. But not all investors concurred. The very first investor Mukesh pitched to in January 2007 with an idea for a personalized gifting site would ask him summarily to go find a great IT job, have a good life, and forget all about starting up. Mukesh isn't certain what discomfited him more, the unsolicited advice or the stream of cigarette smoke blown in his direction. In hindsight, it was just the zeitgeist of those times. Everyone was excited, including investors and founders, as they tried to figure out the best path. None of them had all the information or an understanding of the entire context.

When he moved back to India in 2007, Mukesh was looking to be the early bird. His thoughts on entrepreneurship dated back to his college days at IIT Kanpur, where he had read of Sam Walton and Akio Morita.

But in the India of the noughties, he could see 'a lot of energy in the air, it was just a visceral feeling; every time I visited, I would get more excited'. Casting doubts aside, he launched the online gifting venture he had thought of, along with two classmates from IIT Kanpur. It would metamorphose into a rollicking adventure. Tasked to deliver a batch of personalized T-shirts for a gang of bikers, the team struggled to complete the order on time. This led to the aggrieved customers showing up unannounced at their office one morning to demand immediate delivery. To the utter amazement of the bikers, they found the startup's employees engaged in a game of gully cricket. After twenty minutes of heated exchanges, frayed tempers cooled. The reasons for the delay were explained and a new delivery plan was drawn up. The bikers then joined in the cricket session. But it wasn't all fun and games. On another occasion, charged with delivering an order of 'Amazon'-inscribed T-shirts by 6 a.m., Mukesh would stun the customer by arriving at his doorstep at 3 a.m. to deliver the complete batch. The blue-chip engineer who could code with the best was rolling up his sleeves and getting his hands dirty in the rough and tumble of India.

His startup had by then raised a seed round from Accel, which was still going by the moniker of Erasmic Venture in those days. Soon, two more funds, IndoUS Ventures and IDG, joined in for the Series A investment in 2008. But the business wasn't going anywhere with the personalization model. And the years 2007 to 2010 were very difficult.

It was a common lament. India lacked internet connectivity and had no proven digital modes of payment or a countrywide postal service that could deliver parcels to doorsteps. Unlike the US, where Amazon and even Netflix in its DVD avatar were built on rock-solid freight movement systems—led by the US Postal Service. Among the most trying challenges in India was the low internet penetration. It grew at an abysmal rate from 2.81 per cent of the population in 2006 to 5.12 per cent in 2009.

Casting about for inspiration to grow his business, Mukesh travelled to shopping venues across metros. On one such trip to Pune, he chanced upon a deserted mall stocked with top fashion brands. It occurred to him that moving these products online would stem the colossal waste of resources and time. He had already begun hawking branded sports jerseys by then; the move to fashion was therefore a natural next step.

That pivot would end up as one of the most famous in Indian startup lore. The team was experimenting with the whole gamut of Indian Premier League (IPL) jerseys and Team India jerseys. Following the World T20 success, the launch of the iconic IPL brought the taste of mega money into Indian cricket.

Fixel soon became interested in the entire online sports-based commerce scene in India, leading him into Myntra's life. Tiger Global had invested in a similar venture called NetShoes in Brazil; clearly, it was an idea that could be replicated in India.

In 2010, Fixel took his first bet on Myntra. True to style, he packed Mukesh off to Brazil and then China to get a view of the scale. Not only was Fixel's understanding of e-commerce way ahead of his Indian counterparts', he could open doors and forge ties for Indian entrepreneurs with global counterparts. On his trip to China, Bansal got to partner with numerous companies there through 2011–12; he discovered that while Myntra was perhaps shipping 500 orders a day, in China companies were shipping 100,000 shipments a day. Just seeing the scale and the operating model in China proved to be an eye-opening experience.

For the Bansals of Flipkart, as well as for Myntra's Mukesh, it was Fixel who galvanized them to really think big while he backed it up with serious capital. It helped also that Fixel could provide follow-on rounds of funding in quick time. He had decision-making authority and his willingness to take big risks stemmed from this freedom.

Moreover, his firm did not have the same time constraints that venture funds had to deal with. Typically, venture funds, which pool capital from LPs, have to deliver returns within a specified time frame of between five to seven or ten years. That crucial difference would come to shape a lot of consumer internet activity in India in the future.

While the Indian internet ecosystem would have grown one way or the other, Fixel certainly advanced it by a few years. So much so that an investment banker who witnessed the explosion of energy in the Indian internet ecosystem first-hand declared with fervour, 'Fixel must be given the Bharat Ratna.'[9] Meanwhile, a part-amused, part-exasperated contemporary defines his investing style as 'going around looking for sparks that he could pour gasoline on to light a fire'.

Fixel putting money into Flipkart was akin to putting money in the hands of Indian consumers. It was this deluge of investor money which stoked the risk-capital-driven discounting model for Indian consumers, while solidifying a hitherto unknown model of internet commerce in the country—where businesses had to grow at the speed of light and profits had to wait.

It would take a decade more for most startup founders to realize that the business model of growth at any cost was the aberration and not the norm. By then, billions had been spent and many businesses had seen a spectacular implosion. But during the years 2010 to 2015, Fixel would have an outside influence on the entire Indian startup ecosystem, turbocharging it with both 'big mindset and the big capital'.[10]

This din and disruption of the internet era would sweep along with it the mega ambitions of the Flipkart Bansals as well that of others watching this spectacle. None more than two young entrepreneurs in Delhi: Kunal Bahl and Rohit Bansal. The rivalry between Snapdeal, the online marketplace they would launch, and Flipkart will remain one of the defining duels of the early phase of Indian internet commerce.

Bahl and Bansal, who met as classmates at Delhi Public School in RK Puram, sat next to each other right through classes 11 and 12. Since then, the two inseparables have forged an enduring partnership with few parallels in an industry where flame-outs between co-founders have been more the norm. Some years after they left school and acquired a couple of degrees—Bahl at the University of Pennsylvania's Wharton School of Business and Bansal at IIT Delhi—they decided to revive the early promise of starting up together. This was an idea seeded during holidays spent chilling together including at eat-all-you can buffets that served up the Indo-Chinese fare that both relished.

It wasn't as if everyone in their vicinity was diving into entrepreneurship. On the contrary, there was still 'severe adverse selection' associated with it, recalls Bahl.[11] But for the two of them it was always a certainty, the only questions being 'when' and 'what', never 'if'.

They thought of starting a movie-ticket-booking portal, but Mumbai-based BookMyShow already had a head start in that space. So they began by selling coupon books but made little headway. A pivot to hawking discount cards helped make the fledgling venture self-sustaining.

Around that time, they began hearing the noise around online couponing in the US, particularly about a Chicago-based venture called Groupon that was launched in 2008. The merchants they dealt with also kept pushing the idea at them. A few such ventures had already come up in India and were tapping retailers to subscribe to the model. In the US, Groupon would quickly gain fame for being an acquisition target for Google, thereby sealing the popularity of the online couponing model itself.

Enthused, Bahl and Bansal, who had by then drawn seed capital from the Vani Kola–led IndoUS Venture Partners, decided to wade into the online space. They had spent nearly two and a half years building an offline model with little purchase. So they turned online and launched a marketplace by taking the same relationships they had built with offline merchants, as well as the coupons, and putting them on their website. They named the site Snapdeal. This move delivered 'escape velocity' to the young founders, who edged their way into the vast ocean of online commerce through this niche market. As pivots go, it was a dramatic one. Soon the pedigree of the founders would draw deeper investor interest, and in quick succession the fledgling venture raised two rounds of capital.

The first was a $12 million round from an India-focused venture fund, Nexus Venture Partners, and Kola's fund in 2011. It was followed by a $40 million investment in July of the same year from the same investors as well as from Bessemer Venture. Money was definitely flowing Snapdeal's way.

But what stands out is the tryst with serendipity that has lit the path for Bahl and Bansal right through their entrepreneurial journey. While at Wharton, Bahl got acquainted with a visiting professor, Ken Glass, a former Microsoft executive. At the end of an inspiring management lecture, they struck up a conversation and Bahl mentioned that he too was moving to Seattle for his first job at the iconic software maker. Glass, who was also a Wharton graduate, immediately invited him for a catch-up over lunch, an offer that would extend to quarterly meetings for the entire duration of Bahl's stay in Seattle. As it happened, Bahl left the US in quite dramatic fashion a couple of years later, when Microsoft's application for an extension of his H1B work visa was rejected in 2007. Before returning, he caught up with Glass one last time and was quizzed on what he planned to do next. The idea of coupon books was fresh in Bahl's mind and he told Glass that he planned to cofound a startup along with his childhood friend. Without missing a beat, the kindly American, twenty-five years older than Bahl, told him to call if he ever needed help.

It was a promise he would keep by providing the first angel investment for the coupon book venture. It was the shagun, an auspicious first transaction, for the Bahl–Bansal duo's entrepreneurial exploits. Glass remains an investor in Snapdeal a decade and a half later and an ardent supporter of the founders, making plain that business can be about more than money alone.

Meanwhile, business was powering ahead strongly. Snapdeal, the coupon company that was looking to ace the Groupon idea, was gaining traction amongst significant investors. The two rounds of funding it had received from Nexus Venture had been led by Suvir Sujan, one of India's earliest internet entrepreneurs, best known for cofounding the eBay clone Baazee way back in the early years of the new millennium. He was now forging a second avatar as an investor.

Nexus Venture, the 2006 vintage fund he had cofounded with a crack team including former e-Ventures investor Sandeep Singhal and US-based technocrat Naren Gupta, was looking to make a splash in the industry despite having missed an opportunity of investing early in Flipkart. At that time, investors were evaluating two internet commerce models that were dominating the Chinese market. One was the JD.com-inspired inventory model while the second was the Tao Bao–led online marketplace model.

Sujan, a former Boston Consulting Group (BCG) executive, came with his own back story of having founded and run e-commerce venture Baazee.com much before the start of the wave that Bahl and Bansal were riding. A Harvard Business School graduate, he was posted at the BCG's Mumbai office when the talk was all about Satyam Infoway snapping up IndiaWorld. The seminal deal had many observers stoked about the promise of internet commerce in India. Sujan began looking at which of the two prevailing global e-commerce models—Amazon's inventory-led approach or the eBay marketplace model—would work in India. While he tilted towards the marketplace approach, he soon realized that India's giant unorganized retail segment would require its very own model.

Sujan was mulling options with his to-be co-founder at Baazee—Avnish Bajaj, also a Harvard graduate, then at Goldman Sachs—when events overtook them. A senior from business school, Ashish Dhawan, came to stay for a few days at Sujan's apartment in Mumbai. He was looking to launch an India-focused venture firm, Chrys Capital, and was in the process of raising the fund. For Sujan, this would be akin to providence paying a visit; he literally had a VC sitting on his couch as he was preparing his startup plan. Chrys Capital would famously make its first investment in Sujan and Bajaj's online marketplace, marking a key turn in the evolution of early internet commerce in India.

Baazee, which ran for four years, battled a series of challenges that came with being the first mover in a completely nascent market. In a bid to get merchants on to the platform, they would sometimes begin from scratch, showing them what a computer was. For payments, bank transfers and debit cards ruled, as the share of people with credit cards was so minuscule. Drawing from the eBay example of building PayPal in the US, the Baazee team built a rudimentary digital payment service called Paisapay. All the while, the traction for shopping was growing. Jewellery priced at ₹8,000 was a big draw, as were lifestyle products and mobile phones.

But in 2004, the company faced its biggest challenge. Bajaj, who was then co-CEO, was arrested by the Delhi Police over a complaint that an obscene video had been uploaded for auction on Baazee. He was finally acquitted because the website had only provided a platform for buyers and sellers to interact directly. Subsequently the government would amend a section in the Information Technology Act, 2000, providing immunity to intermediaries for content made available on their platform by third parties. This rear-guard action by the government proved to be a game-changer that opened the doors for an explosion of internet commerce in the coming decade.

Bajaj and Sujan soon sold their site to eBay as the American marketplace pioneer was chafing to enter the Indian market. In turn, they moved to becoming VCs. Bajaj launched Matrix Partners, while Sujan at Nexus Venture bet on the next generation of entrepreneurs looking to build an e-commerce marketplace. In January 2011, he had joined the $12 million funding round in Snapdeal, the first of more capital that he pumped into the company.

At the end of that year, Bahl and Bansal travelled to China, where they met scores of people working in the e-commerce space. The experience made plain to them that the future was not in selling coupons but in selling physical products online. They had already begun to discover the limitations of the niche sector and knew they could only be the big fish in a small pond. Physical e-commerce, on the other hand, was a vast, mesmerizing universe, more so when viewed from a Chinese lens. Back in India, they saw that most competitors were buying and selling goods online using the inventory model. There was no India-centric online marketplace that aggregated merchants on one platform, except for eBay, which wasn't very active at that point of time. This, then, would be the sweet spot for the Delhi duo.

In a matter of days or weeks, they pivoted Snapdeal's business from online couponing to an e-commerce marketplace selling physical products. They were already familiar with working with merchants to provide end-customer experience. The bigger challenge they faced was convincing doubtful offline merchants to sell physical products online. They had to offer cash incentives to get them to sell on the marketplace as they feared not being paid for goods sold through online channels. In turn, they quizzed Bahl and Bansal, who appeared well-spoken, educated folk, about their motivation to indulge in such running around in the heat and dust. Bahl reckons they assumed he had either failed at studies or suffered a setback that had forced him to turn to business.[12] Starting up was not yet a common term in middle India. And it certainly cut no ice with the sharp-eyed retailers who had been selling to value-conscious buyers in the bylanes of Chandni Chowk for generations.

For the Snapdeal founders looking to build an online marketplace for those beyond India's Sec A population and targeting consumers who bought value products, not branded goods, the journey was proving to be '100x harder' than anticipated.

They credit 'innocence and naivete and just ignorance' for their bravado. For entrepreneurship is about 'attempting the absolutely unattainable', and sometimes it just works out. As it would in quite spectacular fashion for the ambitious duo.

The Delhi-based online marketplace would soon emerge as the counterpoint to the e-commerce giant taking shape down south. By 2012, Flipkart was counted as a unicorn—valued at over $1 billion, raising funding rounds of up to $150 million, with the likes of South Africa's Naspers co-investing alongside Fixel.[13] Snapdeal, with its marketplace model regarded as more compliant with the country's retail laws, would attract its own fanbase as first eBay and then Masayoshi Son's SoftBank joined its cap table. The bugles would soon be sounded in an all-out war for the Indian consumer's wallet.

3

The Swell of Enterprise

Queueing up to board an international flight in his early years as a founder, technology entrepreneur Girish Mathrubootham noticed a young salesperson trying to sell international SIM cards to travellers. Nine out of his ten overtures would be rebuffed, but the young man with faulty English kept persevering. Intrigued, the Chennai-based founder of Freshworks, an enterprise software maker, decided to hire the young man for his startup.

His reasoning was simple. He needed a salesperson who wouldn't take no for an answer. And he wanted him to interact with European clients, many of whom weren't proficient in the queen's English either. The SIM card salesman would emerge as a star at Freshworks, which primarily sold customer service software to a vast number of small and medium businesses across the world. On video calls with clients, he would use a Notepad to list out parameters; clients would respond in kind. And soon, a deal would result. So much so that he would sometimes close up to twenty-five deals in a month.

Freshworks believed its success rate came out of a unique model that was focused on spotting and honing talent, discovering diamonds in the rough as Mathrubootham would describe it in the industry podcast hosted by Accel Partners. He picked up three aspects from the chance encounter with the SIM card salesman. A relentless aspiration to sell in order to make a living. An ability to face rejection and not quail under its impact. A thick skin and an ability to return to battle after having failed.

These were the gritty attributes prized by the small venture that began life in what was then a backwater in the startup world. Its founders did not sport elite degrees from the IITs that could work as talent magnets. Instead, Mathrubootham was cultivating a model of identifying specific attributes in potential hires and ensuring they were placed in matching roles. A team with Sachin Tendulkar in it would want to have him batting and not bowling is how the founder terms it.

Born in a small city in Tamil Nadu, Mathrubootham, now forty-seven, refers to himself as an 'outstanding student', one who spent most of his time 'standing outside the class'. Nevertheless, he went on to acquire an engineering degree and later an MBA from Madras University. He switched a few jobs before opening an institute where he taught the programming language Java. But he was singed by the cyclical nature of the business and had to shut the venture down. Joining software exporter HCL, he moved to the US. To onlookers it appeared to be the end of a hard-scrabbled start for the young professional with provincial roots. Mathrubootham, however, had different ambitions. A year into his cushy life in the US, he gave it all up to return to Chennai in search of work that was more challenging than software coding.

He joined a pioneering venture called Advent Net which was launched by brothers Sridhar Vembu and Kumar Vembu and was selling software products built in India to businesses in the West. It would prove to be a career-defining move. He spent more than nine years at the company that would later come to be known as Zoho, one of India's best-known technology startups that is completely bootstrapped—that is, unsupported by any outside capital. Mentored by Kumar Vembu, Mathrubootham would go on to be a product manager known for his pioneering bet to build a suite of software products entirely out of India.

In time he would leave to start up on his own. Frustrated by poor customer service during the purchase of a household gadget, Mathrubootham started to think of the need for robust customer service for buyers of software products globally. He joined hands with a colleague, Shan Krishnasamy, to launch Freshdesk from a small 700 square foot office in Chennai with some six employees.

The business picked up steam but Mathrubootham realized he would need outside capital to compete on equal terms with dominant rivals like Zendesk in the US. A consummate storyteller, he entered blog-writing contests, telling the tale of how he was building a lean startup. One such post on Hacker News went viral and attracted the attention of an interesting person in the Silicon Valley startup ecosystem: Naval Ravikant, the founder of the US website AngelList. Ravikant had launched it in 2010, and it worked as an introduction tool for technology startups in want of venture funding. Impressed by the Chennai team's profile, he offered to introduce its founders to venture investors in India. Ravikant emailed Anand Daniel, who had returned from the US to join the investing team at Accel.

It would prove to be as serendipitous a connection as any that peppers the world of startups, where the adage that success is as much due to luck as it is from effort plays out on a daily basis.

Riding high on its winning bet on Flipkart, Accel Ventures was now looking out to see what could be the next big bet in the world of technology investing. The partners had brought in technology executive Shekhar Kirani from Verisign to beef up its enterprise software practice. Kirani had seen the boom in subscription software at close quarters and knew this was the next big deal developing in India's software export story.

Kirani's gaze would turn to Chennai, where the bootstrapped company Zoho was making waves as a seller of software products to small businesses across the globe. But its founder, the iconoclastic Sridhar Vembu, was not in the market for venture funding.

Meanwhile, Kirani was meeting scores of startup founders. Along the way, he made a fervent presentation to his partners at Accel, arguing the case that SaaS—software as a service—would be the next big, big thing from India. Mitra, Prashanth and Mahendran were keen to back him. The fund had an entrepreneurial culture and were always keen to experiment.

Daniel would share Ravikant's lead about an interesting SaaS startup in Chennai with Shekhar Kirani. Meanwhile, Freshworks had listed itself independently on AngelList.[1] But Indian venture investors were still doubtful. It was a shot in the dark. Chennai was then off centre in the startup wave, the founder Mathrubootham had listed a degree from the little-known Sastra University and an MBA from the Department of Management Studies at the University of Madras. To parse this required lateral thinking from VCs attuned to evaluating founders from IITs who had worked at Amazon, Google and Yahoo. Mathrubootham's was an offbeat CV in the venture world of 2010.

Still, for Kirani one point leapt out. It was a SaaS company and the founder had earlier worked at Zoho before starting out on his own. That was all Kirani needed. He got on a plane to Chennai and to the Freshdesk office in record time. In a no-frills room, he found about six engineers, including the founder, all working on a shiny line of Apple Mac computers. Intrigued, he asked the founder why he had spent on computers and not on furniture. Mathrubootham's answer was spare—tools for work should be of the highest order; everything else can be functional. Kirani spent an entire day there understanding how they worked and what they thought.

The Freshdesk team had prepared a pitch deck—a compilation of past and present information plus future aspirations—that founders use to tell their story to venture investors. However, Mathrubootham failed to include the most pertinent portion—what it was that he had done at Zoho that made him confident of venturing out on his own. The Vembu-led company at that point ran its engineering and quality assurance in India, while all product management and marketing was run out of its US offices. This was the accepted model of the times. Mathrubootham, hired as one of the first product managers in the company, had turned this around and instead built a team where the entire product lifecycle happened in India—it would go on to be called the ManageEngine division. A family of products would thus be created and establish the kernel of the SaaS rise.

Looking back, Mathrubootham credits that phase of his career as the spur to believing that complete products could be built from Chennai for the world. Kirani discovered this through interactions, not from the pitch deck at the presentation. A strong learner, Mathrubootham had spent time working in the US before starting up and used his spare hours to teach programming to students in Chennai. That he could tell when a student was nodding without understanding what was being taught was part of the office lore.

To the Accel partner, he was the real deal with his strong industry know-how, global experience and first-hand execution skills. Kirani gave Mathrubootham a term sheet for a first round of funding. The founder was also evaluating term sheets from other venture investors because word had quickly got around that Accel was courting him. Finally, the clincher for choosing Accel turned out to be quite simple. Mathrubootham's two colleagues who sat around him at their one-room office were sharp observers. They would tell him that while other investors were eager to agree with all he said in his presentation, nodding their heads in assent, Kirani had asked tough questions. The astute Freshdesk team chose Accel.

It helped that Kirani was a native in the global subscription software industry. Until he spotted them, this was largely an unknown business. There was little competition for the deal. Still he would do his background checks. Accel partner Sameer Gandhi, who was visiting Bengaluru, was asked if he thought it was an investment worth making and he said a resounding yes. Once in, Kirani would go all out to open further doors for the company. He had acquired a little over a fifth of it and would urge other investors to take a look as well. But to no avail. That is, until Fixel arrived on one of his periodic visits to Bengaluru. Kirani urged Mitra and Prashanth to allow time for a presentation to him about Freshdesk. The American investor was definitely interested in this SaaS startup that also had Zoho lineage. He knew about Vembu's firm and had tried to invest in it, but Vembu had stayed firm with his bootstrap ideology.

So, at the breakfast meeting, Accel would make a presentation about the Chennai-based Freshdesk. As it happened Fixel, who rarely travelled beyond Bangalore and Delhi, was also making a rare trip to Chennai in January of 2012. Recounting that visit nearly a decade later, Mathrubhootham reckons that Fixel was there to meet a little-known online jeweller CaratLane. Tiger Global would turn out to be the only venture investor in the low-profile jewellery portal that would make waves in 2023 when it was bought out by industry leader Titan in a deal that valued CaratLane at a whopping ₹17,000 crore.

Meanwhile, the Freshworks (then Freshdesk) CEO would meet Fixel and make a pitch. Two days later the American investor would call back and say he was ready to start the due diligence. No term sheet, no protracted negotiations, leaving an astonished Mathrubootham to quiz Kirani on why he, on the other hand, had asked so many questions, right down to the reason for the colour of his shirt.

The Freshdesk investment would also mark Fixel's foray beyond e-commerce into the SaaS sector. Freshdesk's rise made clear the stirrings of a second wave of democratization being unleashed by the expansion of India's startup culture. If the first wave had opened doors for professionals from elite colleges, this second wave was ushering in the brightest and the best from places beyond the metropolitan hot spots. Many of these aspiring founders would also be nurtured by a new wave of industry groupings that would start taking shape in 2010, such as the NASSCOM Product Forum, Indian Software Product Industry Round Table (iSPIRT) and finally SaaSBoomi.[2]

Meanwhile, news of Accel's winning bets was stirring ripples of angst in the larger investor community. At one such gathering of a horde of VCs in Mumbai, 'as the evening progressed, tales of how each had evaluated but not signed up with Flipkart grew longer and more morose'.[3] Flipkart had become the one deal that should not have been lost and would remain as such for most of the decade. Elsewhere, blue-chip venture firm Sequoia Capital, which had set up its Indian base by merging with home-grown venture team Westbridge Capital, would launch an aggressive campaign scouting out the next wave of internet startups. The team would zero in on a spate of deals including in education services, a sector that it had seen success in by backing a Bengaluru-based startup, TutorVista. It would back another edtech venture, Byju's, and in 2014 put its first dibs on the Mumbai-based startup Ola founded by a band of IIT Bombay graduates that was linking drivers with potential ride-seekers. This heralded what is widely regarded as India's tryst with ride-hailing apps.

Ola, cofounded by the mercurial Bhavish Aggarwal, would go on to become one of the poster children of the internet revolution of the 2010s. It would grab headlines, big money and square up in a riveting battle with American ride-hailing major Uber in the years to come.

Its beginnings, as is the case with so many entrepreneurial forays, had more than a touch of adventure. Hailing from Ludhiana, Aggarwal had put in a stint at the Microsoft Research centre in Bengaluru. He was on a trip to Karnataka's wildlife hot spot, Bandipur. En route, the cab driver bailed out, leaving him stranded and deeply conscious of the need for a reliable transport service. Ola was launched in December 2010. As luck would have it, at a business conference in Mumbai, Aggarwal had walked up to Kunal Bahl of Snapdeal and asked if he could show him his presentation for an intercity taxi service. So taken was Bahl with the fresh-faced youngster's approach that he made his first angel investment in the fledgling venture, setting in motion the journey of India's largest ride-hailing service.

These were the deals shaping a new landscape fashioned by outsize ambition, money to back it and technical prowess to power the burgeoning dreams of hundreds of aspiring entrepreneurs.

Despite all the flurry around venture-led entrepreneurship and the high-decibel coverage of it in mainstream media, starting up even in 2012 was a big-city phenomenon. It could be argued that even within that cohort it was further limited to the products of elite education. It was a clubby network where friends backed each other's ventures, connected them to others of their ilk, opened doors and closed deals for each other. So much so that investors who didn't get a look in on a great deal or founders who failed to get five minutes of a VC's time would complain that they had been allotted the wrong hostel building at IIT. Sure, scores of middle-class Indians were wading into the startup pond. But at the start of the twenty-first century's second decade and for quite a while later it would remain an elite pond. That's why the unlikely tale of an entrepreneur from Kerala's commercial hub Kochi who rose to establish one of India's most talked about startups evokes disbelief.

One of the most serendipitous encounters in the startup space took place in Manipal, the university town on the country's south-west coast. It was a meeting between Ranjan Pai, scion of the education and medical powerhouse Manipal Education and Medical Group, and a little-known twenty-eight-year-old from Kerala who was making waves in student circles for cracking the code to the famed IIMs. Byju Raveendran was not a name that rang a bell for Pai when he walked into a teeming crowd of students at his family-owned hotel Valley View in the university town.

Pai asked the steward what the excitement was about and was told that a young man was being mobbed by the students. When asked if he would like to meet him, the curious doctor-entrepreneur answered in the affirmative. Byju's, the eponymous edtech venture, which within a decade would go on to briefly become one of India's most valued startup before courting controversy for alleged accounting and governance missteps, was at that time still an enterprise that offered offline coaching classes, albeit with a twist. The classes, led by Raveendran himself, were conducted within massive stadiums, and students would flock to hear him tell, among other things, how he had turned down a seat at an IIM.

In aspirational middle-class homes, that was pretty much heresy. For millions who dreamt of clawing their way up to prosperity from the backwaters of Indian towns and cities, professional education was the one lodestar. To turn down an IIM spot and a one-way ticket to the good life was beyond radical—it made Raveendran a folk hero for youngsters.

Pai was intrigued by the unusual entrepreneur. He also wasn't clear why Raveendran was keen to raise money directly from him during that first meeting in Manipal. Pai had partnered with former Infosys chief financial officer (CFO) Mohandas Pai to set up venture fund Aarin Capital.

Weeks later, when they met again at his office in Bengaluru, Pai was amazed at the surging confidence in the young man. He was keen to go digital, riding on the VSAT network for distance education that was ubiquitous by then. He wanted Pai to invest ₹50 crore. This shocked the Manipal chief and he checked back with Mohandas Pai. The former Infosys CFO and Pai would agree to invest but only in tranches linked to specific business milestones. They would decide to drip-feed the edtech venture for two years.

But they had not foreseen the sheer enormity of Raveendran's ambition. In his deal book, he had already crafted a three-year buyback and exit for Pai. And he stuck to it, buying out Pai's stake and leaving him with less than 1 per cent stake in the company.

Just as with the Pais of Aarin Capital, also notable in this period was the rise of angel networks dominated by big-name Indian-origin entrepreneurs in groupings such as TiE. There were also city-centric groups such as the Mumbai Angels where high net worth Indians would get their chance to participate in the ongoing startup boom.

In Mumbai, the angel investment network was seeded by the scion of a business family, Sasha Mirchandani, whose family was the promoter of the once-aspirational consumer electronic brand Onida. One of the group's first investments was in a business-to-business startup in 2007 called InMobi. Later, celebrated American venture firm Kleiner Perkins, Caufield & Byers (KPCB) as well as Sherpalo Ventures, founded by legendary Google investor Ram Shriram, would back the mobile advertising technology startup founded by Harvard Business School graduate Naveen Tewari.

The startup would begin life as mKhoj, an SMS-based search service focused on hyperlocal information, but the idea had to be abandoned within a few months owing to poor traction. It would move to building a mobile advertising technology, navigating months of uncertainty, the lack of any paying customers and its existence as a business run on the credit cards of team members. However, once KPCB and Sherpalo backed the venture, its headcount grew to about seventy-five people with four offices worldwide in just over a year, when it rebranded itself as InMobi. A year later, in 2010, US investors ploughed in more cash, providing a bumper exit to early backers Mumbai Angels. The grouping recorded the biggest-ever return on investment by an angel group in India at that time, earning a return of over twenty times its $500,000 investment made in 2007.[4]

InMobi's star, already on the ascendant, would peak in 2011, when it emerged as India's first unicorn backed by Japanese investment powerhouse SoftBank. The $200 million splashed on the Tewari-led firm valued it at over a billion dollars. Tewari has been quoted as saying that he asked the SoftBank supremo to invest $250 million in his startup, which until then had received about $15 million.[5] It was an early signal to those reading the tea leaves that very big money was on its way into the Indian startup ecosystem.

One extremely powerful thing that India did have was talent, a thriving breed of young, bright and ambitious entrepreneurs whose journey was only just beginning.

4

Exits, Ahoy!

In the summer of 2010, Krishnan Ganesh and Meena, among the best-known and arguably one of the most successful couples in the world of Indian startups, were on a Mediterranean cruise. It was their silver wedding anniversary and they had much to celebrate. Their startup TutorVista, which provided online maths tuitions by Indian teachers for American kids, was attracting huge interest from investors. Just months ago, British publishing major Pearson had bought a 17 per cent stake in the four-year-old venture while leaving the door open for further negotiations.

On board the cruise ship, Ganesh was working out on the treadmill with a desultory eye on the CNN News telecast on the screen in front of him. To his amazement, a familiar face appeared on screen with a flash announcing the successful NASDAQ listing by Indian travel company MakeMyTrip. Ganesh could barely contain his excitement and nearly 'fell off the treadmill', as Meena and he watched MMT founder Deep Kalra discuss his firm's spectacular opening.[1] The euphoria was justified, for what they were witnessing was the start of a momentous era for India's nascent internet ecosystem.

Kalra's decade-old startup, which had weathered a near-death experience after the dotcom crash, was now recording a dream public listing. It would 'pop', as trading lore goes, with its American depository receipts gaining as much as 75 per cent on debut. In India, it was a moment of validation for the internet sector that until then was mostly running on the promise of future riches and few actual payouts. The MMT IPO moved the needle forward significantly. It would raise $70 million by selling

5 million shares to US investors. At an offer price of $14 per share, it was valued at close to $480 million prior to the listing. But after the surge in stock price the valuation jumped to around $800 million.[2]

The Delhi company's dazzle would launch a thousand entrepreneurial dreams back home and stoke even deeper interest in key investors about the potential for digital growth in the South Asian nation. Including Tiger Global's Fixel. The New York firm which had bought a stake in MMT in 2008 earned handsome returns on its investment of about $8 million.

MMT's journey to its IPO had already underlined the depth of the market for internet-based services in India. In 2005, when SAIF Partners made its first investment (MMT was already profitable by then), it coincided with the launch of domestic travel services by the Delhi company. Until then, it had mostly focused on travel bookings for the Indian diaspora. In five years, from 2005 to 2010, the company grew twenty-five-fold with gross bookings leaping from 25 million to 500 million. It went for an IPO on the back of this spectacular growth. Even after it shifted to growth mode, it rarely slipped below negative unit economics and never lost money on a single transaction. Internet entrepreneurs at that time were still learning to wrap their heads around the business model of using investor capital to offer discounts to customers in order to boost growth, while delaying profitability. The unspoken rule then was that a business could discount but not lose money on every transaction. Indian entrepreneurs had only bitten off a small slice of the forbidden apple. It was only after Chinese e-commerce companies built on a gargantuan scale changed the rules for internet commerce in the coming decade that Indian startups followed suit.

So for Kalra the big decision was whether to go the IPO way at all. And if yes, whether to list in India or overseas. As the founder, he was certain about the need for an IPO, and his team wanted to build the company further. However, on the question of where, the MMT board would find itself split down the middle. By then, Info Edge—Naukri.com's parent—had been a public company for four years, having listed in the domestic market. Bikhchandani, the Info Edge founder, was an independent member of MMT's board. But there was a difference in the business profile of the two companies. Naukri offered a hybrid model, combining both offline and online commerce, while MMT had a pure internet-first model.

Kalra felt he needed time to evaluate his options clearly. He asked the company's board to give him a week's time to think. He would use that period to sound out others who had gone down the IPO route, including Mohandas Pai, then CFO of Infosys, which had listed on NASDAQ a decade ago. Finally, he would be convinced that an overseas listing suited his online business better as Indian bourses were not yet well disposed to the idea of loss-making e-commerce ventures chasing growth.

In contrast, in the US market there were models to compare with. Expedia, as well as China's Ctrip, was listed on American markets. Kalra could position his company as the Expedia of India. Once the die was cast, he moved quickly. In February 2010, MMT kicked off meetings with lawyers, bankers and investors, and within six months it was a public company. The listing on 12 August proved to be a dream one, with its stock ending the day at $27, up from the opening price of $14. Indian internet commerce had arrived on the global stage.

Ganesh—who, with Meena, was among the first to dial Kalra and congratulate him—is no mean player himself in the exit stakes. In startup circles, he is referred to as the 'exitpreneur'. At a time when an investment was the prized outcome for a startup founder and an exit for the investor was a rarity, Ganesh had delivered not just one but four exits by the end of 2011.

He had started early. Way back in 1990, as a young IIM graduate he pooled together savings to launch IT&T, which offered computer maintenance and networking services for businesses. The couple, who had met at management school, had good jobs in the IT sector: Ganesh at HCL and Meena at NIIT. Their firstborn was then just a year old.

Much to their family's consternation, Ganesh decided to quit and start up.

Casting around for bank loans, Ganesh quickly realized it would be an uphill climb without assets to offer as collateral. An acquaintance mentioned there was a company in Bengaluru offering venture capital that required no collateral or guarantee in return for funding. Intrigued, the thirty-year-old got on a train and travelled south from Delhi. It was his first trip to the technology city he had heard so much about.

The central Majestic area where his train halted in Bengaluru was home to thirty cinemas, all in one square block. But Ganesh had work to do and made a beeline to the offices of Technology Development Corporation of India. This was India's very first venture capital fund set up as a joint venture between ICICI Ltd and the Unit Trust of India. Ganesh reached there with suitcase in hand and met Kiran Nadkarni, who had moved from ICICI to lead operations, as well as G. Sabarinathan, an IIM professor.

The two found Ganesh's idea of a computer maintenance services business interesting and told him they would offer capital to start up but in return would want 25–30 per cent equity. Hours of discussion later, the rookie entrepreneur remained unconvinced and passed up the chance of venture funding, choosing instead to bootstrap the business. A few years in, he would discover the going was tough. Meena, who had continued with corporate work, had joined Microsoft India in 1995, where she had a five-year stint leading multiple initiatives. Ganesh, meanwhile, went on to head the Wipro and British Telecom joint venture. He kept the business going and eventually sold it to software exporter iGate.

Meanwhile, the internet boom around them was building, and the couple's startup instincts were beginning to stir once more. In 2000, they quit their jobs yet again to start up a second time. Conscious that he had missed the software boom by focusing on providing services for computer hardware maintenance at IT&T, Ganesh was determined to make good this time. He noticed the boom in outsourced technology services and set up Customer Asset as an internet-led venture, which would offer email support and not voice-based services for global companies.

This time, Meena and he decided they would seek venture funding. They raised a first round from the newly launched fund eVentures and kick-started operations. But as luck would have it, the fledgling startup drove right into the global rout in technology businesses. All the internet companies they thought would be their clients 'vaporized' as the impact of the dotcom meltdown became more visible. The couple had to rapidly switch tracks. They went back to the traditional business process outsourcing (BPO) model offering call centre and data-processing services. But this was a capital-intensive model that required far more capital than the young venture had. The chances of raising fresh capital was slim as investors were also rapidly retreating. This meant that negotiating a buyout with a deeper-pocketed competitor was the only way out. Four years after starting up, Customer Asset was acquired by NYSE-listed ICICI Bank and is now publicly listed in India as First Source Solutions.

Meena returned to the corporate world, heading Tesco's back-office operations. The British retailer had turned to India to set up its engineering and technical support, one of scores of global corporations doing so. By then, the couple, who had made Bengaluru their hometown, was making a name as technology entrepreneurs with the skill of garnering handsome exits or returns from each of their startups. While the sale of IT&T had netted them some ₹60 crore, the sale of Customer Asset brought in about $23 million.

Ganesh was well and truly hooked to startup entrepreneurship and looking out to see what he would do next. To think of a new business and the high that comes with the first cheque, the first order or the first customer to him was 'like a drug'. But he was certain he would no longer aim for low-hanging fruit. He went on to cofound a high-end data analytics startup called Marketics with three others in 2003. It offered market research and analysis for some of the world's biggest corporations like Coca-Cola and Procter

& Gamble from centres in Bengaluru and Coimbatore. Four years later when it was sold to BPO giant WNS, the startup fetched a price of $63.5 million. Hawking back-end services had certainly paid off for Ganesh.

He describes himself as an entrepreneur who is passionate about his dreams and foolish enough to believe they will work out. He is also not one to let the grass grow under his feet. Even before the Marketics buyout gathered steam, Ganesh was already on to his fourth venture. It helped also that he was the chairman of the knowledge process outsourcing (KPO) firm while operations were led by other co-founders. This freed up Ganesh, who teamed up with IIM Calcutta classmate Srinivas Anumolu to set up his fourth venture, a unique model offering online education services.

Ganesh's entrepreneurial career until then had been all about providing back-end technology services. This time round, the forty-five-year-old repeat entrepreneur was certain it would be different. He wanted to build a brand from India. Scouting around for an entry point led him to an obvious strength that India offered: education. Internet commerce was all the rage, and Ganesh was not immune to its charms. He combined the two to develop a unique model where Indian teachers would offer online maths tuition to American kids.

It was an idea that quickly found favour with the most exacting of investors, with its first institutional capital coming from blue-chip firm Sequoia Capital. The Silicon Valley firm had merged with a local Indian venture fund called Westbridge Capital and was an aggressive early investor. This first deal set the tone for TutorVista as it provided the venture with enormous validity that Ganesh would parley to great effect.

At an industry event that brought a large contingent of overseas investors and founders to Bengaluru in 2006—akin to what Lilani had earlier helmed—Ganesh met an investor from Lightspeed Venture, another Silicon Valley firm. Half in jest, he quizzed him on whether he was there to see the Taj Mahal or invest in Indian startups. Taken aback, the investor, Ravi Mhatre, asked Ganesh if he was in the market for funds. On being told that TutorVista had just raised money from Sequoia Capital, he urged Ganesh to call while raising the next round. As investor pitches go, this was certainly unique.

Ganesh's unconventional fundraising methods bore more fruit as TutorVista raised over $90 million by the time it was acquired by Pearson. By then, Meena had joined the company and helped launch a series of services focused on the Indian market. This domestic footprint is what drew Pearson to the company and resulted in the $213 million buyout in 2011. The landmark deal would deliver a near sevenfold return on investment for Sequoia Capital, boosting the blue-chip firm's commitment to the fast-growing Indian startup sector.

In a market starved for meaningful exits for VCs, the ebullient Ganesh had carved out a special niche while sealing his reputation as an 'exitpreneur'. It would take another two years before another blockbuster exit further energized the Indian internet sector. The sale of ticketing venture redBus to a larger travel firm, GoIbibo, heralded the real explosion of internet enterprise in the country. If MMT's IPO was the equivalent of a midfield goal, in footballing terms, redBus's sale for $130 million was a blinder from left field. It came at a time when a drought of big-bang returns had led to faltering interest among internet investors. GoIbibo's daring buyout reignited belief in the Indian startup ecosystem and led to a fresh flood of capital from a diverse set of investors in the next two years.

This ebb and flow of investor interest was not something that twenty-six-year-old Phanindra Sama was aware of when he set out to build his bus-ticketing venture way back in 2005. The gold rush of venture capital to India had begun by then. For Sama, the lure of big money was not the hook. It was the inability to get a ticket to ride back home that spurred his startup ambitions. The BITS Pilani graduate, looking for a ticket to get home for Deepavali, was told by every bus operator he approached that they were all sold out.

Low-cost airlines like Air Deccan were selling tickets online; for train tickets, there was the sarkari portal IRCTC; why was there no online portal for bus tickets, he asked his flatmates. Being geeky engineers, they decided to answer the question by designing an online booking service for bus tickets that began as an open-source software platform. Sama and his friends had found a problem and were focused on delivering a solution. Building a business was not what they had originally intended to do. They trudged from one bus operator to another, coaxing them to install the software, only to realize that none of them were interested. Fleet operators gained nothing from what they viewed as new-fangled software; they wanted to sell tickets, not ease the pain of travellers looking to book tickets ahead of time.

Sama was disheartened by the lack of response. But he was still intrigued enough by the swell of enterprise around him to explore further. He signed up for a mentoring session at the newly formed industry grouping the Indus Entrepreneurs (TiE) Network that was just spreading its wings in the country. He had heard of it from chatter at his workplace, Texas Instruments. Much before globalization became a buzzword, this semiconductor major headquartered in Dallas was drawn by India's engineering talent to set up a development centre at Bengaluru in 1985. It was a hotbed of technology research and had seeded entrepreneurial ambitions in scores of its engineers. Most famously, in 2001, its then managing director Srini Rajam quit to launch his own venture-backed video technology services startup, Ittiam. The enterprising Sama had clearly found his way to the right place at the right time.

He signed up for a mentoring session at TiE and met early-stage investor Sanjay Anandaram. This would prove to be a fortuitous development that changed the game for the young engineers from Texas Instruments. Anandaram was a seasoned technology investor. As early as 1998, he had set up a cross-border investment firm, Jumpstartup, which was an early investor in Netkraft, the startup cofounded by Accel's Prakash. As a former Wipro executive, his connections in the technology industry ran deep. He urged Sama to go back and speak to the bus operators and ask them what they actually wanted.

To their surprise, Sama and his team discovered that the bus operators wanted something very simple. 'Khaali hamare tickets bech do,' they were told. That's when the penny dropped for the young engineers. They went back and built a direct-to-consumer system that would allow travellers to book and operators to sell bus tickets online. Thus, redBus was born.

They were still part of the mentoring programme, and TiE had put out their names on its newsletter for members. This resulted in enquiries from three venture capital funds: Sequoia, Seedfund and Yahoo's corporate venture arm. Sama asked his mentor which one to pick. He was directed to Seedfund, a small fund that famously counted Google as one of its limited partners. In addition to an investment, it could also provide time for mentoring that would not be forthcoming from larger setups, he was told.

In his meeting with Bharati Jacob, a partner at Seedfund, Sama asked for ₹30 lakh in return for 30 per cent equity stake in his venture. To his utter amazement, Jacob accepted the offer of 30 per cent equity but in return gave him ₹3 crore. Sama counts that moment as a defining one in the journey of redBus and his own as an entrepreneur. He remembers his folks back home being astounded that somebody who didn't know anything about him—apart from his business plan—and with no collateral requirement was giving him that kind of money. A stranger to Bengaluru who didn't know anybody in the city and had just come there to work, Sama had ended up raising venture capital on the strength of just an idea.

From then, things moved in a blur, at warp speed almost. From a topline of about ₹50 lakh in the first year to ₹5 crore in the second year and ₹30 crore in the third year, redBus declared ₹600 crore of revenue in 2012.

But the founders, with little exposure to how a venture-funded company ran, had literally exchanged one workplace for another. They operated less as entrepreneurs and more as employees, applying for leave and being schooled by the board that the end game for the venture was to provide an exit. To wit, every six months, the startup was bombarded with buyout offers from the exploding line-up of travel portals, from MMT to Cleartrip, Yatra and Travel Guru, all of whom were riding the explosion of interest in online travel services.

But in 2012, business circles were stunned by a legislation introduced by the government that would gain infamy as the retrospective tax. In a clarification to the Income Tax (I-T) Act, 1961, the Centre virtually amended the law to make cross-border transactions such as the $11.08 billion buyout of telecom operator Hutchison Essar by British telecom major Vodafone in 2007 liable for capital gains tax. It seriously dampened the attractiveness of Indian businesses in the eyes of overseas buyers.[3]

So when GoIbibo dangled the bait, the redBus investors were more than inclined to bite. They didn't know when such a meaty offer would come again. The deal was sealed at a value of about $130 million. GoIbibo also came with interesting pedigree. It was backed by South African conglomerate Naspers, best known for its bet on Chinese internet commerce star Tencent. As it happened Naspers would go on to take a bet on India's rising e-commerce startup Flipkart, propelling the Tiger Global–backed firm to unicorn status.

In the hyper-competitive world of global venture capital, these are signs that don't go unnoticed. Naspers's bets spurred an explosion of interest in Indian internet commerce. Asian firms like SoftBank and Alibaba would soon flood Indian startups with billions of dollars, remaking the nascent industry beyond recognition.

Thirty-two-year-old Sama would hang up his boots after the exit. It was the year in which he also welcomed his firstborn. In the ensuing years, the hunt for new things to engage with would take the entrepreneur far, including a stint as chief technology officer (CTO) of his home state, Telangana. He also signed up for a continuing education module at Stanford University and did a deep dive into mentoring entrepreneurs and in philanthropy. It was exhilarating stuff for the engineer who unlike most peers had well and truly made his fortune and retired in his early thirties. So much so that his wife would remark that his young son had never seen 'daddy go to office in the morning'.

The redBus imprint is unique because it took the story of Indian internet commerce global in a way that few other startups have done. At a time when the goal for an entrepreneur was to build the Google of India or the Amazon of India, redBus carved out a different niche, one that other founders in Southeast Asia, Africa and even the US have gone on to emulate. This has given rise to the phrases 'redBus of America' and 'redBus of Africa'.

To onlookers, it could well appear that the country's nascent startup industry had dropped down a rabbit hole into an alternate universe, one of irrational optimism. However, the redBus saga was born out of the forces of disintermediation being let loose by the internet. This tectonic shift was moving the Indian retail consumer to the centre of the technology universe, just as it was doing for customers across the globe. Coupled with the lower cost of starting up, this shift to internet-led entrepreneurship would open the doors for thousands from the Indian middle class, who now had a realistic chance to be their own boss. Just as it had for Sama.

India in 2013 was at the cusp of transformational change. The national debate had shifted to impatience with the status quo and a rising hunger for change that could help millions more benefit from the demographic advantage that had long been touted as the country's trump card.

The 1991 reforms had pulled millions out of poverty and into the middle class. The United Nations Development Programme (UNDP) estimated that 271 million Indians were lifted out of extreme poverty between 2005–06 and 2015–16.[4] Coupled with the coming of the internet, the period from 1991 to the noughties and beyond had stoked the creation of—among other things—the $150 billion IT services industry, and brought mobile phones into the hands of over 500 million Indians.

While these tectonic shifts were underway, a new generation of twenty-somethings had come of age. They carried no legacy, no awareness of the licence permit raj or of shortages. They were the 'have cash, must spend' generation, or 'have an idea, want to startup' tribe. The line 'the first paycheque is equal to Dad's final one' no longer made sense for this generation of Indians. Their dreams, ambitions and goals were of a different order, steeped in global mores and fired by ambition that would not wait. They were about changing the world and dominating it. To them, Cisco was not meant to change the world, Tesla was.

On the ground, there were a minefield of challenges. Capital was turning scarce, internet penetration stayed on a slow track and regulatory overhang lengthened. In the 2013 Union Budget, Finance Minister Palanivel Chidambaram used the word 'startup' while announcing a series of measures for the sector. It was the first official nod to a bubbling cauldron of activity, enterprise and energy.

Globally, it was the year of the infamous taper tantrums, the collective panic that gripped markets the world over when the American Federal Reserve began to gradually ease the quantitative easing that had pumped money into the economy following the Lehman Brothers bankruptcy in 2008. Estimates showed that between 2008 and 2013, the Fed had tripled the size of its balance sheet from around \$1 trillion to around \$3 trillion by purchasing almost \$2 trillion in Treasury bonds and other financial assets to prop up the market.[5] The threat of a pullback from this policy led to investors exiting emerging markets, including India. The rupee fell by over 15 per cent between late May and late August 2013. This forced the Reserve Bank of India (RBI) to raise interest rates to try to stem the outflow.[6]

In the startup world, it led to a drying up of what had once been plentiful risk capital. So much so that the plethora of Silicon Valley funds that had made a beeline to the country in 2007 quite unceremoniously packed up to leave. Among those who left were Canaan, KPCB and Sherpalo Ventures, led by the famed Indian American Ram Shriram, best known for his early bet on Google.

For everyone who left, however, there was still a second and a third investor waiting in the wings—the lure of India never dimmed. Speaking to *The Economic Times* in 2013, Vinod Khosla, the famed Silicon Valley investor, said, 'India is very nascent when it comes to startups. There's a lot more work to be done in the way of developing an ecosystem that supports entrepreneurship, from having enough investors willing to take risks to veteran entrepreneurs who have been around the block providing mentorship and guidance.'

But it was what he said in closing that sums up the zeitgeist of those times. 'One extremely powerful thing that India does have is talent. There's a new breed of young, bright, ambitious, and socially minded techies.'

5

The Gig Economy

In the India of 2010, young engineers with savings in the bank and a cohort of like-minded friends would most likely dream of just one thing: starting up. Twenty-four-year-old Sahil Barua was no different. He had spent a couple of years working at Bain Consulting and the prospect of rising through its ranks did not excite him. He had no clear idea of what else he wanted to do. But the thought of working with friends to build something new was an exciting prospect. So he quit, along with two colleagues, Mohit Tandon and Suraj Saharan. Barua already had a management degree from IIM Bangalore while Tandon and Saharan, IIT graduates, were of a mind to go back to management school. The next six months were spent exploring different ideas and writing essays for business school admissions. They were testing the waters while also keeping an eye out for what peers were doing.

Just months before they quit, two seniors from Bain, Deepinder Goyal and Pankaj Chaddha, had also left to start up. They had been struck by the demand for restaurant menus and food ordering by colleagues while at work. Sensing an opportunity, Goyal and Chadha had set up FoodieBay, a restaurant listing website. They were catering to a new customer base that was developing across urban centres. For the first time in independent India, there was the perfect confluence of a young, globally aware population which had cash in hand and was keen to spend. In the country's technology hot spots—Bengaluru, Pune, Chennai, Hyderabad, Gurugram and Powai—a growing number of millennials were focused on instant, not deferred, gratification. This was a cohort that didn't want to wait before it began spending on eating out, holidays, apparel and gadgets. The reigning mantra was 'have money, will spend'.

This fundamental sociological shift underpinned the explosion of entrepreneurial energy in the decade ahead. It triggered the launch of hundreds of ventures that aimed to satiate this voracious appetite for everything from consumer goods to lifestyle products and financial, educational and entertainment services.

Barua and his friends gravitated to Gurugram, where they met Goyal. The FoodieBay team had raised seed funding from Bikhchandani's Info Edge and moved from operating in an apartment to a small office. Barua recalls quizzing Goyal and Chaddha about why they were stopping at linking customers and restaurants. Why not deliver the food also, he asked. But the two entrepreneurs were vehement in their assertion that they were not inclined to travel down that road as it would mean owning the entire customer experience. Conceding the argument, Barua posed a further question. If he and his friends were to set up a back-end delivery service, would they introduce them to the restaurants on their website? Goyal and Chaddha agreed to do so, marking the launch of a pure-play food delivery company called Delhivery.

They began by taking orders on the phone, relaying them to restaurants, picking them up and delivering to the customer. They would do about half a dozen orders a day. 'We were Swiggy on a telephone' is how Barua describes those salad days. Soon the service would begin to be recognized locally.

As luck would have it, one of two people who would alter the trajectory of the fledgling startup arrived in Gurugram. Abhishek Goyal, best known as the sutradhaar who urged Accel to make the first seed investment in Flipkart, had quit the venture firm. He was starting up on his own and had set up a lifestyle e-commerce venture aimed at women called Urban Touch. He needed a quick and efficient delivery network and asked Barua and his friends if they were game. His thesis was simple. If the Delhivery team could deliver food in thirty minutes, they could also deliver shipments from his warehouse in Sector 44 to neighbourhood customers. Barua's company picked up the gauntlet and they were off.

By then, the team was already engaging with investors ranging from Canaan Partners to Sequoia Capital. But the crucial break came from a meeting with Anshoo Sharma of Lightspeed Venture, who too was a senior from Bain. He pointed out that delivering just food was not the big game; it was delivering for the exploding e-commerce market.

Clearly, e-commerce was going to be the big game for the decade. The latest funding round for Flipkart was all the news. Equally clear was the yawning gap in the entire e-commerce cycle from warehouse to customer. The journey from computer screen to doorstep was yet to be figured out. Not least by the logistics companies tasked with taking orders to customers. Even the Bansals, when they began in 2007, had picked books as the commodity of least resistance; one that courier companies would agree to deliver without complaint. India Plaza, the original competitor to Flipkart, was best known for its selection of books online much before the Bansals had even thought up a name for their 'everything store'. However, by 2011, more than just books were zipping along on the e-commerce highways. Smartphones at crazy discounts were fast emerging as the top-selling product on these sites, along with a variety of other consumables, clothes and electronic gadgets. The need for a robust e-commerce delivery network was crystal clear. The picks and shovels were growing to be as important as they were in the original California Gold Rush.

Intrigued, the nerdy founders at Delhivery began thinking of the structure for an e-commerce delivery network at a first-principle level. The food-delivery business would go on. Alongside, the team—now numbering five founders—was working on preparing a 'mathematical paper' for a logistics network for India. It helped that they had the experience of working on a similar sort of problem while at Bain. Where should a telecom tower be placed to provide maximum coverage was the question they had been tasked to answer as India embarked on a massive phase of telecom expansion in the final years of the noughties.[1]

Barua and his team soon realized that the plan for a telecom, networking and communication infrastructure rollout had several similarities to rolling out a logistics network for the country. They debated the problem, wrote the solution and in six months had a paper ready. The question then was how to execute and test it. For instance, among the challenges that kept Barua awake at night was the thought of the taxation and regulatory compliances he would have to navigate with delivering across India. This was the pre-GST era, and waiting for GST to kick in was like waiting for Godot.[2]

Even in the absence of a national tax framework, a logistics network for e-commerce was still possible. So the team dived into it while keeping the plan for a general all-purpose network on hold. Next up they needed cash to start up. They met multiple investors, only to be blown off by either their disbelief in the size of the opportunity and its feasibility or their scepticism about the capability of a bunch of twenty-five-year-olds to pull it off.

Determined to start up, Barua and team pooled in collective savings of ₹10 lakh apiece. Goyal came in with an additional ₹5 lakh as an angel investment, playing a part much like he did with Flipkart. Barua describes Goyal as the 'chess master who saw trends playing out long before anybody else did' in the Indian internet saga.

The team had technically raised a seed round of about $100,000, 95 per cent of which came from the founders themselves. They went on to bootstrap the venture for another eighteen months before receiving their first institutional investment from Times Internet. On the ground, though, the team discovered that execution was as complex as what some of the early investors who had reviewed their business plan had told them. Barua points to missteps such as a poor understanding of local regulations, where to position and build warehouses, deal with the police, worker strikes and a plethora of other challenges that led to the learning curve being quite steep right up until 2015. To test their mettle, they chose to build their first network outside Gurugram, in Chennai, a city where they didn't know anyone, or the language and customs. Seeing that business stabilize is now counted as a milestone in the company's early journey.

By then, Nexus Capital, led by Suvir Sujan, had also invested in the company. But the high point, as Barua sees it, came when Renuka Ramnath–led Multiples Asset Management closed a $35 million round in early 2014. A seasoned private equity investor, Ramnath is credited with having turned ICICI Venture into a name to reckon with in the Indian risk capital industry. For Barua, she was an uber investor to have on Delhivery's cap table. He travelled to Mumbai to meet her and was offered dinner at her office after the discussions. Ramnath closed the meeting by telling Barua that she would get back to him. But within half an hour, she called to say that she was ready to invest $35 million in the company. An ecstatic Barua, who had travelled without his co-founders for the meeting, called them all up immediately. In the absence of a video-conference facility, the group of five co-founders dialled in from individual locations to raise a toast that night. It wasn't a premature celebration.

Close on the heels of the Multiples investment, Fixel himself took his first bet on the company. He led an investment round of $85 million, putting in about $60 million in the company that was then valued at close to $300 million. Boosted by the investor validation, the Delhivery team made their first big hire, bringing in their former boss from Bain, Sandeep Barasia, as co-managing director. This combination of young founders, senior managers and blue-chip investors would drive this small company to become one of India's largest e-commerce logistics networks in quick time.

Meanwhile, also in Gurugram, the Foodie Bay founders had gone through their own cycle of evolution. A year after Goyal, Chadha and a third co-founder, Gunjan Patidar, had quit their jobs to focus on the startup, it had 8,000 restaurants across five Indian cities on the website, as well as a first round of venture investment. Fired by the promise, Goyal was looking to go international and offer more than just restaurant listings on the site. The goal was to build a recommendation engine that would throw up best options for home delivery, dining out and even where to find the best places to go to for an evening's entertainment. With ambitions beyond food, the founders renamed the company Zomato in late 2010.

In quick succession, it raised the next round of funding from Info Edge, and in 2013 again raised a $37 million round that would power its international expansion plans. With money at his disposal, Goyal listed a target of twenty-two countries where he planned to launch Zomato's services. The startup had already begun drawing about a third of its traffic from overseas markets, including the UAE and the UK. It was not just its global ambitions that made the company unique; it was also reporting profits in specific markets, including on home territory. As a restaurant discovery service, it was adding features such as one to help users find a particular dish in a restaurant. This was an addition to its original startup model where menus collected from restaurants would be scanned and uploaded on to its website for consumers to choose from. Now, they could parse through photos and costing for specific eateries, and leave reviews and ratings. So much so that by the time of the initial Sequoia investment, Zomato's founders would maintain that theirs was a business of 'search', that their company was in the 'business of Google for food'.[3]

The young company was also focused on rapidly expanding its footprint to gain scale. India's urban markets, limited to a few of the top metros at that time, offered a finite market opportunity. To acquire scale with its core offering of restaurant discovery, Zomato had to look outward. It aggressively cast its net overseas. In addition to the score of countries it operated in, the big target was to launch in the United States. Goyal was acutely aware of the challenge of entering a sophisticated consumer market like the US where he would have to go head-on with market leader Yelp, a publicly listed company that connects people with local businesses. Meanwhile, he went on an aggressive buying spree in other markets worldwide to gain size and prepare for the upcoming battle in the US. In one breathless wave, the Gurugram company acquired Italian search service Cibando, Menu Mania in New Zealand, Lunchtime in the Czech Republic, Obedovat in Slovakia and Gastronauci in Poland in the final months of 2014. In November 2014, it also raised further capital with a new funding round of up to $60 million. This added further heft to its buying power.

Since the time of Zomato, Goyal has cultivated a direct line of communication with customers. Every new company development would be conveyed through blogs written in his trademark chatty style or later through witty posts and threads on Twitter. In the midst of the company's gigantic shopping spree in 2014, he told his readers that Zomato was built to foster 'conversations over great meals'.[4] From his perspective, the startup had grown from just restaurant discovery and menus to a 'vast global community driven by social interactions'.

In January 2015, he splashed nearly all the money raised months ago to enter the US market in style—by acquiring Urbanspoon. For this Indian company with outsize global ambitions, the buyout came with more than just the key to the US and Canadian markets. The website and mobile application listed information and reviews on restaurants in six other countries. In one swoop, the company had expanded nearly threefold. The deal was widely pegged as the largest buyout of an American venture by an Indian internet startup, heralding the growing maturity as well as ambition of the country's technology entrepreneurs. Zomato, with its aggressive global rollout, played a huge role in spreading the word that India was a startup nation on the move.

For the company, this rapid pace—Urbanspoon was its sixth buyout in six months—would bring up challenges of integration. By 2016, Zomato found that it had spread itself too thin, being in a battle with competitors across multiple markets. By its own admission, it was caught between taking on entrenched rivals and building new markets by changing user behaviour.[5] More ominously for the company, even as it was traversing the globe, back home an interesting rival was taking shape.

Sriharsha Majety is in many ways an archetypal example of the societal upheaval that was underway in the mid-2010s. India was by then wide awake to the power of the internet. Consumers had sampled the delights of buying online and hailing cabs to their doorstep, and were in the mood for more. Twenty-eight-year-old Majety, who graduated from the Birla Institute of Technology in Pilani, was the son of a doctor who ran her own clinic and an entrepreneur with his own restaurant in Vijayawada. Growing up, he noticed with keen appreciation the freedom his parents enjoyed from being self-employed. The freedom to make one's own choices was something that his college would also foster. Widely regarded as the bastion of counterculture, BITS famously does not require students to log in attendance. It was situated nearly 300 km from the nearest urban hot spots, with students perforce having to learn to entertain themselves. Majety would dabble in quizzing and photography and develop a taste for travel, beginning with exploring Rajasthan in groups, then backpacking and finally travelling solo. Opting out of campus placements, he dipped into the ₹40,000 he had earned from an internship to travel alone through Southeast Asia. He met people who were doing likewise, picking up new skills or taking a gap year and learning new arts, all of which fascinated the young engineer.[6]

On his return, he opted for an MBA at IIM Calcutta. He ran the campus placement committee there, which gave him a chance to hone his negotiation skills and manage complexity and chaos. He was hired by the investment bank Nomura International, where he got the opportunity to test his financial mettle in London. He stayed for a year on the trading desk to discover that London was fun but the job not so much. He needed more exciting work to get stuck into. In August 2012, he took the hard decision to return to India with no clear plan about the future.

As he had done before, he again turned to travel to find the answers. The next six months delivered the best trip of his life. First on a bicycle and later through a mix of backpacking and hitchhiking, he travelled solo from Portugal to Turkey, a journey of some 4,000 km, and from there on to Kazakhstan. It was certainly not a trip without incident. In fact, he received the first and most exacting jolt on the very first day of the journey.

In the scorching heat of the Mediterranean—45 degrees in the sun—Majety found himself completely dehydrated and way off course within just 30 km of starting out. His host during that leg, a local farmer, drove some 60 km to pick him up and provide sustenance for the next few days. Majety would recoup by harvesting beans on his host's farm while gathering strength and courage to return to the road. He learnt to stop worrying about the risk and instead began worrying about how to enjoy the trip—a lesson that would come in handy on his return when he dived straight into the cauldron of Indian internet commerce.

Once back home, Majety began tapping into his network. No one within his immediate circle was starting up. But someone he knew very well had done so to great effect. redBus founder Phanindra Sama, a senior from BITS Pilani, had just closed one of the biggest exits for the Indian internet startups of that time. He had sold it to global travel firm GoIbibo for an enterprise value of $130 million.[7] The bumper exit offered early validation of the internet opportunity in India. For those looking to found their own startups, Sama had emerged as a role model. Even better, from Majety's perspective, Sama had been a fellow member of a hallowed club on campus, the Department of Photography—or 'Dopey' in Pilani jargon. As had another friend, Nandan Reddy, two years Majety's junior. Majety began 'jamming' with both, looking for ideas to start up with. While Sama's was an outside-in view, for Reddy, the stakes were higher. He formally teamed up with Majety to set off on an entrepreneurial journey.

E-commerce was the flavour of the season, but all the consumer internet bets appeared taken. Flipkart had raised about $360 million in 2013, led by South African conglomerate Naspers. It was then valued at $1.6 billion. Snapdeal, which was the marketplace incumbent, had also received an ₹830 crore fund infusion from investors led by US e-commerce marketplace eBay. Amazon, after testing the waters with comparison site Junglee, had launched e-commerce operations in India in June 2013. In a little under a year, it had expanded into eighteen product categories and was setting up logistics and warehouse facilities across the country.

To find an entry point into this world, Majety and Reddy turned to B2B commerce. They soon discovered that there were millions of small enterprises looking to sell to other businesses online. These companies required logistics, payments and marketing support. Typically, they would have their own websites and attempt to attract traffic to it on their own. Often, they would struggle to connect with logistics providers. And if they did, they were unable to negotiate best prices.

Majety and Reddy realized there was a robust opportunity here to build a logistics network for businesses looking to go online—one that could quickly ship from 'Salem to Darjeeling'.[8] They pooled resources and set up Bundl Technologies. In the coming months, they spent time in Hyderabad looking for a third co-founder who could build out the technology backbone of the company. Meanwhile, the duo would focus on sales. But nine months after starting out, they realized they were not getting anywhere. The opportunity cost of turning dross into gold was way too high. The two had a frugal operation, had no investors and no other liabilities. It was easy to cut their losses and shut shop. It was a decision the two young entrepreneurs would go on to rate as one of their best.

The failed venture provided them with perfect clarity on what they were best suited for: the consumer internet business. They had by then moved to Bengaluru in search of technology talent. Reddy briefly considered retuning to the job market while Majety began hunting out new ideas once more. He had learnt a few things by then. He knew the business he wanted to start must be at the intersection of logistics and technology, and that it must create customer delight.

It was 2014, and the ride-hailing space was in full swing across Indian metros. At the push of a button, consumers could summon a cab to their doorstep. Majety was struck by this and wondered why consumers couldn't press a button and order food that would arrive in quick time too.

E-commerce deliveries at that point could take up to three to five shipping days. A super-fast urban delivery service was clearly a requirement. Globally, this was something that China's Meituan, for instance, was already doing. Closer home, Domino's was delivering food at speed in hyperlocal markets. In June 2014, Reddy and Majety began work on a new hyperlocal delivery startup.

The goal was to build a consumer-focused intracity delivery service for anything ranging from food, grocery to pharmacy. As bachelors, they knew first-hand the demand for quick food delivery. They also knew that if they were to build a food-delivery platform as a logistics-first business they could crack the problem.

Over a couple of beers at the popular Arbor Brewery in downtown Bengaluru, they firmed up the name: Swiggy. It was designed as a logistics company that would use technology to create consumer delight. They would sign up fifteen to sixteen restaurants, hire five or six delivery partners and use the city's startup hub Koramangala as a test-bed to begin from. Majety and Reddy began handing out pamphlets announcing their service around the neighbourhood college, Jyoti Nivas. One day, they asked a friend who worked at Flipkart to post these details on the company's internal messaging system. Within days, this raised thirty-odd queries. The demand was becoming startlingly clear to the founders.

Soon word of this quick and smooth food-delivery service travelled to the office of venture capitalists Accel, also located in Koramangala. There, a partner, Anand Daniel, immediately smelled a new opportunity. He was just coming off an intense few months where his early investment in the cab rental service TaxiforSure had closed with a mega buyout. Ola had acquired its local rival, turning India's ride-hailing business into a two-pronged race between itself and Uber.

Daniel had been looking for the next opportunity when he heard about Swiggy. The idea was fresh and the execution simple and effective, with the team doing about a hundred deliveries a day. Majety also provided a clear view of how the business could earn profits at the unit level even while scaling up.

The VC looked around for overseas matches but was hard-pressed to locate any other. At home, Zomato was still a search and marketing platform. The idea of food delivered hot in thirty minutes was an exciting idea for someone accustomed to waiting for over an hour and a half for lunch to be delivered after church every Sunday. Swiggy was offering trust and convenience at a price point that was affordable. Others were sniffing around the startup too, including SAIF Partners, one of the earliest investors in Indian internet. Daniel moved quickly once he heard of SAIF's interest, and the two funds together took the first seed bet on Swiggy.

Coming as it did on the back of the huge taxi app wave that was taking off in India, Swiggy's advent would open the doors to the gig economy. Within a year, the business had grown to about 3,000 orders a day. From employing thirty to forty people, it had a workforce in the hundreds within six months. A third co-founder, Rahul Jaimini, also joined the young team as its CTO. Looking at the rear-view mirror, Majety later pointed to missteps on the way, including the delay in hiring a CFO. In a 2020 podcast beamed by Accel, Majety described the early days at Swiggy as 'a bit of the Wild West', conceding that it could have done with more financial prudence.

Elsewhere, in a rough industrial suburb of Delhi, a very different kind of company was taking shape, one where the founder quizzed a prospective investor on why he wanted to back his startup. It was the start of 2015, and Abhinav Chaturvedi, a partner at Accel, had set up a call with a co-founder whose pitch he had found interesting. He was returning from the US and had asked for an early-morning call. A few minutes in, Chaturvedi found himself standing up to continue the conversation, so taken was he by the level of preparedness and clarity from the caller, Varun Khaitan. Along with his co-founders, Khaitan was aggregating informal home and personal services on a digital platform they would call UrbanClap, now known as Urban Company. Chaturvedi, looking to move quickly, offered to set up a video call with his partners at Accel India as the startup was a Delhi-based venture.

Instead, the founders—Khaitan, CEO Abhiraj Singh Bhal and CTO Raghav Chandra—said they would travel south to meet the Accel team in person.[9] Their plan to offer an asset-light marketplace with services across some fifty to seventy verticals—ranging from carpenters, electricians, technicians, beauty and grooming services to home-building, wedding and event management—found immediate favour. This was the height of the internet commerce wave in India and massive unorganized businesses were all being aggregated online.

To speed up the engagement, Accel dispatched Chaturvedi for an on-ground recce of UrbanClap's office in Delhi for a due diligence of the startup's technology stack. Landing at the 110 square foot office in Bhikaiji Cama Place, Chaturvedi was asked to find a seat in a room that could seat only four—there wasn't place for a fifth. Soon Bhal rounded up the group and offered to buy them lunch, which to Chaturvedi's further surprise was chhole kulche at a dhaba where truckers and others were eating too. Along the way, he was asked by Bhal why he wanted to work with them and invest in their startup.

Bhal didn't start out being contrarian. The son of a naval officer who grew up in Tirunelveli, Visakhapatnam and Mumbai, he had ticked all the right boxes: a degree from IIT Kanpur, followed by one from IIM Ahmedabad, and a consulting job at BCG in Mumbai as his first job. It was only three years after that textbook start that he decided to re-evaluate his choices. His proposition was simple: he wanted to be the one building the next Fortune 500 company, and not the one consulting for them.

It was a shift in perspective that had been building up. A sporty kid growing up, he had landed in IIT as a matter of routine. His father, grandfather as well as his sister were all engineers. But once there, he found this path held no special appeal for him. He graduated in the middle of his class and remained in search of what to do next. It was the stint at management school, where he worked sixteen hours a day, and finally the stint at BCG that changed his worldview. Thrown into close proximity with some of the world's biggest corporate leaders, he discovered that everyone had started somewhere small, as he would recount in an industry podcast.[10]

Bhal renewed conversations with dear friend and IIT college mate Khaitan, who was also working at BCG in New York. They soon came around to appreciate that value creation could happen by starting an enterprise. Bhal lists two big gains from the BCG stint that he terms as his 'real world MBA': a toolkit for structured problem-solving and the confidence to engage with anyone on equal terms.

Quitting their consulting jobs, the two of them returned to India and started tooling around with different ideas. Six months on, they were introduced to Raghav Chandra, an engineer from the University of California at Berkeley who had worked as an engineer at Twitter. Chandra was trying to start up too. The unemployed startup aspirants gathered in a living room and began throwing out ideas.

With one failed venture each, they were extra careful about which space to choose next. It had to offer a large market opportunity. They soon gravitated towards the home and personal services market and spent a lot of time trying to understand problems on the ground while speaking to customers and service providers.

Consumers wanted reliable and efficient services. Meanwhile, the plumber, carpenter and mason were shackled by middlemen in a low-margin business. They were demotivated and could earn only so much as ₹10,000–₹15000 every month. Bhal and his co-founders realized this was a perfect seeding ground for a tech-enabled marketplace. For sure, there were at least twenty others attempting to do the same thing, but none of them had built the scale that these founders were seeking.

Accel and Elevation Capital (then Saif Partners) backed the founders on the strength of the idea and the potential of the team.

Bhal and his co-founders were off. The all-purpose marketplace offering services across some fifty to seventy verticals would scale rapidly. It was a deeply fragmented market that could keep them busy for decades. By the end of 2015, the startup would have soaked up nearly half of all funding directed at hyperlocal startups. It raised $35 million in three rounds out of an industry total of $75 million raised by the sector overall.

Then something remarkable began to take shape. Business was growing at a steady trot; there was money in the bank and calm in the boardroom. But the founders knew that to build for the future they would have to disrupt themselves. Instead of being all things to all people, the company decided to concentrate on five core business lines. To test the argument, they picked beauty services, which had repeat customers every six weeks, compared to five years for home-painting and maybe a year or so for home improvements.

The business boomed from zero to a few million dollars in record time. The company bit the bullet and put an end to its original model that accounted for 50 per cent of revenue. It went all out in across four categories: beauty, appliance repair, handymen and cleaning service.

From then on, it was rapid growth, with international expansion to the Middle East in 2018 and Singapore in 2020. In January 2020, it rebranded itself as Urban Company.[11] To investors, it was a was a 'no-drama company' that only focused on execution, not promises to execute. But it was the impact it had on India's rapidly evolving gig economy that makes this one of the country's most consequential internet startups. Working directly with beauticians, electricians and carpenters on its platform, it allows them to retain 75 per cent of what the consumer pays and not the minuscule 10–15 per cent that a contactor would have given. Its stated goal is to provide a middle-class income for these gig workers, nearly a third of whom are women.

If India's gig economy expands to be worth $455 billion by 2023—as forecast by industry groupings—Urban Company, would have played a key part in priming its growth.

Part II:

2003–18

6

The Big-Money Game

There are years when nothing much happens. Then comes a year after which nothing remains the same again. For India and for Indian startups, 2014 was one such year.

It began quietly enough, with talk of a possible union between online retailer Flipkart and fashion portal Myntra. It wasn't only that a trio of Bansals helmed these businesses; they also had common investors. Very influential investors at that, who were keen to see the two companies join forces. And they wanted it to happen sooner rather than later. Fashion was becoming the most sticky of all online commerce categories. Consumers were flocking to buy branded clothing at hefty discounts and were also picking up sizeable numbers of trendy private-label designs sold exclusively with robust margins. Electronics and mobile phones brought in the big volumes for e-commerce platforms but at a high cost, while fashion offered the chance of breaking even. India's e-commerce contest was shaping up to be a three-cornered race—led by Flipkart, Amazon and Snapdeal. All three were shopping around for a fashion portal that could lend ballast to their corner.

Myntra's Bansal, backed by his early investors—IndoUS Venture Partners and IDG Ventures—had other ideas, though. In the previous two years, Indian startups had weathered a slowdown in venture capital inflow into the country. But for Myntra, money was available, even if not in plenty. Tiger Global's Fixel, who first invested in Myntra in 2012 and followed up with another round in 2013, stepped in with a bridge round of financing for the fast-growing company. The question for Bansal, therefore, was whether to brave it through the winter knowing that summer will arrive or accept the shelter proffered by a larger rival. There was also the looming threat posed by Amazon, which was becoming increasingly aggressive in the Indian market. In just over a year since it went live with its marketplace in June 2013, the US online retail giant had launched twenty-eight categories of products, hosting about 8,500 merchants.[1]

To hold his own, Myntra's Bansal needed to keep raising ever-larger rounds of financing at regular intervals, just as its larger suitor Flipkart was doing. Towards the end of 2013, Mukesh Bansal met up with Flipkart's Sachin Bansal and then IDG Ventures' Sudhir Sethi at a suburban hotel. The Grand Mercure in Bengaluru's Koramangala is tucked away in a quiet lane. But on any given day, its coffee shop is abuzz with the chatter of valuations, funding, hiring and more as founders and investors gravitate there to negotiate away from prying eyes. It was no different for the Bansals and Sethi who met at a corner table in the hotel's patio.

Sethi, a bustling man with over two decades of experience in venture-investing, was no stranger to the cut and thrust of dealmaking. He had earned a management degree at Delhi and then put in a twelve-year stint at Wipro Limited that left him steeped in knowledge of the global technology services space. And as the first wave of internet enterprise blew into India, Sethi was among the first to move into the sunrise sector of venture-investing. He became the country manager for Walden International, a Silicon Valley firm that was one of the earliest to set up an Indian arm. By 2006, Sethi moved again to lead IDG Ventures as it joined the gold rush of venture funds chasing the Indian startup dream. Along with Vani Kola of IndoUS Venture, he took the very first bet on Myntra, investing as early as 2008 when the startup was still a personalized gifting portal. So, at the negotiating table with the Bansals, he came with both industry heft and a real stake to ensure the fashion portal got its due.

From a starting price of $190 million, the negotiations continued for nearly nine months. Myntra was battling challenges ranging from supply-chain disruptions to the need for big money for the battles ahead. But the attractiveness of the portal was only growing stronger. Premji Invest, the family office of the Wipro founder-chairman Azim Premji, was among those drawn to its promise. In January 2014, the firm led a $50 million round in the company, valuing Myntra at a little over $200 million.[2]

That round also saw the entry of Belgium-based family office Sofina on to the Myntra cap table, months after it had invested in Flipkart. The taps were opening for venture capital into India, yet again. Emboldened, in February, the fashion retailer entered the market for another round of funding, this time for up to $40 million. All this while the two biggest investors in the company, Accel Partners and Fixel's Tiger Global, stayed away from the nitty-gritty of the negotiations with Flipkart, with good reason. They were top investors in both companies, and while they favoured a merger, the decision by their rulebook had to be made by the founder himself. So Myntra board meetings would end up being awkward occasions with only Sethi, Kola and Bansal taking part, while Fixel and Accel's Subrata Mitra would stay at arm's length.

As the weeks sped by and Myntra's value was being reset with cash infusions from eager investors, Flipkart was in a hurry to close the deal. The asking price reportedly rose to $370 million, but the companies did not publicly disclose the sale value when it was finally sealed in May 2014. It was the biggest e-commerce purchase of its time, and it cemented Flipkart's position as the country's largest online retailer.[3]

Although it was a 100 per cent buyout, Mukesh Bansal and his team continued to run Myntra as an independent entity. They brought in a hip, new fashion quotient to the parent company. At a fashion show hosted by Myntra, Flipkart's Bansals were coaxed to walk the ramp. To be sure, fashion is fun, but for e-commerce companies its worth is derived from the hard cash it brings to the business—something that even Amazon would become keenly aware of. The US company sent out feelers to the only other fashion portal of note in the market: Jabong. With the coming of the festive season, it threw out the lure of a buyout. Jabong, which was backed by the German technology investment firm Rocket Internet, didn't take the bait. Amazon's fashion dreams had to be on hold.[4]

Two years later, the Flipkart–Myntra combine kept the Jeff Bezos–led company successfully at bay in a renewed contest for the portal. Making a late entry, Flipkart executives sealed the deal in a record three days, paying just $70 million for Jabong.[5]

The Indian e-commerce company's dominance over the online fashion retail market was complete.

So how did winning become a habit at Flipkart? Sure, the Bansals were talented, they attracted the right amounts of capital at the right time and found a powerful mentor in Fixel. But much of the company's early success can be traced back to two unique initiatives begun just three years after starting up. At that time, Indians were buying online, but barely a fraction of the population had credit cards. For an e-commerce company, this was not an optimum situation. Determined to break through, Flipkart offered customers the option to pay by cash-on-delivery at their doorstep. It was a gamble that paid off bigtime for the young company, and what's more, it established online commerce as a viable retail channel. So much so that even a decade later, in 2022, when digital payments were a common byword, nearly 50 per cent of all e-commerce purchases in the country were still being paid for in cash. For Flipkart, it also led to their second innovation, an in-house logistics network that could handle cash and ensure top-drawer customer service. From a pilot programme tested out in small neighbourhoods, the eKart delivery service soon became a mainstay of the Flipkart brand.

Introducing cash-on-delivery in a market where credit-card penetration was low and digital payments were yet to earn the trust of consumers was the big game-changer for the business. But the scale it unlocked for both Flipkart and Indian internet commerce also led to unintended consequences. For a while, brick-and-mortar retailers had been complaining that e-commerce portals were enjoying an unfair advantage. It was alleged that the portals stocked inventory in contravention of FDI rules that prevent those with overseas capital from selling directly to Indians. In 2013, the Enforcement Directorate began an investigation into Flipkart. That company, founded by Sachin and Binny Bansal in 2009, accounted for a large share of Flipkart's revenue in the early years. Following the regulatory scrutiny and the need to gain full compliance with the law, Flipkart transformed its original inventory-led business model into an online marketplace in 2013.

These run-ins with regulators took their toll on the founders. Sachin largely withdrew from everyday operations to focus on the investigation, leaving the running of the company to Binny. It was also during this phase that a top executive from its investor Tiger Global, Kalyan Krishnamurthy, was appointed as the company's interim sales chief and finance head.

Despite the regulatory overhang, on the ground, business was growing at a blinding pace. This was both a measure of the vibrancy in the Indian e-commerce space and the momentum the young startup had built. In 2014, the Indian e-commerce market was estimated to be worth $14 billion, a near-fourfold increase from the base of $3.8 billion in 2009 when the Bansals were starting out. To be sure, online travel services still dominated the sector, accounting for an overwhelming 70 per cent of market share. But the key statistic for number-crunchers was the fast pace being set by the online retail segment. From accounting for just a tenth of all e-commerce sales in 2009, online retail was clocking 18 per cent share by 2013. Without question, it was Flipkart that was driving a huge chunk of that growth.

In March 2014, Flipkart said it had recorded $1 billion in gross merchandise value or GMV. It was a milestone for the young company. And for a bemused audience, it marked the introduction to a term that typifies the 'growth now, profit later' mantra of internet commerce. Online retailers would measure themselves by the gross value of merchandise sold on their platforms. This number denotes the scale and size of a business. Flipkart had notched up the magic $1 billion GMV number a year ahead of its own forecast. Myntra and Snapdeal, meanwhile, said they too would reach that milestone in 2015. India's e-commerce sector was growing at a red-hot pace.

In turn, it was providing validation for the methods employed by Tiger Global's Fixel. The dominant internet investor of that period, he had sunk nearly $1 billion into a slew of startups from Flipkart to Myntra, Ola, Freshworks and more. He had been investing in India for nearly seven years. But it was only after the pick of his portfolio—Flipkart—began showing results that sentiment towards him turned from incredulity to awe. Fixel, who until then was regarded as an 'impulsive outsider', would begin to truly appear like the king of the jungle.

Just days after announcing the acquisition of Myntra, Flipkart closed its first funding round for that calendar year. It was a $210 million investment led by the billionaire Yuri Milner's investment firm DST Global. Moscow-born Milner is counted as Russia's most influential technology investor and was an early backer of some of the world's largest internet companies including Facebook, Twitter and Alibaba. Named after Yuri Gagarin, the first human to go to space, Milner is also a science philanthropist who has backed initiatives searching for extra-terrestrial intelligence. At the time when he was investing in Flipkart, his other big e-commerce bet, Alibaba, was preparing to list on the US markets. The ripple effect from the Chinese firm's blockbuster IPO later that September would be felt keenly across India's internet ecosystem.

If classic venture capital from blue-chip Silicon Valley firms had scripted the initial chapters of India's internet story, the narrative in the middle chapters would be taken up by a swarm of hedge funds and an eclectic cast of Asian investment firms grown rich on returns earned from China's internet behemoths. Their entry also delivered a strong signal to Amazon that India's e-commerce market would not yield easily to the Bezos-led company. Milner's bet was the first inkling of the coming tsunami of risk capital that would flood India's internet economy.

Within Flipkart's swarming offices—adjacent buildings dotted around the startup neighbourhoods of Bengaluru—the mood from mid-2014 onward could only be described as electric. The Bansals and their army of top-notch engineers, including the company's very first few employees such as Amod Malviya, Sujeet Kumar, Mekin Maheshwari and soon the talented Mukesh Bansal, were all on mission mode. The aim, among other things, was to move Flipkart from website to mobile phone. By 2014, India already had some 25 million mobile internet users compared to about 15 million broadband users. The trajectory was clear. The Bansals were intent on riding that mobile curve. Smartphone prices were dropping, internet access was growing. Schooled by Fixel to think of the macro changes ahead over the trends prevailing at present, they were plotting, planning and preparing for the coming explosion of internet access driven by cheap data plans.

In July, the company hosted a mega coming-of-age party. The Bansals raised $1 billion in the biggest round of funding by an Indian internet firm at that time. Singapore's sovereign wealth fund GIC became the latest investor to put faith in India's largest online retailer by participating in a round which valued the seven-year-old company at about $7 billion. Sachin, who had launched Flipkart as a twenty-six-year-old, would say, 'We were a little kid waiting to grow up. Now, we have grown up with this funding.'[6]

Nothing would ever remain the same for Flipkart and Indian e-commerce after that. To be sure, Flipkart has exerted a transformational influence on the Indian startup space like no other company has. But the changes underway in the industry were being driven also by deeper and wider impulses. For instance, at the start of the Indian internet startup wave in 2007, entrepreneurs were led by fairly conservative ambitions. It was deemed important to make businesses capital-efficient so that they reach the finish line having raised maybe $30 million from some three investors. Entrepreneurs were starting up with the aspiration of building a $100 million company. Even the Bansals believed that was their goal. It was no different for the investors. The first set of India-focused funds launched in 2006 would have begun with a corpus of $100 million–$250 million. Their biggest ambition would be to clock a $200 million–$300 million exit in a company where they owned a fifth of the stake. This was their goalpost and they would go about investing in line with it.

Fixel's advent threw that modest copybook out of the window. Seven years on, Flipkart's meteoric rise was stoking the entrepreneurial ambitions of thousands of Indians. So much so that trade body NASSCOM declared that startups were blooming in India like butterflies in spring.

Drawn by this effulgence of enterprise, a new band of opportunistic investors entered the market. Iconic venture funds from Accel to Sequoia would feel the pressure as a host of newer investment firms such as Steadview and Falcon Edge began dominating cap tables. Their aggressive hustle accelerated the speed of dealmaking and triggered ballooning valuations for even nascent internet startups. Falcon Edge, now known as Alpha Wave Capital, and Steadview formed part of a second generation of tiger cubs, or firms that mirrored the investment philosophy of legendary US investor Julian Robertson. Fixel's Tiger Global was a first-generation product from that same school of investing. These firms had all gained handsomely from early punts they had made on the massive Chinese e-commerce wave. They were intent on parleying those models and the money they had earned into India's startup ecosystem.

Steadview, founded in 2009 by Indian-origin entrepreneur Ravi Mehta, created a splash in the country's internet market in mid-2014. His firm took an aggressive lead in a $250 million round of funding for ride-hailing startup Ola Cabs. It was a significant deal as it marked the start of the fast and furious battle that would ensue for leadership in India's mobility market. Ola would later attract investment from yet another tiger cub, Falcon Edge, cofounded by Navroz Udwadia in 2012. That firm landed in India in 2014, with its first investment in the country being in student-led startup Housing.com alongside the big daddy of them all: Japan's SoftBank. The Masayoshi Son–led firm came armed with a war chest bulging with returns from the spectacular listing of China's e-commerce juggernaut Alibaba.

In the saga of global internet business, September 2014 will go down as a seminal month. Alibaba, China's then-largest e-commerce and cloud company, priced its shares on the US NASDAQ stock exchange at $68 per share on 19 September. It raised a staggering $25 billion and overtook Meta Platforms (then Facebook) as the largest-ever IPO in the US. Founded in 2000 by Jack Ma, who was famously an English teacher in the Chinese city of Shenzhen, the sprawling conglomerate had dazzled American investors. Its TaoBao and Tmall marketplaces listed millions of merchants on their platforms. Shoppers on these sites would typically make payments through Alipay, the digital payments platform also founded by Ma. And just like Bezos's Amazon, the Chinese company too had its own cloud infrastructure platform.

Son, the CEO of SoftBank, had invested $20 million in Ma's fledgling startup at the height of the dotcom era in 2000. When Alibaba listed in 2014, his firm owned about 32 per cent of the Chinese company. Based on the opening price for the Alibaba scrip on listing day, SoftBank's share was worth a staggering $75 billion. The Chinese digital empire spanning the gamut from a wholesale portal to an investment platform for online shoppers had delivered a fortune to both Son and founder Ma. In the weeks and months ahead, significant chunks of that fortune would find its way to Indian internet startups.

However, before the Japanese–Korean investment giant could touch down, another heavyweight contender was already on Indian shores. Jeff Bezos, then owner of an 18.5 per cent stake in the digital commerce juggernaut he had founded, arrived in India in the final week of September to mark Amazon's first full year of business in the country.

His battle was defined. South Africa's Naspers, Tiger Global and GIC had already boosted the cap table of India's online juggernaut: Flipkart. In just three months, the startup had raised $1.2 billion or ₹7,200 crore. To compete, Bezos would have to not just match but exceed that number. Standing atop a yellow painted truck in downtown Bengaluru, Bezos waved a $2 billion cheque that he handed over to his Indian team for further investments in the country.

Indians who shopped online regularly had by then enjoyed the benefit of the initial skirmishes between the Bansals and Bezos. The two companies had tried to outdo each other with discounts on everything from apparel to electronics. They were competing to deliver goods within a day, while expanding rapidly across India. This was just the beginning of an epic rivalry. Those watching from the sidelines declared that the Indian consumer would soon be enjoying some seriously 'achhe din' around Diwali in 2014.

The catchy phrase was a take on the election slogan from earlier that year which had swept a new dispensation into power in India. Narendra Modi had wooed both business and citizens with the promise of better days ahead to win a landslide victory for his party. Truth to tell, the ballooning of the money pile for Indian startups was in large part boosted by the rise in business confidence with the advent of the BJP at the helm of the Indian government as much as from global pools of money looking for a new home. Quantitative easing by the US Federal Reserve in the aftermath of the great financial crisis of 2008 had helped boost the first cycle of startup investment in India. Now it was the turn of hordes of investors who had gained from the explosion of China's digital commerce.

It was also the turn of one entrepreneur whose ambitions in China had been thwarted. In an interview with *The Economic Times* during his India visit, Bezos pointed to his company's practice of not obsessing over and thinking much of competitors, declaring he had 'never felt pressure from Alibaba's rise'.[7]

But Bezos's plans for dominance of the Indian e-commerce market would soon be challenged by companies bolstered by funding from Alibaba's largest investor and from the Chinese giant itself.

A fortnight after the Amazon CEO's landmark visit, India hosted yet another aspirant to the country's e-commerce crown, SoftBank's Son. To be fair, Son was in India to be a kingmaker and not the king himself. He did not come alone. India-born Nikesh Arora had been appointed as chief of SoftBank's Internet and Media Inc. in 2014. He was slated to lead the Japanese firm's investments in India. The son of an Indian Air Force officer, Arora had quit as chief business officer at Google after a ten-year stint at the search giant. Son and he had come to Delhi armed with not one but two blockbuster deal announcements. The Japanese investment firm would pump in $210 million into ride-hailing app Ola and $627 million into online marketplace Snapdeal.

Until then, the Japanese telecommunications and internet group's big-ticket investment in India had been the $200 million it had put into Naveen Tewari's InMobi in 2011. The gamble on Bahl's online marketplace and Bhavish Aggarwal's Ola took Son's cumulative investments in Indian startups to over $1 billion. It would become, by far, the top backer of Indian internet entrepreneurship. It was an October like no other for the Indian startup ecosystem, with the reverberations of the announcements in that week set to alter the shape of the industry. An early-stage investor[8] visiting Fixel in New York that week recalls him remarking that Son had done in a week what had taken Fixel nearly a decade.

He wasn't wrong. In absolute terms, the nearly $1 billion that Fixel had invested was spread across a slew of startups beginning from his first punt on Flipkart in 2009. But what Tiger Global's investments had done along with that of the early investors was place the building blocks for explosive internet growth in India. The startups he had backed from Flipkart to Delhivery and Myntra had begun when there were only rudimentary delivery networks, no digital payments systems and no mobile internet networks. These companies would pave the way for those who came later.

By the time Son came on the scene, Indian internet had entered adulthood. Son, a famously maverick investor who has been quoted as saying that he invests 'based on his sense of smell',[9] was also fast with his decision-making. An oft-repeated industry joke has it that founders meeting the uber investor would be out in twenty minutes if they didn't gain his favour. If they did, Son would click a selfie with the chosen one and hand out a cheque. Those who did business with the man say 'it was all about chemistry'.[10]

Son believed that India was at a turning point in its development and was hoping to replicate the success he had enjoyed in China. SoftBank Internet and Media Inc., the unit headed by Arora, became the largest shareholder in Snapdeal. The Delhi-based online marketplace would begin to aggressively compete with Amazon and Flipkart. Arora took a seat on the Snapdeal board. Neither company disclosed valuation, but estimates pointed to Bahl's company having snagged a $2 billion valuation with SoftBank estimated to have acquired about a 30 per cent stake. In keeping with Son's trademark style, the Snapdeal investment too was finally sealed in a record three weeks, tracing an arc literally from Alibaba's listing in September to Son's announcement in New Delhi in end-October.

But the prep work for it had happened at least two months prior. When Son and Arora landed in Delhi that October, they met a record forty entrepreneurs in the space of two days. That blitzkrieg startup pitch would yield some of SoftBank's subsequent investments, including hotel-room aggregator Oyo.

For Snapdeal, the SoftBank funding would be transformative on several fronts, most of all with regard to the cash required to compete on an even keel with well-funded rivals Flipkart and Amazon. In the course of 2014, the company raised a total of about $1 billion, including the largesse from SoftBank and multiple funding rounds from varied investors. In comparison, since its launch in 2007 the startup had raised a grand total of $150 million. It was as dramatic a change in fortune as any startup would experience. Bahl, speaking after the SoftBank investment, pointed out that until then his company had spent just $100 million through its lifetime, simply because it did not have much money before. In a market where capital was a necessary condition for success, Snapdeal had always operated at a disadvantage.

Now, with ample cash in the bank, it was the third contender in the great Indian e-commerce battle, a contest which Bahl would frame as one aimed at gaining a greater share of India's overall consumption pie, estimated to be about 70 per cent of GDP at that time. E-commerce accounted for just about 0.05 per cent of that market, making plain that there was no limit for growth. With belief in entrepreneurship at an all-time high—even if the valuation of several ventures evoked incredulity—Startup India was entering an epochal phase.

The other company to have caught the fancy of Son was the four-year-old ride-hailing startup founded by the swashbuckling IIT graduate Aggarwal. A researcher at Microsoft with patents to his name, Aggarwal also fit that rare personality of hustling businessman. As early as 2010, he had teamed up with batchmates to set up a taxi service using call centres. He was now competing to win against two rivals: desi taxi aggregator TaxiforSure as well as global competitor Uber.

Just as he had with Snapdeal's Bahl, Arora would be instrumental in getting Aggarwal to close the deal with SoftBank. He arranged for the Ola founder to fly to Tokyo for dinner with Son. In October, the SoftBank chief announced his investment in the startup being primed to take on global and local rivals. Along with Son, Ola's existing investors, Tiger Global, Steadview Capital and Matrix Partners, participated in what was then a mega-funding round for the Bengaluru-based company. It would be valued at about $650 million and SoftBank would become its largest shareholder. As the app economy gained pace, Aggarwal and Travis Kalanick's Uber would square up in one of the most epic rivalries in the Indian internet space.

But before that, Ola's newly acquired dollar arsenal stoked one of the toughest fights among Indian startups. Within a few months of the SoftBank funding, Ola captured a thriving rival, the Accel Partners–backed TaxiforSure. TFS, as it was widely known, was set up by two IIM Ahmedabad graduates, Aprameya Radhakrishna and Raghunandan G. in 2010. The son of a professor father and a homemaker mother, Aprameya was a stranger to enterprise. No one in his family had run a business, and those who had tried to set up small ventures had failed. Business was not something that was encouraged in their household. As a result, the young management graduate had a simple formula: get a good corporate job, work maybe for forty years in eight companies—about five years in each company. That was how he had mapped out his career trajectory. True to plan, on graduating he joined realty consultant Jones Lang LaSalle as business development head. That was when something began to change. He got a good view of how businesses were being built up close.

After having stayed away from all startup seminars on campus or recruitment pitches by new ventures, he slowly started reading business literature. He read about Sanjeev Bikhchandani's Info Edge and Deep Kalra's MMT, both of whom were celebrated alumni of IIM-A. Frustrated by corporate work, he began tapping into his network of friends to check what they were doing. Soon he had linked up with college-mate Raghunandan to toss ideas around. Over a meal at a Bengaluru restaurant, the two ended up discussing an everyday problem both were facing: the daily commute in India's technology capital. What if we clicked a button and the nearest cab turned up at our doorstep, they asked each other. In a tried and tested startup method, they drew up a blueprint for a business on a paper napkin. They didn't know about Uber or Ola; their research didn't reveal any other operators either. Dipstick surveys of daily commuters querying the need for such a service came up with a resounding yes, as did a survey of drivers who said they could do with more business.

The two friends quit their jobs and took their business plan for a review to college senior Kalra of MMT. Aprameya recounts being told that it was a 'great idea and you guys should do it'.[11] Kalra connected the two raw entrepreneurs with investors he was familiar with. Such connections and the privilege of being able to tap into them underscores once more the very tribal nature of the Indian startup ecosystem in its infancy and pretty much well into its teens.

However, while connections could help a raw entrepreneur get a foot in through the door, it was chance, luck or even sheer merit that decided the outcome. Among the early pitches they made included one to Info Edge's Bikhchandani and Naukri CEO Hitesh Oberoi. In Aprameya's telling, they were 'hammered'. The two beginners had no answers to a ton of questions ranging from cost of customer acquisition to how to run an internet venture. Abashed, they returned to Bengaluru. They decided to stop talking to investors and instead start building the business. They set up a website and started talking to cab operators and drivers to onboard them. Finding no purchase from big players like Meru and Mega Cabs, they decided to focus on local operators. Pooling in personal savings of ₹4 lakh apiece they started out to address a very specific pain point. Getting from Point A to point B within Bengaluru. They built a website, got some cabs on board, hired an engineer for the tech framework—and they were off. That was when they first began hearing of Mumbai-based startup Ola. But caught up with concerns for their own survival, they paid little attention to a business in another city.

Within six months of starting up, they realized they needed outside capital to take the business ahead. They started reaching out once more to investors, which brought them in touch with the chief investment officer (CIO) for city-based education venture Jain Group. Serendipity took over after that point. The CIO, Hemachandran Seshadri, happened to be a neighbour of a VC who had just moved to Bengaluru, Anand Daniel of Accel Partners. The Jain Group was not interested in seeding the new venture but he had an inkling that Daniel might be interested. One day, he called Aprameya and told him that Daniel was in his office and asked if he would like to come and pitch to him. The TFS founders needed no second invitation. They drove to Jain

College in the city centre in twelve minutes flat. They would get a further ten minutes to make their pitch to Daniel.

This time round, the entrepreneurs clearly did a more polished job. Impressed by the business, Daniel asked them to meet his colleagues, including senior partner Prashanth Prakash. The firm had already been researching the mobility space. Unlike the TFS founders, they had identified at least ten companies operating in it. But within the first ten minutes of listening to their pitch, Daniel knew that Appu and Raghu—as he refers to them—were thinking differently. Accel would go on to co-invest, along with Helion Venture Partners. Fittingly enough for a deal born out of serendipity, TFS's parent holding company was called Serendipity Infolabs.

However, for TFS, the journey from startup to sale spanned three and a half years. Several factors played into that outcome—to start with, the conflict between running a profitable business and the approach of growth at all costs adopted by rivals. TFS, weaned on the conservative approach defined by their traditional venture investors, was playing the slow but steady growth game. SoftBank's $210 million infusion into Ola changed that equation.

TFS was forced to up the ante, and it did so. It wanted to raise $80 million or so in response. The startup gathered commitments of up to $60 million, and had an option to keep running and then raise money yet again.

Until the unfortunate incident of a passenger allegedly being molested by an Uber driver in December of that year sent regulators into a tizzy and put the future of the ride-hailing business itself in question. Investors spooked by the developments dithered, and TFS slowly began dying from want of cash. Then Ola came calling, as did Uber. Looking at the three options, the TFS founders decided to sell, a decision that in hindsight Aprameya believes was the right one, though painful. As he saw it, 'across the world, there is an Uber and a local player. Either Uber has won or the local player has won. There are no two local players anywhere that have won.'[12]

In India, with SoftBank in the fray backing Ola, there was little doubt as to who the winning player from the local team would be. In March 2015, Ola bought TFS for ₹1,237 crore or $200 million in a cash-and-stock deal that set the stage for a battle between Ola and Uber in the coming years.

Reporting on the transaction, *The Economic Times* said that TFS shareholders would get one Ola share for every seven TFS shares.[13] It would rank as the second-largest deal in the Indian internet startup space at that time.

7

Railroads for Commerce

For a few hours in May 2009, Nandan Nilekani was close to becoming India's human resources development minister. Then co-chairman of iconic software exporter Infosys, he received a call from the ruling Congress party one morning, asking if he would take the job. Following a few quick consultations with colleagues, Nilekani accepted the offer. But by noon on the day of the swearing-in he would be told that he was no longer being considered. The Bengaluru resident did not travel to Delhi.

Nilekani may have lost a ministership, but India had gained a CTO. In the ensuing weeks, he declined an offer to join the Planning Commission. Instead, he asked for the chance to lead an initiative tasked with providing a digital identity for all Indian residents. The idea of a unique identity number which the government could use to directly deliver financial benefits like scholarships, pension and unemployment benefits had been discussed in 2006. If the state wanted financial inclusion, citizens required a proof of identity document that could be their passport to a better life. Millions who in an earlier time would have spent their lives in a single village were on the move looking for newer opportunities. Most did not even have a basic birth certificate. They required government-issued identification to access jobs, transport and other services. In January 2009, the Union cabinet approved the project. By mid-year, Nilekani was appointed chairman of the Unique Identification Authority of India (UIDAI).[1]

For Indians, as much as for the then fifty-four-year-old IIT Bombay graduate, it would prove to be a seminal appointment.

In 2007, Nilekani had stepped down as chief executive of the IT services firm he had cofounded with seven other colleagues. He had turned to thinking about the big ideas that could shape a nation, writing about it in his first book, *Imagining India*. Amid discussions on labour reform, language and globalization, it included a chapter on digital identity. Nilekani's penchant for societal and urban issues was evident even during his time in the corporate boardroom. He had served on an urban task force in his hometown and contributed to the Jawaharlal Nehru National Urban Renewal Mission while he was still chief of Infosys. By the time he took charge of the country's digital identity project, his thoughts on why civil society, government and business must collaborate to deliver change at 'population scale' were fairly advanced.

Aadhaar, the unique identity number which he would help to architect, was born as a digital tool to solve the problem of financial inclusion. At the time it was taking shape, less than a fifth of adult Indians had a bank account. The cost of verifying the identity of prospective customers in far-flung locations was neither logistically nor economically viable for most of the formal banking sector. So Aadhaar took shape as a tool for the government to directly transfer benefits to bank accounts that were opened by using the unique ID. The first direct-benefit transfers (DBTs) in January 2013 would be on a modest scale, covering seven welfare schemes. In seven years, that number grew to 420 schemes across fifty-six ministries. By 2020, nearly 60 per cent of all central welfare and subsidies would be routed through Aadhaar-seeded bank accounts. In that time, the world's largest biometric identification number would have traversed a tumultuous path of legal and political challenges to emerge as one of the most ubiquitous facets of modern Indian life.

To begin with, it helped that the enrolment process itself was stunning in its simplicity. A person provides four demographic data points: name, address, date of birth and gender. And three biometric data points: a facial photograph, iris scans and fingerprints. Once the system confirms there is no duplication, a unique identity number is issued. This tactile design was intentional.

The world over, identity numbers are conflated with citizenship. India's Aadhaar exercise was uniquely designed from the get-go as a tool for economic inclusion. An Aadhaar number can be allotted to anyone resident in India; it does not bestow citizenship. What it does is allow an Aadhaar holder to authenticate her identity in return for a vast array of services from opening a bank account to getting a mobile connection or applying for a loan. And of course to receiving financial benefits from the government. In turn, this had the potential to help the country bridge the yawning digital divide.

In the 1950s, the construction of large hydel power dams had proclaimed the economic ambitions of a newly independent nation. In time, public sector units in sectors ranging from aeronautics, heavy engineering and space to oil and natural gas would deepen the country's industrial footprint. But finally, it was the economic liberalization of 1991 that unshackled the aspirations of a surging middle class, stoking an unprecedented wave of technology-led entrepreneurship. To have a fighting chance in a world that was entering the information era, India would need transformative technology that could help her leapfrog the developmental backlog of decades.

From the vantage point of 2009, it was clear that internet adoption would only grow deeper and stronger. Connectivity was improving with more sophisticated telecommunication infrastructure while the cost of smartphones was dipping. For the team at UIDAI, the writing was on the wall: their design had to be built from first principles and could not mimic something that already existed. They had to work with a view to where the 'trend was headed'.[2]

For that to happen, the twelve-digit Aadhaar number had to be more than just a pipeline for government benefits. It needed to evolve such that ambitious private innovators could also build atop the network to create newer solutions. It had to be a product that offered both inclusion and efficiency. No one person or group could singly drive such an initiative. Neither the government nor the private sector could do this by itself. It required someone who could combine the best of each to create a new entity.

New to Delhi and the ways of government, Nilekani would gather a veritable army of volunteers, professionals and career bureaucrats who could take the idea forward. Among the swarm of people joining up were young PhD holders and also mid-career professionals who had earned their stock options. They were signing up to work for country rather than for company.

Among those leading the charge was top bureaucrat Ram Sewak Sharma. A Jharkhand cadre bureaucrat, he would go on to head India's telecom watchdog, the Telecom Regulatory Authority of India (TRAI), before becoming the country's IT Secretary. He was brilliant at the helm of UIDAI according to those who worked closely with him, including computer scientist Viral B. Shah, best known for being a co-creator of the Julia programming language.

In 2007, Shah had finished his PhD and was working for a US-based startup in the area of supercomputing that would go on to be acquired by Microsoft. 'Foolishly', he had decided to pursue a second PhD in finance and economics that would lead to a chance encounter with Nilekani. Accompanying his professor Rajnish Mehra to present a paper at the India Policy Forum in July 2009, Shah found himself in New Delhi. At the sidelines of the event, he ran into Nilekani, who asked him if he would consider joining his new team. Assuming it was just a casual remark by a government official, Shah recalls being certain that Nilekani wouldn't turn up at the appointed time for the meeting at a Delhi coffee shop. To his amazement, not only did the UIDAI chairman turn up on time, he wasn't surrounded by a platoon of aides either. A fifteen-minute conversation was all it took to get Shah on board.

From deeply committed bureaucrats like Sharma to idealistic engineers like Shah, everyone involved would revel in this culture of innovation within a government crucible.

As did Pramod Varma, the computer scientist who would go on to become the chief architect of several products within India Stack, a collection of digital public infrastructure tools that would take shape in coming years. Varma had joined Infosys in 1994 before moving on to the company's Boston-based management solutions spin-off, Yantra Corp, three years later. In 2005, that unit was sold to Sterling Commerce. Varma would continue to work at the US company for the next five years. In signing up for UIDAI in 2009, he returned to work at a Nilekani-led initiative for the second time in his career, a move that would turn out to be propitious for the engineer whom Nilekani credits with the ability to think at 'population scale' to build the digital products required for 1.3 billion people. In time, they would collaborate and create what is now regarded as a fully made-in-India trifecta of digital innovation that spans citizen identity, payments and data.

There was a combination of factors that would make this possible. First and most important, there was political will. Both from the United Progressive Alliance (UPA) government led by Manmohan Singh, which would drive the ideation and early adoption of Aadhaar, and later from the Narendra Modi government that came to power in 2014, which would accelerate the adoption of digital public goods and stoke the creation of newer networks.

India's central bank, regarded as one of its most progressive institutions, played its part in providing the regulatory frameworks essential to the rollout of a slew of financial products. Ranging from the Aadhaar-enabled payment bridge and payments system to the iconic Unified Payment Interface, UPI.

And in the background, the technology infrastructure would be built by the likes of Varma and scores of others. These volunteers crafted what is now widely known as India Stack: a slew of digital networks built on open application programming interfaces (APIs), the software interface that allows two or more computer programmes to communicate with each other. This open architecture allowed a range of products to be built on the foundation of identity, triggering a uniquely Indian digital revolution that twins the public goal of financial inclusion alongside private innovation by technology entrepreneurs.

Nilekani told the Centre that in five years he would enrol 60 crore Indians on Aadhaar, a target that UIDAI would meet when he stepped down from his post in March 2014.[3]

Aadhaar enrolled people faster than WhatsApp enrolled users. By 2022, as India emerged from the COVID-19 pandemic, nearly 1.3 billion people had Aadhaar numbers.

At the start, however, there was no copybook for what the UIDAI team was attempting. It had to be simple and scalable. It had to work for the government and the ambitious entrepreneur. While they were creating the framework for Aadhaar, the team already had examples of citizen identity to draw from within developed countries, including that of the US Social Security Number. They were inspired also by the public funding for technology research in the US that had delivered defining platforms like the internet itself.

The global system of computer networks linked through telecommunication and optical networking was first developed by the US Defense Department in the 1960s. Techno visionary Vinton G. Cerf, credited with having collaboratively written the protocols that allow computers to connect with each other, has for long held that his interest in the internet was stoked in part by the hearing loss he suffered as a child. Communicating via the internet, in his words, provided a level playing field for deaf people. In time, the English computer scientist Tim Berners-Lee would credit Cerf's design, which allowed future technologies to be built atop the internet, as the spur to his creation in 1989 of the World Wide Web, the information system which allows documents and all downloadable media to be accessed over the internet.[4]

It would take another five years after Berners-Lee's creation of the World Wide Web for the internet to be harnessed for commercial use. Marc Andreesen, a young computer science student at the University of Illinois Urbana-Champaign, teamed up with others at the National Centre for Supercomputing

Applications to develop a web browser called Mosaic in 1993. It combined text and images, providing the first graphical web browser. On graduating, Andreesen moved to California and teamed up with another visionary technologist, Jim Clark, the founder of Silicon Graphics. Clark would urge Andreesen to see the commercial possibilities of Mosaic and cofound an internet software firm. Their firm's launch of the Netscape Navigator marked the first strike in the commercial opening up of internet technology that has left no part of the world unchanged.

This arc of public investment that served to create the early internet inspired the UIDAI team. Over a decade after Andreesen's Netscape took the world by storm, in Delhi, the UIDAI team knew this was their moment to create public digital infrastructure for India that would deliver both public good and commercial opportunity. And while they would look at what others had done with regard to identity, there was no masterplan they were looking to draw from. They were not out to build the 'x' of India, like aspiring internet entrepreneurs who were setting out to create either the Amazon of India or the Alibaba of India.

Looking back, a snapshot of India's technology landscape in mid-2009 can appear almost cinematic. In two distant cities, vastly differing forces were taking shape. In Bengaluru, a cradle for private enterprise, Tiger Global's Fixel was taking his first bet on homegrown e-commerce upstart Flipkart. His bold infusion of $9 million while valuing the two-year-old startup at $50 million forever changed the pace and trajectory of private internet entrepreneurship in India.

At the same time, in Delhi, Nilekani and his band of dreamers were taking the first step to creating public digital infrastructure for an aspirational developing country. India Stack, which would emerge from their efforts, has defined the unique evolution of India's internet economy like nothing else. It has done this even while transforming the economic fortunes of millions at the lower end of the population pyramid.

To many in India's startup ecosystem, these two happenings—disparate and widely separate—have come to signify what is now being spoken of as Indian technology enterprise's Yamuna–Kaveri corridor. Early-stage investor Sajith Pai, who coined the term in an annual overview of the Indian startup ecosystem, credits the confluence of these two vastly different forces of change—one seeded in Delhi on the banks of the Yamuna and the other germinating in Bengaluru, which draws its water from the mighty Kaveri—with having shaped and moulded India's pulsating startup ecosystem.[5]

To be sure, Aadhaar was seeded as an identity tool. But for the team building it, the ID was something to be harnessed for development as well. Unlike some existing systems the world over that viewed identity as a security measure by and for governments, the UIDAI team fashioned it for inclusion and development. They approached the problem as mathematicians looking at it from the perspective of necessary conditions and sufficient conditions.

To them, digital public infrastructure—or DPI, as they termed it—was a necessary condition. It was not an option but an essential framework to provide access to financial services, education, healthcare and employment. By then, it was also clear that digital pathways would be the ones to deliver access to unbanked Indians, to those living outside the organized economy. Internet penetration was low, but growing at a steady clip. Smartphones had been launched and it was evident there was purchase for them in the Indian market. With an affordable smartphone in hand, most Indians would have a full fledged computer at their fingertips. The Aadhaar ecosystem would be built with a view to where this trend was headed.

Varma, a member of the early core group that designed India's PDI framework, maintains that even they didn't quite anticipate the pace and extent at which India would adopt these tools in the years after the launch of Aadhaar. They were certain that the digital identity could open access to the formal economy for millions of the unbanked. Once the friction to access was removed, millions more than just those at the top of the population pyramid could access digital products and services. And so, they aimed for the long shot.

They began building Aadhaar as a digital pipeline atop which other innovators could build newer products and services. In 2009, such thinking was based on equal parts anticipation and optimism. But in practice it has turned out to be a startlingly persuasive story, where the rollout of public digital infrastructure has stoked unprecedented private enterprise in financial services, triggering in its wake phenomenal economic tailwinds.

But first, the transformative influence of the biometric identity number would become apparent in the speed and scope of financial inclusion. When UIDAI was launched, just 17 per cent of Indians had bank accounts. In a December 2019 note, the Bank for International Settlements estimated that India would have taken 47 years to achieve 80 per cent of adults with a bank account had India solely relied on traditional growth processes.

Much of this can be traced to the launch of two things. As Aadhaar was a digital number, it could be verified and authenticated online—providing both efficiency and speed. Atop this came the electronic know your customer (eKYC) system that Aadhaar facilitated. This could be used to open a bank account or a mobile phone. Second, the opening of the no-frills Jan Dhan Yojana (savings) account launched in 2014, for which using eKYC as a verification tool several hundred million accounts were opened.

Typically, opening bank accounts requires documentation to first establish the identity, location and occupation of applicants. Those without such papers—most often the poor—have remained outside the formal financial system to their long-term disadvantage while also dragging down the larger economy and the country in its quest to rise from being a low-income nation.

One of the primary hurdles—identity—was something that Aadhaar successfully dealt with as it allowed bank accounts to be opened within two minutes with biometric identification included, leading to a dramatic collapse in the cost of KYC regulations. As this was a digital tool, verification and authentication could even be done at agent locations. The cost of KYC dropped from ₹1,500 to ₹20 per person.

Several hundred million bank accounts were opened through the Jan Dhan Yojana starting in 2014 when it was launched. Official estimates peg the amount of money transferred since inception through DBTs up until 2022 at about ₹24.8 lakh crore.

Even as the government-to-person (G2P) pipeline began gaining traction, the team at UIDAI began to notice an interesting development. Remittances from urban to rural India are among the biggest small-value, large-volume transactions in the country. Migrant workers would earlier pay up to 4–5 per cent as transaction fees to money transfer entities including the likes of Western Union to send money back home, specifically where neither sender nor receiver had a formal bank account. Or they would move money in suitcases or make bulk transfers through agents who would distribute cash at the receiver's end. It was cumbersome, leakage-heavy and grossly inefficient. The emergence of Aadhaar and Jan Dhan provided a breakthrough in this person-to-person financial channel as well.

To the UIDAI team, this was further proof of the power of digital infrastructure. Once a person had linked their Aadhaar number with their bank account, DBTs would reach that account, as would LPG subsidies. Suddenly, for the larger population, Aadhaar became more than just an ID.

As Varma recalls, it is not as if he and his peers had envisioned the entire suite of digital tools that would be built under the umbrella of India Stack. They were literally learning on the go.

The alignment of forces that led to the housing of this project under the Ministry of Electronics and Information Technology (MEITy) also played a cardinal role in defining the future trajectory of Aadhaar. Across the world, identity, regarded as a security tool, is housed under the aegis of the home and security ministries. Aadhaar is unique in that it is overseen by India's technology regulators.

It also helped that Aadhaar was not designed to confer nationality—anybody resident in India for more than 182 days in a calendar year can get an Aadhaar number. Even more powerful was its design—the open architecture makes it possible for other innovators to build products and services atop it. This open-platform approach would mark a first for a government-led programme. By drawing on the identity, verification and authentication that Aadhaar provided, it would trigger the creation of a suite of products.

To begin with, in 2011, along with R.S. Sharma, Varma would begin ideating on how they could further the journey begun with creating an identity number. They mooted the idea of the DigiLocker, an electronic vault where citizens could store all their certificates—driving licences, college diplomas, PAN cards, vehicle registration papers—offering digital credentials for easier transactions. Along with this came the idea of a digital signature: eSign.

This had its own interesting backstory. As early as 2000, digital signatures had been given legal status in India. The Information Technology Act, 2000 defined digital signatures as the authentication of any electronic record using digital signing, making e-signed certificates issued by certifying authorities legal. Businesses would use this to sign invoices, tax certificates and reports, agreements and other documents. But it had not gained widespread acceptance for a simple reason. Private individuals did not have a way to digitally authenticate identity as this was before the launch of Aadhaar.

This was an illustration of how despite being an early adopter of digital technology, India was yet to capitalize on the enormous efficiency it could bestow. The technocrats at UIDAI would pick this gap in the techno-legal chain. It spurred Varma on to think about how an Aadhaar-enabled digital signature framework could be built. The eSign draft that emerged from this was submitted to the Controller of Certifying Authorities (CCA) housed within MEITy. Formed in 2000 under the umbrella of the IT Act, it was tasked with promoting e-commerce and e-governance in the country by widening the use of e-signatures. The CCA adopted the eSign framework, marking the first of a suite of tools to emerge out of the Aadhaar ecosystem.

Close on the heels of the digital signature tool would come the plan for a digital certification framework. Varma's early scribblings on the DigiLocker idea was fine-tuned by a focused team of volunteers. In 2015, it was unveiled as part of the larger Digital India campaign launched by the Narendra Modi government. Among those who volunteered to architect this digital storage 'container' was Amit Ranjan. The technology entrepreneur had earlier cofounded SlideShare, a platform to share professional content, along with his US-based sister Rashmi Sinha and Jonathan Boutelle, the startup's CEO. The $119 million acquisition of the venture by LinkedIn was among the most high-profile tech buyouts of that era involving Indian entrepreneurs.

Ranjan worked with LinkedIn for over two years before making a transition to join the government in 2015. He had volunteered with industry groupings including the NASSCOM Product Conclave and its later offshoot iSPIRT. Once in, he would be part of the team that would take DigiLocker from its introduction in 2015 to the formal launch in mid-2016.

Building the technology framework was regarded as the easier part by this cohort of talented techies. It was the rollout of what they referred to as 'use cases'—actually getting organizations and people to use these tools—which would challenge, uplift and engage them.

In the case of DigiLocker, the first task was to get the storage container notified by the Central Transport Authority as a valid repository for driving licence and vehicle registration papers. With transport being part of the concurrent list—with oversight by both central and state governments—the next step was to get all Indian states and union territories to do the same.

The identity number may have been birthed as a value-add to governance but in practice it was fast morphing into a strategic platform for multiple uses in both the public and private spheres. The digital ID, digital signature and digital locker would be the first set of APIs opened out for innovation. By the start of 2023, nearly 150 million people across the country were storing their documents electronically.[7]

But even as these forces were gathering speed, there were rumblings around the reach of Aadhaar. Fears arose about implications on citizen privacy and even misuse of the powerful biometric-based identity number. In 2012, a retired judge of the Karnataka High Court challenged the government on making Aadhaar mandatory and its plans to link the biometric identity with various schemes. Justice K.S. Puttaswamy's writ petition in the Supreme Court argued that Aadhaar violated the Fundamental Rights of equality and privacy granted to citizens under the Constitution. In the following five-odd years, nearly twenty-six more petitions were tagged along with his. The legal battle raged for another six years, riddled with multiple twists and turns. Embroiled in these hurdles, Aadhaar's ambitious goal of growing beyond identity appeared to have dropped into limbo.

In the early years, the Supreme Court restricted the use of Aadhaar to LPG and public distribution schemes (PDS) in an August 2015 ruling. Two months later, it expanded the scope to include the Prime Minister's Jan Dhan Yojana, the Employee Provident Fund and the unemployment payout through MNREGA, among others.

In what is regarded as a seminal event in the history of Aadhaar, Nilekani sought a meeting with the new prime minister in July 2014. He had by then stepped down as chairman of UIDAI, and contested and lost an election to the Lok Sabha in the summer of 2014. He was even more determined to see his transformative work at UIDAI reach a rightful conclusion. Prime Minister Modi would provide backing for the digital ID, but with a caveat: whatever improvements were required had to be made and all legal challenges had to be resolved. Equally fortuitous, from the perspective of DPI's votaries, was the appointment of UIDAI chief executive Sharma as India's IT Secretary.

The Centre was preparing to launch Digital India, a flagship programme to catapult India into the knowledge economy. An important centrepiece of this programme was 'cradle to grave digital identity that is unique, lifelong, online and able to authenticate every citizen'. In 2015, two products from the UIDAI stable—eSign and DigiLocker—were introduced at the formal launch of the Digital India programme. Early in 2016, the Lok Sabha passed the Aadhaar Bill, and with the President providing consent, the Aadhaar Act was notified in the Gazette of India.

Still, it wasn't until 2018 that the legal overhang over Aadhaar would dissipate. In August 2017, the Supreme Court upheld the Right to Privacy as a Fundamental Right. The ruling stemmed from the multiple petitions challenging the constitutional validity of Aadhaar. But it wouldn't impact the legal standing of the ID itself. The 2017 ruling in actual terms cleared the field for further court hearings on the petitions themselves. Finally, in January 2018, a five-judge Constitution bench of the Supreme Court would begin hearings on the constitutional validity of linking Aadhaar with several government schemes. They would continue until May 2018.

On 26 September 2018, the Supreme Court delivered its judgement upholding the Aadhaar Act as constitutionally valid, a verdict that would be affirmed with a majority of 4:1 by a Constitution Bench in January 2021.[8]

The court directed the government to establish a robust legislative framework for data protection and privacy and ruled that Aadhaar could not be mandatory to open a bank account, get a mobile connection or school admission. It noted, however, that it was a robust tool to foster financial inclusion. In the *State of Aadhaar Report* released in 2019, Aadhaar-enabled payment systems were found to be responsible for 100 million transactions a month. Aadhaar, so to speak, was finally on course.

During the battle over the validity of the digital ID, much had transpired on the ground. The combination of public digital infrastructure and private enterprise was transforming the landscape of financial services, telecom connectivity and technology entrepreneurship across India.

On 1 December 2016, in a much-awaited press conference, Mukesh Ambani, Reliance Industries chairman, announced that his company's cellphone service Jio had snagged 50 million subscribers in just eighty-three days, making it the world's fastest-growing technology company, surpassing even the likes of Meta's social network Facebook and messaging app WhatsApp.[9]

Multiple factors had coalesced to produce this astounding feat—most importantly, the development of digital verification platform eKYC. Reliance Jio rode this wave to add 6 lakh subscribers per day with nearly the entire user base verified through eKYC, allowing a mobile SIM to be activated in less than five minutes.

But more than just ease of verification was at work here. Jio's rapid climb to 100 million subscribers was driven also by the sharp discounts offered to customers by the oil and gas conglomerate. It was leaving no stone unturned in its efforts to transform towards a digital future. Building a robust telecom brand was the first step in the overhaul of its DNA.

The Reliance scion had been offering a clear indication his company would bring to Indian homes and offices online connectivity of an order of magnitude unseen till then. A quantum increase in connectivity and a matching drop in prices would mean that businesses could easily harness the power of online authentication. Add to this a drop in smartphone prices and biometrics. In sum, it was game, set, match—only the players needed to take guard.

The only missing piece was cheap data.

The average revenue per user (ARPU) during 2005–08 was broadly at ₹130–₹140 at the lowest end—and it was voice only—and at the higher end the ARPU could go up to ₹240. The launch of Reliance Jio triggered a massive pricing overhaul while boosting the average ARPU to about ₹150 for voice+1 GB data. That equation has further turned in favour of the user, who now pays about the same price, adjusted for inflation, but gets around 30 GB of data every month.

Jio offered free voice and data calls over its 4G network, driving a price war overnight that drove rivals to scramble in order to stay apace. At the end of 2021, Jio had more than 400 million subscribers. Years earlier, the architects of Aadhaar had planned their design for where the trend was headed: cheap connectivity, blistering internet adoption and affordable smartphones. Across Startup India, there is little doubt that those trends were stoked and directed by Ambani's Jio. So much so that it appears foolish to have imagined that India would board the digital train without low-cost data. Sure, cheap and powerful phones were widely available in India. But what could people do with a cheap phone without cheap data on it? Ambani's economy-altering gamble provided a definitive answer to such questions.

Finally, it would take a combination of private enterprise and government initiative to propel India into the digital future. While Jio was a private initiative, Aadhaar and later the National Payments Corporation of India's (NPCI) UPI were more sarkari. But both were indubitably at population scale. While Jio fixed the connectivity problem for the common man, collapsed the cost of data and brought in 4G, solving the demand conundrum, Aadhaar and eKYC transformed the supply side. The two gigantic initiatives harnessed technology to widen access, backed by political will from diverse parties. In the case of Aadhaar, it was first the Congress Party–led UPA and then from 2014 onward the BJP's National Democratic Alliance (NDA). The unique ID would survive and grow through the transition of governments. Today, it is not just part of everyday life, but part of popular culture.

Paying Power

In 2016, as smartphones turned ubiquitous—driven by two factors, cheaper handsets and cheaper data—Indians began to consume social media, entertainment and shopping. Meanwhile, within newly formed government circles, the idea of digitizing India was firmly embedded. The buildout of Aadhaar at a mammoth scale had already been done, with nearly half the country's population enrolled. Just as US government institutions had laid the foundations of the internet, so also in India a collaborative digital framework was being crafted.

These were interesting times. From Google to Amazon and Facebook, the examples of phenomenally successful corporations built atop the internet were common lore. For those within government, a constant question was how these corporations were building mammoth scale products at relatively low costs. The answer was in front of them. Aadhaar itself had been built on open architecture and open source, and had opened out APIs atop which others could innovate.

The idea that a country's digitization could be led by volunteers and such networks could then be opened out for private innovators to build on was startlingly new and powerful. Indian officialdom's embrace of this marks the singular most important aspect of India's journey into the information age, of the evolution of a Digital India.

However, from the perspective of the country's aspiring tech entrepreneurs, the big benefit that Aadhaar delivered was an electronically lubricated way of customer acquisition at scale and speed via the electronic customer verification service eKYC. As Reliance Jio had demonstrated, eKYC was a powerful identity tool that could be harnessed to provide a plethora of consumer services. Digital payments pioneer Paytm would also emerge as one of the biggest users of eKYC, going on to launch its now ubiquitous digital wallet.

But by far, the biggest tectonic change that India's digital identity unleashed would come from the payments network that it seeded: the Unified Payment Interface, UPI. While Aadhaar and Jio set the stage, the definitive development that widened India's railroads for digital commerce was unquestionably the UPI. It was built on a simple tenet: allow a user to pay in real time from her bank account without swiping a card.

As it often happens, this most exponential of ideas began on a quiet note. In September 2013, Nilekani and Varma met with Dilip Asbe in Bengaluru. The London School of Economics alumnus was then chief operating officer (COO) of the NPCI.

Among other things, he had overseen the deployment of a real-time inter-bank payment system—immediate payment service (IMPS)—marking yet another digital first for India.

The NPCI itself was a seminal organization. A year before Aadhaar took shape in Delhi, this not-for-profit entity was set up in Mumbai, backed by the RBI and the Indian Bank Association to operate retail payments and settlement systems. It began with a mandate to manage ATM networks but evolved to set up a string of innovative financial products ranging from the early IMPS to the national toll collection initiative FastTag, domestic payment card RuPay, to the now-blockbuster UPI. The Delhi-based government organization UIDAI and the Mumbai-based non-profit NPCI were all led by corporate executives, people from the world of business. They hit it off very well.

At the meeting, which took place in a sarkari venue—Khanija Bhavan on the city's arterial Race Course Road—Asbe discussed the fast clip at which IMPS was growing. The UIDAI executives were intrigued by the possibilities. They were already seeing Aadhaar-enabled no-frill accounts being opened and smartphones becoming ubiquitous. On the ground, events were gathering speed. People were withdrawing cash in villages through an Aadhaar payment bridge. Benefits were going into Aadhaar-linked bank accounts. EKYC was making it possible for bank accounts to be opened in two minutes.

The galloping pace set by IMPS spurred the thought of a comprehensive digital payments system. What could be the next payment infrastructure combining government-to-person, person-to-person and person-to-merchant in the era of smartphones is the question the three would debate in that fateful September meeting.

They let the idea germinate for the next eight to nine months before picking up the threads of the discussion again. This time, Varma would collaborate with Asbe and others on his team. Also volunteering in the discussions was Sanjay Jain, IIT Bombay alumnus who at that time was working at Khosla Labs, a startup incubator and innovation lab backed by Silicon

Valley VC Vinod Khosla. There, he had set up Novopay—a core banking platform for large banks and financial institutions. More pertinently, Jain had also put in a two-year stint as chief product officer at UIDAI, helping to build Aadhaar. This was after several years spent at Google where among other things he helped launch Mapmaker, where 170 countries would come on to Google Maps on the back of crowdsourced data. You could say Jain knew a thing or two about working at 'population scale', much like Varma. And equally enough about collaborating with government.

This crack team would get together to build the initial protocols for UPI. One year after the first discussion with Nilekani, the team had the UPI protocol ready, in September 2014. It wasn't a hefty document, just a short, sharp, to-the-point discussion paper. What the exercise proved once again was that to build enduring institutions, you didn't actually need an army of thousands. A hundred good people could take an idea forward, and build and rebuild, as Nilekani pointed out in his book *Reimagining India*.

That is literally what happened. The vision of a few leaders delivered a suite of products unlike anything built anywhere else in the world—the result of an era of cooperation between the government, the RBI, the NPCI and the UIDAI. Such partnerships were leading to 'combinatorial innovation', where public digital infrastructure acts as the foundation for private enterprise innovations.

The UPI protocol to facilitate and speed up inter-bank, person-to-person and person-to-merchant transactions was designed in September 2014. Varma and his peers had crafted the highway; they were providing the infrastructure, not driving the bus. For UPI to be populated with traffic, there was a need for an anchor institution that could catalyse adoption of the real-time payment interface, which was regulated by the RBI.

The robustness of UPI's growth can be traced back to its being anchored in a regulated market and being offered to users as a bank-led product. The Payment and Settlements (PSS) Act in

2007 had established the RBI as the regulator and overseer of the entire national payments system and all financial ventures offering payments. It was the PSS act which allowed the establishment of entities like the NPCI. As a result, it was entirely natural for the UPI to be housed within the Mumbai-headquartered non-profit company that was backed by the government and the country's top banks.

Meanwhile, Nilekani, who had returned to Bengaluru, was increasing his interactions with the fast-growing startup ecosystem in the city. He met with venture investors, founders and a rash of engineers working on the next new thing in and around the city's entrepreneurial hot spot, Koramangala. This hip neighbourhood was also fortuitously where he had his home. Among those he met were members of technology think tank iSPIRT, cofounded by former Yahoo research and development (R&D) chief Sharad Sharma.

Among the most influential people in the Indian technology space, Sharma had put in stints at corporations such as Lucent Technologies and worked in the US technology sector in the early 2000s before returning to India. A graduate of the Delhi College of Engineering, his time at Yahoo coincided with the rise of technology entrepreneurship in India. He was also active within the country's apex IT grouping, NASSCOM, the two-decade-old industry lobby that had gained fame for playing a huge part in boosting the fortunes of India's IT services sector. It was the voice of the then $785 billion industry both locally and globally. In response to India's growing ambition to emerge as a software product centre, it had set up a sub-grouping, the NASSCOM Product Council. Sharma went on to chair this grouping, emerging as an evangelist of note for the sector. Sometime in 2013, even as India's startup ambitions were growing fast, Sharma and a score of others who worked to organize the NASSCOM Product Conclave felt the need for a more focused grouping to deepen what they regarded as a veritable revolution. They broke away to launch iSPIRT, or the Indian Software Product Industry Round Table.

It had a clear agenda. With an initial membership of about thirty individuals and organizations, it aimed to direct government policy, increase market awareness and help product entrepreneurs build large-scale software product companies out of India. Soon this unique network based in Bengaluru would evolve into a hive of conversations and policy interventions while mentoring and catalysing software product activity. It would stand out for another detail as well: iSPIRT has never maintained a physical office. Long before the COVID-19 pandemic ushered in work from anywhere (WFA), this grouping of technology evangelists had made WFA their calling card. If they required an office, any one of the member companies or someone from the larger community typically provided them with one. In local parlance, iSPIRT's demeanour could be described as 'hatke'. It was designed as a grouping high on intellectual debate, low on bureaucracy, high on future innovation, low on legacy.

It proved to be a natural breeding ground for next-generation technologists, and a magnet for the high-quality band of technology volunteers who had built India's first public digital infrastructure networks from Aadhaar to eSign, DigiLocker, and the most lustrous of them all, UPI. Much of this thinking would arise from iSPIRT's stated raison d'etre as a grouping looking to support collaborative solutions to solve India's 'hard problems'. It argued that answers to India's development questions were beyond the efforts of any one single entity—market, public or non-profit.

With Nilekani and many more from his UIDAI team now back in Bengaluru, the India Stack conversations deepened. The most dominant theme in 2015 was how to craft an ecosystem for the commercial launch of UPI. Asbe, then CTO at NPCI, organized the first UPI workshop at the Cricket Club of India in Mumbai. Twenty to thirty of the country's top bankers turned up to hear about the brand-new digital payments interface.

In Bengaluru, iSPIRT organized UPI 'sandboxes' or hackathons—calling on technology entrepreneurs to build solutions on the network and to hear from the architects,

Nilekani, Varma and others. This was the market outreach piece. Simultaneously, the non-profit recognized that it had to up the visibility for UPI among regulators.

Sure, Asbe at the NPCI was parenting the payment interface, and Sharma's MEITy was a co-parent, but the country's central bank was yet to sign off on the network. The largest banks were wary of joining the network; there were also technology upgradations required for them to meet the NPCI stipulations.

In February 2015, determined to break the impasse, iSPIRT volunteers led by former Infosys CFO Mohandas Pai and others made a spirited pitch to then RBI governor Raghuram Rajan in Bengaluru. Rajan, who was in the city to deliver a lecture at the Indian Institute of Science, spoke of the gains from the Aadhaar-driven DBT programme which had made it easy to channel targeted subsidies. The India Stack votaries urged him to turn his attention to the newest offering from the stable: UPI. A meeting in Mumbai between Rajan and Nilekani that year would also be important in convincing the central bank to approve UPI in its current form.

In the following months, Rajan pushed the banking ecosystem to sign up for the platform. Finally, in April 2016, the RBI announced the beta launch of UPI with twenty-one banks. It took another six months for the commercial launch of the iconic payment service. UPI grew manifold on the back of the undercurrents set off by the events of 8 November 2016, when in one swoop, the Union government outlawed currency notes of ₹500 and ₹1,000. The demonetization set off waves of change that engulfed the country as people scrambled to shift from paper money to digital modes of transaction. Digital wallet provider Paytm rode the wave, with corner stores selling India's trademark drink of choice—nariyal pani—paid for by a Paytm-emblazoned QR code. Indians of a particular generation who had never used a phone to do more than chat were now asking offspring what a QR code was.

For internet entrepreneurs, this conflation of Jio's data blitz with UPI summed up what the country is witnessing today: a digital payment revolution. Jio brought a lot of users online, while UPI and the entire fintech stack created pockets of disruption. In a little over three years since demonetization, in October 2019, UPI had grown to processing a billion transactions a month. It had also stoked the launch of a myriad array of payment solutions from Google Pay to Walmart's PhonePe to BHIM (Bharat Interface for Money) itself, triggering a payment revolution that has become central to the public digital infrastructure ecosystem rated as unique to India. It helps also that UPI is completely free—you pay ₹10, you get ₹10.

Three years later, in October 2022, India's flagship digital payments platform recorded a staggering 7 billion transactions in a single month estimated to be worth about ₹12.11 trillion. This in a country where a little over a decade ago less than a fifth of its citizens had bank accounts.

Varma likens this saga to one of Indian mythology's best-loved tales in the Ramayana—of how the monkey god Hanuman was oblivious of his power to fly, that is, until he is reminded by the wise bear Jambavan that as a child he could easily fly even up to the sun. Aadhaar, to the India Stack votaries, was an affirmation of the potential and power stemming from a country's belief in its own capabilities. And living proof of what India could achieve while working at 'population scale'.

Economists estimate that for every 10 per cent density of a population coming on board with voice mobility, infrastructure was naturally created for GDP growth to push up by 1 per cent. From the vantage point of the 2020s, it's easy to see why this has proven true as more than 500 million Indians now own smartphones, making it the second-largest smartphone market in the world after China. With a penetration rate of less than 50 per cent, there is still room to grow.

Broadly, it was assumed that businesses in India would grow as per capita GDP grows. As people get richer, they would buy more, just as they had in China. But India saw a different trajectory—here, the masses would get data-rich before they became financially rich. In 2010, fewer than 2 per cent of

Indians had smartphones. In the decade since, that has changed to hundreds of millions of Indians coming online. With a smartphone in every hand, an ordinary Indian's digital footprint is far more than his financial wealth.

This is lending itself to the creation of the third leg in the India Stack trifecta of financial inclusion. In the first—the identity stack—it was Aadhaar, eKYC and eSign. In the second stack—payments—it was UPI and the Aadhaar-enabled payment bridge and payment services. Now, as millions transact online, the account aggregator network seeded under India Stack is looking to help individuals and businesses gain control over their own data and use it to transact for a range of financial services.

It was an idea that was seeded in 2015 when the Financial Sector Development Committee led by the country's finance minister called for unified, consented data-sharing ability for consumers. This was backed by all the top financial regulators including the central bank. More so in an era when over 2.5 billion people globally own a smartphone. India alone was adding upwards of 100 million smartphones a year. Two years later, at an industry presentation, Nilekani laid out the argument on data democracy—why it was important for an individual to have control over their own data and not rely on either a private company or a government to keep it safe. He argued that India with its advantage of having built a robust digital public infrastructure could offer an alternative to the Western model where corporations parse individual data to deliver targeted advertisements. Instead, an individual with access to her own data should be able to share it safely with anyone. He termed this 'an inversion of the usage and ownership of data'.[10]

In the months thereafter, iSPIRT volunteers would take this idea and run with it. They defined the protocol for an account aggregator network. In July 2021, as India emerged out of a pandemic-bruised economy, the government launched the account aggregator network with nine licenced aggregators and eight top banks.

The system works like this. Typically, a consumer or a small business seeking a loan is required to provide collateral. But today, with a store of personal and business information available through his GST transactions, income tax records and bank transaction statements available digitally, could this verified data be used as collateral? The account aggregator network could make this happen.

A consumer or business provides consent to a licensed account aggregator to query a financial information provider for specific data—for example, GST returns. This is delivered in an encrypted format to the financial information user, like a bank or lender, who can use this data to make decisions based on the consent of the applicant.

Newer business models will emerge that take this digital wealth and convert it into economic wealth, triggering an economic cycle of trickle-up rather than the conventional trickle-down theory. If Aadhaar was about eKYC and UPI about digital payments, arguably the most consequential will come from the developing story of account aggregator systems.

8

The Fintech Boom

As early as 2010, when internet commerce was still regarded a novelty across much of urban India, a young technology entrepreneur in Noida would think otherwise. Vijay Shekhar Sharma, a spunky founder who had by then built a robust business selling value-added services for mobiles and had raised capital from blue-chip investors, was now casting about for the next innovation. The mobile, he was certain, would come to be used for more than just communication. He launched Paytm—an acronym for pay through mobile.

Elsewhere, another founder, Kunal Shah, would team up with his friend Sandeep Tandon to set up a recharging service for mobile phones called Freecharge, also in 2010. In time, Paytm and to a lesser extent Freecharge would go on to play an outsize role in the evolution of online payments in India. But that was still in the future.

In just about a year after the two startups were launched, a buyout of a small Mumbai-based content firm by Flipkart drew a trio of engineer-entrepreneurs into the vortex of internet commerce. The team would later combine to deliver a fintech startup—PhonePe—that has become the byword for paying online as much as Sharma's earlier gambit.

It all began in 2011, when a small digital content platform in Mumbai received a look-in from a co-founder of the country's hottest startup at the time, Flipkart. As meetings went, it turned out to be sharp and decisive. Binny Bansal, along with colleagues Amod Malviya and Mekin Maheshwari, spent half a day speaking to the co-founders of the venture that acted as a bridge between music content companies and publishers. The two-year-old venture had an interesting business model. It would tie up with content owners such as music label Saregama and in turn provide APIs for publishers like Gaana.com to stream this encrypted content. For Flipkart, which was then on a mission to broaden its offerings, this digital distribution platform was a snug fit.

The bigger hook for Binny Bansal, however, was the quality of the founding team that had both deep technical skills and business chops. The team of Sameer Nigam, Rahul Chari and Burzin Engineer would then meet up with Sachin Bansal. In a thirty-minute presentation, the Flipkart CEO laid out his vision of how e-commerce could be a $20 billion–$30 billion business in India by 2020. A decade later, recounting the incident in an industry podcast, Nigam said that he and his co-founders were stunned by the 'amazingly bold' vision.[1] Engineer, the oldest of the trio, remarked that either the Flipkart team was 'crazy or that they'd change the world'. Intrigued, Nigam and his mates decided to cast their lot with the ambitious Bansals and the star-studded team surrounding them. Flipkart made a 100 per cent acquisition of Mime360 in a part-cash, part-stock deal.[2]

The three co-founders joined the e-commerce company and took up digs on a particular floor in its Bengaluru office that would acquire cult status in the years ahead. Some of the biggest names in the Indian technology startup space, from business to business commerce venture Udaan's Sujeet Kumar, Malviya and Maheshwari were all Flipkarters first before starting out on their own. They had their desks on that floor. Nigam, Chari and Engineer joined this elite grouping. Later, Myntra's Mukesh Bansal would move in after the fashion portal was acquired by Flipkart. The young company was unwittingly becoming an advanced university for entrepreneurial education.

Nigam began by heading the engineering function in the years when Flipkart was growing at rocket speed. It was a unique culture where a horde of engineers, mostly in their mid-twenties, nerdy, ambitious and uber confident, were building businesses for the next couple of decades. The go-for broke attitude that was the zeitgeist in its hallways spurred the creation of some of today's best-known startups from Udaan to Bansal's Cult and Nigam's PhonePe.

These businesses had something in common: they were products of a brand-new era of internet entrepreneurship, one that began around 2014 and stretched all the way until the turn of the decade. The forces that shaped them were vastly different from those which birthed the likes of Flipkart. For one, they would have the benefit of being repeat entrepreneurs who had started at least one venture before setting out again. There was precedent to refer back to for anything from a human resource crisis to a regulatory challenge or investor conflict. If not directly, they would at least know of a peer who had dealt with such issues. More importantly, their businesses would cater to consumers already conversant with transacting online. As serial entrepreneurs they would know much more about what in their parlance is commonly termed as product–market fit.

But all that was for later. Newly inducted into one of the country's fastest-growing technology startups—which had moved beyond books to selling mobile phones, consumer electronics, music CDs and DVDs—the goal for Nigam and his team was to build a digital music store which would be called Flyte. They had prior experience in going direct-to-consumer. Before building Mime360 as a platform connecting content owners with publishers, they had tried their hand at building a music streaming store, but had to shut it down in the face of competition from larger companies. At Flipkart, which was experimenting with various ideas, this was another chance to go directly to the consumer.

Soon it was clear that Indian consumers were going online mostly to buy electronics and mobile phones. It was the start of the great Indian romance with smartphones. Flipkart, with its smart tie-ups with handset makers, was offering Indians the best deals for the choicest handsets. The Bansals were going big and everything around them was designed to drive that single-minded goal. As phones and consumer electronics began to be the fastest items flying off digital store shelves, the focus turned to driving that business. At the heart of their quest was scale. By 2014, boosted by a record capital infusion, the company aimed for its Big Billion Day sale. It was an engineering and technical challenge for the young startup and it faced a slew of challenges from managing scale to meeting customer expectations. But the most glaring gap was the lack of a robust digital payment system.

Flipkart had broken away from the pack to become India's leading digital store on the back of its prescient move to offer consumers the option of cash-on-delivery. It had good reason to do so. Cards accounted for just 5 per cent of personal spending compared to between 30 and 50 per cent in developed markets. But if the e-commerce company was to reach the scale it was aiming for there had to be a quick, easy, secure way to pay online. In 2015, nothing like that existed at the size and scale required to transform the payment landscape of the country. Even with Flyte, which required users to make small, single-digit purchases as low as ₹3 for a song download, it was the lack of a scalable micro-payment service that did it in.

It was not only Flipkart that felt this need. India was on the cusp of mega transformation. Flipkart and Amazon were leading the charge to get more people to buy online. Their growth had led to the creation of logistic networks, supply chains and rising appetite among offline merchants to join the gold rush. Cash could hardly be the engine to drive such growth; neither could it be driven by just credit. There needed to be more.

In the aftermath of the global financial crisis of 2008, triggered by the collapse of the subprime mortgage lending business in the US, caution had become a watchword for bankers worldwide. In India, credit had become tight for both businesses and consumers. Credit-card penetration, which had reached a high of about 27 million cards in 2008, arguably on the back of aggressive selling practices, dropped to a low of about 18 million cards before growing to about 21 million cards by 2015.

Debit cards, meanwhile, were growing. In the five years up to 2015, debit-card transactions grew at a compounded rate of 36.5 per cent while credit cards expanded by 21.3 per cent. The spike in debit-card growth was also a result of the ambitious push by the Centre to widen access to banking services itself. The Jan Dhan Yojana, backed by Aadhaar eKYC, launched in 2014, had led to the opening of new bank accounts with debit cards issued as default, leading to an increase in overall debit-card growth by nearly 40 per cent, according to industry estimates.

Meanwhile, with even small-value items being sold online, e-transaction volumes were set to increase. An industry report in 2014–15 found that mobile wallets and prepaid cash cards accounted for about 3 per cent of all digital transactions in India. A robust card network, as well as the buildout of digital payment options like PayPal in the US and Alipay in China had contributed in no small measure to the expansion of online commerce in those markets. India, by the same reckoning, was ripe for a rapid innovation in payment systems.

But this is where the story diverges for India—and in quite spectacular fashion. The impact of India Stack, the collection of open programming software interfaces created by government-backed volunteers, unlike anything else anywhere in the world, would start to become evident. Fashioned in a manner that private innovators could build new solutions on top, this set of APIs were only then beginning to draw attention, and indeed rising curiosity among India's ambitious cohort of technology entrepreneurs. Its remit spanned from identity, through the unique ID number Aadhaar and the eSign application, to data via the DigiLocker platform to store personal and professional identity certificates. But the crown jewel in the open API stack was the payment network: the Unified Payment Interface, UPI.

In Bengaluru, where the chatter about the payment interface was rising, the India Stack volunteers as well as the NPCI—the public–private non-profit championing digital payments—would set up UPI sandboxes. The votaries for public digital infrastructure would introduce the platform, and techies would get to experiment and build products atop it.

Nigam, Chari and Engineer, meanwhile, had decided to move on from Flipkart after the proposed digital music store Flyte was shut down in 2014. They wanted to start up again. But this time as true-blue engineers, they wanted to build something that had technology at its core, not just as an enabler, Nigam said in a podcast hosted by the investment firm Matrix Partners. Secondly, they wanted to build a large and impactful venture. The stint at Flipkart had taught them a thing or two about scale, of going big with an idea.

They had seen first-hand the big gap in the e-commerce chain: the lack of a robust digital payment product. Building a technology-led payment product was an attractive option for sure. They explored IMPS, launched by the NPCI a few years earlier, but were chary of competing with incumbent banks. It was around this time in 2015 that they found themselves at a UPI event. They got to hear directly from Nilekani, as well as from Pramod Varma and Sanjay Jain—who had built the UPI protocol—what the big fuss was all about. More importantly, they heard from NPCI top boss Dilip Asbe himself. They got to know of the central bank's backing for the product and saw for themselves how excited Asbe was by the potential of UPI.

By then, some of the first few banks which would back UPI were already on board. This, to Nigam and his peers, was indication enough of how seriously it was being viewed by regulators and bankers. In a way, the argument was simple. Demand for online commerce was rising at a rapid pace. Data consumption was also set to explode in tandem with falling data prices and increasing mobile penetration. The Jan Dhan programme by the government was escalating the number of Indians with bank accounts at a massive rate. The missing piece was an easy technology interface linking banks that a consumer could use to make quick, easy payments using an app.

Four-way interoperability was key to UPI's uniqueness. It was an entity agnostic network. For instance, a consumer using

Payment App A could link his account on it to his savings bank and in turn send money to a merchant or individual with an entirely different Payment App B linked to a savings account in a different bank. The entire transaction was designed to take no longer than a minute or two.

The core of the UPI proposition was that any service built atop it would have to remain within the banking system, with apps acting only as the intervening link. This is where it differed from a digital wallet that stored consumer money. On a UPI app, money remained within the consumer's bank account, the app would only help him draw the money and pay a merchant or an individual in real time. Just like physical currency, except this was digital money. What's more, it had the blessing of the regulators.

To Nigam and his peers, this was the equivalent of a moonshot. If it clicked, it would be bigger than anything they had seen. They dived in, and in December 2015, PhonePe was incorporated. It would attract a significant amount of investor attention, not least for the quality of its experienced founders. Rivals such as digital wallet Paytm were drawing in mega pools of capital from the likes of Alipay, the fintech arm of the Alibaba Group, as well as from Japan's SoftBank. Another startup, Freecharge, acquired by e-commerce player Snapdeal in March 2015, was also on an upbeat mode. SoftBank was a large investor in Snapdeal.

From Flipkart's perspective, a digital payment arm was needed, and badly. By then, Binny Bansal had moved to become the Flipkart CEO. He had a good equation with Nigam and Chari, having been the one to initiate the buyout of their first startup. He assured the PhonePe founders that the unit would be treated as an independent entity within Flipkart. For the return entrepreneurs, it was also the aura of familiarity that Flipkart came with and the assurance of the deep pockets that PhonePe would need to stave off challenges from the likes of Paytm and Freecharge. In April 2016, Flipkart acquired the young startup in an all-stock transaction.[3]

Nigam would go on to become CEO of the venture that was run as a separate unit under the umbrella of the Flipkart Group.

By his own telling, Nigam and his team chose to build the new venture as a startup and not as the arm of a large company. They wouldn't share office space with Flipkart, unlike in their first tryst with the e-commerce major. Instead, they had their own setup in an adjacent neighbourhood. They linked their compensation to specific targets to be met by the business, in effect taking on the risk–reward matrix that comes with a high-potential startup.

Also in April, the NPCI had launched a pilot of the payment interface to be tested across twenty-one of its member banks. With then RBI governor Raghuram Rajan inaugurating it, official sanction for UPI was clear. In August 2016, PhonePe tied up with private sector lender Yes Bank to launch a UPI-based payment app. Events would move in a blur from then on. Within three months of the launch, the app would be downloaded by 1 crore users. It proved to be the harbinger of explosive growth in digital payments that would irrevocably transform the way Indians deal with everyday money.

Much of this spectacular revolution was triggered by the events of a single evening. At 8 p.m. on 8 November 2016, Prime Minister Modi in a nationally televised address announced that currency notes valued at ₹500 and ₹1,000 were no longer legal tender. His government offered new ₹500 and ₹2,000 notes as replacements for the demonetized ones in a bid to crack down on black money. The societal upheaval this occasioned would range from cash shortages at ATMs to a drop in industrial output, a crash in farmyard prices and a cut in GDP growth forecasts by global analysts.

One sector, though, thrived as a result of this catalytic action. Among the stated objectives of demonetization was the spurt it would provide for the adoption of digital payments. While the effect of notebandi, the colloquial term for demonetization, across sectors remains a matter of debate, opinion with regard to its impact on digital payments is unequivocally positive. Indians would use the UPI mobile payments platform for 3,00,000 transactions adding up to about ₹90 crore in November 2016. By 25 December, such transactions would balloon to 1.4 million, worth about ₹480 crore.

PhonePe wasn't the only beneficiary of this growth spurt. In Noida, Paytm, the near-ubiquitous brand emblazoned on shopfronts and at vegetable carts, was borne upwards by the sharp spike in demand for digital payments. It was founded in 2010 by the ebullient entrepreneur Vijay Shekhar Sharma, a small-town boy who had made the big city his own.

His is a story that will resonate with many across the country's small towns and cities who made their way in the rough and tumble of urban India, and with nearly anyone driven by a relentless will to succeed. The son of a schoolteacher, he was an academic prodigy who at age fifteen enrolled for a degree at the Delhi College of Engineering. But the front-row student soon found himself all at sea in his new surroundings. The boy from Aligarh wasn't conversant with English, the medium of instruction.

Disheartened, he drifted to the back of the class, determined to teach himself spoken English. He graduated at age nineteen with the firm conviction that 'formal education was overrated'. There were big learnings he would take from this formative phase of his life. While struggling to pick up English, Sharma discovered a smart trick. He trained himself to think in English and not the reverse—think in Hindi and then translate into English, which is the conventional method that new language learners adopt. It was a hack that would get the enterprising teenager ahead in quick time. This ability to think on his feet and persevere against all odds would in time come to be his biggest calling card.

While still in college, he began learning the ropes of business, setting up a venture with peers to build technology frameworks for clients. For a year, during 1999, he built technology services for publishing giant India Today. By then, he had picked up the nuances of business. His college startup was sold to a New Jersey–based telecom software firm. This stoked the young Sharma's interest in the emerging telecom sector. He was watching the rise of Sunil Bharti Mittal, who was making his telecom service Airtel a household name in the country. Sure, the internet was booming, but to Sharma's mind it was a layer on the underlying telecom infrastructure—that's where he wanted to be. He had set up One97 in 2001 at the height of the dotcom boom. The young startup offered ringtones on mobiles. It was followed up with other value-added services (VAS) for landline phones. Soon, Sharma saw the benefit in working through the telecom operators to offer a mass of subscription-based content including stuff like astrological services.

By 2006, as a flood of overseas capital began to move into the nascent Indian startup ecosystem, Sharma's telephone lines were buzzing. He was interviewed on prime-time television as the founder of one of the country's largest providers of value-added telecom services which was gathering attention from big names in the world of investing. Then twenty-eight-years old, he declared that far from being a small-town boy, he was an engineer fired by the Silicon Valley dream, inspired by the likes of Netscape's Marc Andreesen and Yahoo's Jerry Wang in an interview with a business channel.[4]

But behind the talk lay the glimmerings of a single-minded vision that defined Sharma's entrepreneurial career. India was where he wanted to do business, and he had a spate of new launches up his sleeve, from incoming call management applications to video-on-demand on cellphones. To venture investors, he had declared his asking valuation would be $50 million. For perspective, it is good to remember that this was a time when venture investors would most likely be taking $1 million bets on Indian tech startups while regarding these as staggering valuations. Tiger Global's stupendous $50 million bet on Flipkart was still two years away. And One97 was operating on very, very thin margins. So much so that Sharma in his later years declared that in the first six years after launching it (in 2001) there were many days when he had to get by on just one meal a day.

To those who watch Indian startups closely, the maverick, talented and relentlessly committed Sharma provides no easy comparisons with anyone else in the industry. To his investors, he is an original. Managing partner at Saama Capital Ash

Lilani, who was then leading Silicon Valley Bank's investments in India, and SAIF Partners's Ravi Adusumalli would be the first investors to take a bet on One97 in 2007. The company operated from small, cramped quarters in Delhi's Nehru Place, where investor meetings would happen too. For lunch, there would be rajma chawal from the vendor downstairs. For Lilani, there would be one reason for the deal: 'Vijay was infectious,' he recalls a decade and a half after that seminal investment. The two funds put in about $6 million (about ₹26 crore) in the company in March, following it up with about ₹10 crore at the end of the year.

This proved to be the turning point for the VAS player, which would move on to raising further capital in quick succession, including from Intel Capital. It snagged nearly $30 million over three to four rounds of fundraising in the next two years. In his book *The Moonshot Game*, VC Rahul Chandra has laid out the sheer persuasiveness of Sharma, his vernacular argot and his incredible self-assurance.[5] Chandra's fund Helion Ventures even heard a pitch from the charismatic founder but it would not reach fruition.

In 2010, Sharma tried to take One97 public. It even received a go-ahead from market regulator Securities and Exchange Board of India for a ₹120 crore public issue. However, Sharma decided to pull back and instead raised capital from a private investor. Even more presciently, he had launched Paytm, an acronym for 'pay through mobile', reading rightly the huge shift looming ahead that would see India transition into a mobile-first economy. Years later, he listed it as his biggest and possibly wisest decision. By then, he had followed Airtel's example and made a foray into Africa, launching operations in Nigeria and even in neighbouring Bangladesh. Backed by SAIF, he also launched One97's corporate investment arm, backing other startups in the mobile VAS space.

Lilani recalls that as investors they had little to do with the evolution of One97 into Paytm. It was Sharma who came to them with a slew of new ideas and plans. Margins in the mobile

VAS space had become bone-dry—he wanted to find a way out. He understood the mobile ecosystem and was mulling an option to create a product allowing recharges on the phone. Consumers mostly had prepaid SIM cards in those days, and Paytm would offer a recharge facility—voila, a new business was born.

In a few months, he returned to his investors with more exciting findings. People were not just recharging their phones, they were leaving extra money behind on the app and using it for cash-on-delivery. 'Why don't I ramp it up?' he asked his investors. Sure enough, in no time, he had come back to them with more to show. One day, he urged Adusumalli and Lilani to listen to a 'gaana'. He played a jingle sung by a little girl in a sweet voice, saying, 'Paytm karo.'

These turned out to be seminal moments in the life of the company. Sharma made paying digitally a household thing with the launch of the Paytm wallet. Little kids and elders alike would hum the jingle. India had entered the era of digital payments. Paytm would go on to sponsor the Indian Premier League cricket tournament, further cementing the absolute name recognition that big brands are built on.

By then, Sharma had also entered the big league in capital accumulation. As early as 2011, SAP Ventures had put some $10 million into the company in a round valuing it at $300 million. Meanwhile, SAIF decided to go big on the fast-growing venture, buying out Intel Capital's holding and raising its stake in the digital pioneer to nearly 50 per cent.

In 2014, the year India's digital revolution took flight, Paytm found itself right at the centre of the action. Its digital wallet was picked for integration by the new ride-hailing major Uber. The San Francisco company was launching its India operations and it added the Paytm wallet as one of the payment options on its menu. In a market-defining move, so would the Indian Railways. Sharma's venture had definitively transformed from a mobile and DTH recharge tool to an m-commerce platform. In 2015, it added Delhi Metro card recharges, electricity payments, and gas and water bill payments. In turn, its registered user base grew from 1.18 crore to 10.4 crore in the space of one year from mid-2014 onward.

This was the period of mega capital inflow into India. With Asian giants SoftBank, Alibaba and the horde of Asia-headquartered tiger cubs from Falcon Capital to Steadview Capital flooding the Indian startup space with millions of dollars, Flipkart, Snapdeal and scores of others were raking in the moolah and snagging staggering valuations.

Paytm caught the eye of Chinese giant Alibaba. Sharma met Jack Ma. Ma's group had built a formidable ecosystem with an e-commerce marketplace as well as a payments arm housed under the Ant Financial umbrella. This fintech unit bought a significant stake in Paytm in 2015, buying nearly 40 per cent and valuing the company at about $2 billion, making it India's then-second-most valued-startup behind Flipkart.

Sharma went on to attract more trophy investors. Indian corporate icon Ratan Tata invested in 2015, and two years later Warren Buffet's Berkshire Hathway bought a 3–4 per cent stake in the Noida-headquartered fintech major. In a bid to recreate the vast e-commerce and digital payments ecosystem of Alibaba, he launched Paytm Mall, cementing the successive iterations that had taken a once mobile VAS provider on a journey of transformation into a fintech and e-commerce giant. Sharma's Paytm was fast shaping up to become all things to all people.

Amid the rapid-fire growth, Sharma was called upon to take another seminal call. The first sparks of the UPI revolution were beginning to show, and PhonePe was not yet an idea. Sharma, when asked to consider boarding the UPI express, chose instead to stay with the by-then-near-ubiquitous Paytm wallet.

To be sure, until 2016, the Indian startup ecosystem had grown firmly on the premise of creating either the Amazon, Uber or Alibaba of India. It was following the copybook model with an aim to recreate the zip and zest of the world's largest startup ecosystems. Paytm was a company that had come of age in the pre-Aadhaar, pre-Jio ecosystem. It was modelled on the closed-loop model made famous by the Chinese giants.

However, demonetization proved to be a game-changer for the Paytm wallet as well. In time, its wide basket, beyond just UPI alone, would place the payment pioneer on a sound footing. The company, which had introduced India to digital wallets and QR codes, expanded its oeuvre to include postpaid payments—buy now, pay later—debit and credit cards, net banking and easy money instalments (EMIs), while also taking the lead in providing omnichannel payment choices for offline merchants.

An aerial view of India's startup landscape in 2015 would also reveal brisk buyout activity. Boosted by record inflows of risk capital, Indian startups were embarking on a period of mergers and acquisitions (M&A), splashing cash to buy quicker growth through the inorganic route. Flipkart had already snapped up Myntra and in early 2016 went on to acquire PhonePe. But the biggest deal in the Indian technology landscape in 2015 came from Snapdeal's nearly $400 million buyout of fintech startup Freecharge, announced in the spring of that year.

The fintech company founded in 2010 by two friends, Kunal Shah and Sandeep Tandon, offered mobile recharging services and incentives to consumers for bills paid online. It created an ecosystem that would compete with Paytm in the pre-UPI era. Shah, a college dropout, and Tandon were repeat entrepreneurs who had shut an earlier venture, Paisaback, a promotional discount venture, to set up Freecharge. The move to reward consumers for online transactions would see it snag up a user count and draw the attention of big-ticket investors like Sequoia Capital and Belgian family office Sofina. In early 2015, it was shaping up to be a credible rival to Paytm.

The spring of 2015 was an eventful phase for online retail companies in India. Big money was shaping the contours of the industry, aligning itself behind what it regarded as the likely winners in what by then was indubitably a big-gun battle.

So if Tiger Global and Naspers were ranged behind Flipkart, SoftBank—the newest entrant and arguably the one with the deepest pockets—put Snapdeal in its corner. That left the Chinese giant Alibaba's backing for Paytm. All three were gunning for the chance to emerge as the top rival to Bezos's Amazon.

It was an interesting line-up, each with its own strengths as well as glaring gaps in their portfolios. Flipkart had market dominance, a fashion vertical and momentum on its side. But it lacked a payments arm. Snapdeal, newly revived with SoftBank's backing, was gunning for a payments vertical. Paytm, the original payments company, was looking to acquire e-commerce arsenal.

It was against this background that Snapdeal's Kunal Bahl called up Freecharge's Kunal Shah in late January of that year. The two founders and their teams were all well known to each other, having done business together in the past. This time they agreed to meet in person in Mumbai for a catch-up. Bahl was accompanied by co-founder Rohit Bansal while Shah had Tandon as well as COO Alok Goel with him. The idea for a buyout mooted there moved at lightning speed thereon as each party only saw gains and little to hold back the transaction. In early March, India's largest financial daily *The Economic Times* was the first to report the news of an impending transaction. Days later, the founders of Snapdeal and Freecharge met reporters in Bengaluru to announce the sealing of what at that time was the largest buyout by an Indian internet startup. In time, Snapdeal would sell Freecharge to Axis Bank as the private lender embraced the UPI platform and was looking to quickly build digital heft.

Shah, well known as one of the Indian internet space's most outspoken founders, went on to launch yet another fintech venture, Cred. This time, his focus would be the creamy layer of the population and not the mass market. His premise was to build a differentiated credit information record for high spenders that they could use to parlay for greater benefits. In his new home town of Bengaluru, the startup maven would choose to tool around in a Vespa even as he backed newer ventures by scores of aspiring entrepreneurs. Paying it forward, in his own way.

9

The Era of Reckoning

Those tuned into the startup world in India during the summer of 2015 found their attention gripped by a very public feud. Rahul Yadav, the co-founder and chief executive of online realty portal Housing.com, had locked horns with the board of his company. Just months earlier, the IIT Bombay dropout had made headlines for a very different reason. His two-year-old startup had received an investment of $90 million led by celebrated Japanese investor Masayoshi Son's SoftBank.

Cofounded in 2012 by a group of college mates in their early twenties, the Mumbai startup had started out robustly. It intended to help consumers locate houses to rent or purchase while the portal charged the broker or the builder. It ran on an algorithm built by the in-house engineers. The website was user-friendly, with the look and feel of a product built for the internet-savvy consumer.

Son's investment team in India, led by former Google executive Nikesh Arora, was drawn towards the spunky, technology-led venture and its potential for growth in a large, disaggregated realty market. Weeks after backing online marketplace Snapdeal and mobility app Ola, Arora signed off on the Housing.com deal. In a matter of six weeks, SoftBank invested close to $1 billion in three companies. It was an investment blitzkrieg. Nothing of such scale and speed had ever been witnessed in the Indian startup market until then.

But very soon, events began to go south for the realty portal. Flush with cash, Yadav decided to splurge on a high-decibel advertisement campaign for a reported ₹120 crore. Chastised

Office of Infosys Chairman Nandan Nilekani

Nandan Nilekani (*right*) with RBI Governor Raghuram Rajan during the launch of UPI at Mumbai on 11 April 2016

Info Edge Ventures

The Info Edge Ventures team: Founder Sanjeev Bikhchandani (*standing*, *centre*) with (*to his right*) Kitty Agarwal, partner, Info Edge Ventures

Abhishek Goyal

Tracxn co-founder Abhishek Goyal (*right*) with
Flipkart co-founder Binny Bansal

Abhishek Goyal

Abhishek Goyal of Tracxn (*left*) with Flipkart co-founder Sachin Bansal

Accel India

Accel India's Subrata Mitra (*left*) bags the Midas Touch Award for Best Investor at *The Economic Times* Startup Awards (ETSA) in August 2018, following the spectacular $16 billion purchase of a majority stake in Flipkart by Walmart in May 2018. Accel was the first investor in the ecommerce startup way back in 2009. Mitra is receiving the award from Infosys co-founder and founding chairman, UIDAI, Nandan Nilekani (*right*), who chaired the ETSA jury in 2018. Nilekani is regarded as the architect of Aadhaar, which is seen as the enabling platform for the rise of several fintech startups such as Phone Pe and Zerodha.

Accel India

Accel Partners India at their first office off Bengaluru's Infantry Road, the hub for meetings with a swathe of founders including Flipkart's Bansals. This is in 2009, when the team made their biggest bet in India: a small investment of about $1 million in a startup called Flipkart.

(*Left to right*) Prashanth Prakash, Subrata Mitra, Mahendran Balachandran and Gagan Kumar (who has since moved on from Accel)

Fireside Ventures

Fireside Ventures: Among the earliest venture funds to have raised the bulk of its capital from domestic rupee capital investors. Seen here is the founder, Kanwaljit Singh (*front*, *centre*).

Fireside Ventures

Fireside Ventures' First Annual Conference: This marked a milestone for the domestic rupee capital fund that has backed brands such as BoAt and Mama Earth.

Nasscom

The group that called itself Black Shirts and worked to put together the Nasscom Product Conclave, circa 2010

Freshworks

The founding team of Freshworks (then Freshdesk) at their office in Keelkatalai, Chennai, celebrating the Microsoft Bizsparks award they won, beating over forty startups from all over India. The award was the first validation to the team that their startup had what it takes to make it in the big league. Girish Mathrubootham is third from left.

MakeMyTrip

Deep Kalra of MakeMyTrip (*second from left*), along with co-founders (*left to right*) Keyur Joshi, Rajesh Magow and Sachin Bhatia

MakeMyTrip

Deep Kalra (*left*) and Ravi Adusumalli, founder and co-managing partner of Elevation Capital (earlier SAIF Partners), an early backer of MMT

Chairman Emeritus of the Tata Group Ratan Tata (*left*), an early backer of firms such as Snapdeal and later Ola and Paytm, and Chiratae Ventures founder Sudhir Sethi. Tata is an adviser to the India-based venture firm.

Zerodha

(*Left to right*) Nithin Kamath, Nikhil Kamath, Kailash Nadh, Venu Madhav and Karthik Rangappa of Zerodha

Zerodha

Zerodha CEO Nithin Kamath with CTO Kailash Nadh, who is credited with building the company's technology platform

for it by an industry senior, he would strike back publicly and go on to harangue another VC for purportedly poaching talent from his startup. The social media spectacle that ensued had the company's board concerned enough to begin a formal search for a new CEO. As news of this broke, Yadav tendered his resignation with seven days' notice. It was high-decibel drama and a meltdown in the investor–founder relationship of a kind unseen in the industry until then.

One investor, singed by the entire fracas, described it as a 'come-to-Jesus' moment. It marked a sudden realization or recognition that often comes before a major shift in thinking. The board decided that the CEO had to go—by no means an easy call to take. The investor–entrepreneur equation is a delicate one. Missteps that lead to a rupture can have far-reaching consequences for both parties in a business where reputation precedes all.

Hailing from Alwar, Rajasthan, Yadav had made the big shift from a small town through the tried and tested route of entrance to an IIT. He enrolled in IIT Bombay in 2007 and chose to major in metallurgy. The college was then a breeding ground for startups, the most recent being Bhavish Aggarwal's Ola. In his final year, he dropped out of college to start up with some eleven of his batchmates. The enterprising dozen were having a tough time finding a place to rent in Mumbai. In true-blue techie fashion, the geeks fired up their code-writing skills and built an online site that could ease the problem.

Within three years of its launch, the startup raised a total of nearly $120 million, or about ₹750 crore. But the initial capital for the launch in 2012 had come from Yadav's savings. This earned him the title of CEO among the eleven co-founders. It was an unwieldy number. But those who watched the team from up close would attest to their camaraderie, of the impromptu cricket matches that would break out in the office and the all-night coding sessions that were the staple of techie lives.

In July 2015, when the board decided to formally fire the co-founder and CEO citing 'his behaviour towards investors, ecosystem and the media',[1] it would again be a one-of-a-kind development. To many, the Yadav saga was a cautionary tale.

The investor–founder fracas would also come at a time when the industry was already struggling to deal with the inflationary impact of too much money chasing too few companies able to scale in quick time. This problem of plenty, particularly that of plentiful money, can be a tricky one to solve. In the context of Indian startups it has proven to be a recurring challenge.

For sure, there were macroeconomic factors underlying the surge in capital flow. The US government's quantitative easing, where it increased the money flow in the economy in response to a crisis (first in 2008 following the financial crisis and again in 2020 during the COVID-19 pandemic), would typically lead to an increase in risk capital flows worldwide. In both instances, India saw a sharp spike in venture capital activity.

However, in 2014 and 2015, the spike in venture fund activity would come from a different direction. Firms that had gained handsomely from bets they had taken on Chinese internet startups would begin to deploy that capital in India. Venture returns in Asia's largest economy reached a high with the blockbuster public listing of Alibaba in 2014. Investors who gained by exiting from their investments in Chinese startups channelled that money to the next emerging startup hot spot, India.

Flush with cash, they would power their way on to the cap table of Indian startups, only to discover that barring a few exceptions there just weren't enough companies with experience and talent to handle this volume of money. Even more critically, there wasn't even a market with sufficient depth to absorb the rush of capital. So they would pick two or perhaps three frontrunners and pump in more and more money to create a winner-takes-all market. This bruising model became the default for startup investing in India through much of the era of stupendous growth in the 2010s.

Early-stage investor Sajith Pai, who has co-authored a sweeping study of the country's startup landscape, holds that

India is a nation of browsers 'gorging on content and video calling'.[2] By the start of the 2020s, Indians were consuming about 18.4 GB of data per month compared to a global average of 11.9 GB. The Chinese, who in popular imagination are seen tethered to their smartphones, consume about 14.5 GB. For internet commerce companies, what can be even more worrying is that just a tenth of these browsers are shopping online in India. In comparison, nearly 50 per cent of Chinese internet users are buying online.

What this means—and it was even more pronounced in 2015—is that a very small number of transacting consumers are available to pay for goods and services sold online. Internet commerce startups therefore burn cash to gain growth, luring consumers with deals, discounts and more, literally competing with rivals in a game of who can burn more cash and win more customers. Money is thrown at the problem in a bid to boost the GMV. This measure, of the value of goods sold before deducting expenses, is the default standard used to narrate the growth of internet commerce startups.

Predictably enough, investors would run into the limits of how much private capital they were willing to wager on such loss-making businesses. And this was more in the case of the e-commerce industry. The big-ticket funding may even have continued if it wasn't Amazon that the Indian e-commerce leaders were competing against. The American company, which is publicly listed and has infinite pools of capital, was well placed to play the waiting game. In truth, big money from the tech giants and VCs was flowing into India in the hope that one day the business would be large enough to justify all the marketing dollars.

In such a milieu, the implosion of one of the country's most talked about startups would leave its mark on investors and entrepreneurs alike. Questions would rise as to how much of the blame must rest with investors for the messy denouement. Was it a case of too much money too soon? Did startups led by raw, inexperienced founders require adult supervision?

For long, the Indian startup industry has wrestled with these questions. In the early days of the internet wave when American investment firm Tiger Global's Lee Fixel upended the dynamics of venture capital investing with his bold bet on first-time founders like the Bansals of Flipkart, it would leave rivals in a tough spot. FOMO, the fear of missing out, would drive others to enter the fray. While the Flipkart gambit went on to create startup history, not all such punts would end in glory. Often, it would result in the distortion of markets as it fostered a winner-takes-all model. Instead of capital flowing to multiple ventures and creating a healthy, competitive marketplace, investors would end up privileging the leader in the pack or at best the top two in a market. Money would become the moat to keep rivals at bay. And in turn lead to a pervasive disaffection across the industry. So much so that even SoftBank, which had made its first bets in late 2014, was already looking at 2015 as a time of reckoning. It had sunk in nearly $1 billion in a matter of weeks in late 2014 and it was time to see how the bets were faring[3] in the summer of 2015.

SoftBank's president at the time, Nikesh Arora, who wrote some of the biggest cheques in India's startup scene, cautioned that valuations had raced 'far ahead' of what they should be. In an interview with *The Economic Times* in August 2015, Arora termed the Indian startup ecosystem as 'not mature enough'. He conceded that while valuations of Indian startups may have been reasonable two to three years ago, the country had gone far ahead and was probably rivalling valuations in China and even the US in mid-2015. More people were chasing the same number of investments, and valuations would surge nearly threefold in the space of just one year.[4]

It is likely that until the entry of Amazon with its deep pockets, these investors may even have been indulgent to the likes of Snapdeal and Flipkart. But with staggering amounts of money already invested without any clear exit in sight, any indulgence would soon come to an end. The tone at board meetings and elsewhere became tough and conversations turned rancorous. It was a messy time in the startup trenches in 2015.

Much of the malaise gripping the industry in those days can be traced back directly to a paucity of big-ticket exits in the industry. Investors who had entered the market before the advent of SoftBank were still waiting for returns. Some of these were funds that had placed their bets in the first boom cycle starting from 2008–09 onward and were still waiting to cash out. Their capital had been in play for a long time, and they wanted to see results. This included the biggest investor of that period, Flipkart-backer Tiger Global. Concerningly, well-funded Indian startups weren't delivering the blockbuster exits these funds had become accustomed to in China, for instance.

For founders, this was a real grouse that needed to be addressed. Because if venture capital was stuck in companies for which there were no new takers, it was unlikely that more money would be committed by existing investors. If there was one fly in the Indian startup ointment, it was the absence of a vibrant market to buy and sell companies.

Seen from that perspective, the deluge of money in 2014 delivered at least one welcome outcome. It kicked off the beginning of an M&A market for small as well as mid-size startups in India. So much so that 2015 would go down in startup lore as a watershed year when the bigger startups began to acquire smaller or younger ventures. Tracxn, a startup that tracks dealmaking involving startups, found that in all of 2014, forty-three startups were acquired; by the second half of 2015, forty-one had been bought. The best part was that startups themselves were the most acquisitive of the lot. Of the forty-one transactions, just two were struck by large corporates: Godrej and Mahindra & Mahindra.

This robust dealmaking began in early 2015 with SoftBank-backed Ola snapping up rival TaxiforSure, as we have already seen. By March, Snapdeal had bought Freecharge, paying out over $400 million—the biggest buyout in the Indian startup space at that time. Both transactions by the SoftBank investee companies signalled the power that big money bestows.

No doubt, money was important. But along with the aggressive dealmaking, startups were displaying guts and ambition. They were aiming for faster growth and dealing with the challenges of integration while refreshing and renewing company culture and setting new goals. For example, by acquiring fashion portal Myntra, Flipkart had cemented its position as the market leader. Freecharge was an acquirer before it was bought by Snapdeal in the biggest startup M&A deal yet, demonstrating the dynamism of the market and opening a new revenue opportunity for the Delhi company. These new-economy companies were showing how it was done. They had demonstrated confidence in their businesses and a willingness to take risks.

These deals would also put money in the hands of a large number of founders, employees and early investors. In turn, this money would find its way to backing fledgling ideas as the new rich would turn into mentors and angel investors. India would witness the strengthening of angel investment networks across cities, including in non-metros, as a crucial link in the startup chain.

Some entrepreneurs would also return to set up newer ventures for a second or third time. All this activity would set off a new phase of internet entrepreneurship in the country that would take wing in the age of cheap data. This was made possible by the rollout of competitive data plans by telecom companies led by Reliance Jio, making it possible for millions more to access the internet on very affordable mobile phones.

Not least, the Union government was also catalysing greater startup activity. The Digital India initiative, announced in 2015, was already extending the reach of the unique public digital infrastructure which was seeded by Aadhaar and furthered by the volunteers at India Stack. In January 2016, the government went a step further by introducing the Startup India initiative for infrastructure, regulatory and financial support for startups. This would include the ₹10,000 crore fund-of-funds managed by the Small Industries Development Bank of India, SIDBI. For sure, this was more money coming the way of startups.

But this foray by the government would be different in many ways. For one, this was money for venture funds already registered with the country's market regulator and not for individual startups per se. Second, it would trigger interest among India's wealthy to consider venture capital as an asset class, marking the first step in the creation of a rupee capital base for Indian startups, one that would become stronger and more visible in the years ahead.

These developments, ranging from a wave of homegrown M&As that catalysed the development of angel investment and rupee capital for startups to the government's aggressive backing for technology startups, are not isolated events. They must be seen in unison with the buildout of public digital infrastructure at a time of sharp decline in the cost of data and smartphones. Together, these were the harbingers of what is now being spoken of as the third wave of starting up in India, one that would gain strength and purpose on the back of a maturing base of consumers as well as from founders building unique businesses focused on the needs of Bharat, and not just for urban India as the bulk of their predecessors had done. Startup India was bustling.

In stark contrast, the sector's biggest players were morose. They had less cause for cheer—the clock was ticking for the country's biggest online commerce companies. Investors who had weighed in with the big cheques were not willing to wait any longer for returns. The shadow of Amazon was growing lengthier across the industry and it was clear that Indian online retail would not have place for more than two players at the top. Successive rounds of funding had also created a clear ownership grid across the top three companies of the time: Flipkart, Snapdeal and Paytm.

SoftBank, the biggest investor in Snapdeal, was keen to get a foothold in rival Flipkart, then the country's largest online commerce company valued at about $11 billion at the start of 2017. Beginning with its $200 million investment in mobile advertising network InMobi in early 2011, the investment powerhouse had put in about $1 billion in Snapdeal, Ola and

Housing.com in the space of a few weeks in late 2014. It now had its eyes set on the biggest prize of all, a stake in the country's largest e-commerce company: Flipkart.

Meanwhile, Tiger Global was impatient to cash out from its near $1 billion bet on Flipkart made nearly a decade ago. In some eight years of investing in India, led by the reclusive Fixel, the New York firm had invested over $1.3 billion in some forty companies at that point. As for Paytm, which had first raised strategic capital from Alibaba and its fintech subsidiary Ant Financial in 2014, the fintech brand was now looking to make headway in the e-commerce arena with Paytm Mall. All of this would play out under the giant shadow of Amazon. At that point, Jeff Bezos had committed $5 billion for the India business. He was in no mood to stint. This cauldron of clashing needs, ambitions and goals would shape the coming months in the Indian e-commerce industry.

It began with a rather startling idea: of Snapdeal combining forces with Flipkart. The scrappy third runner in the great e-commerce battle had run into rough weather through the course of 2016. With the winner-takes-all model firmly entrenched in the Indian startup space, internet founders were girded to a tried and tested path. They had to close successive rounds of funding with ever-higher valuations for greater amounts of money, and with near-metronomic consistency, or prepare to perish. As the third player in this brutal marketplace, Snapdeal had begun to fray. It was also being laid low by a general slowdown in e-commerce growth countrywide.

India's e-commerce sector was responding to the economic upheaval set off by demonetization in November 2016. As cash was abruptly sucked out of the system, consumer spending began to slow. For the online retail industry, the impact would show fairly quickly. In the final quarter of fiscal 2017, the industry expanded only by a small 5 per cent, reaching $14.5 billion. Snapdeal, as the third player in a slowing industry, would feel the pain keenly. It had last raised big money in February 2016 when it was valued at $6.5 billion. It found few takers for its renewed need for cash a year later. Investors had dragged its valuation down to $1.5 billion. As the troubles mounted, Snapdeal fired hundreds of employees and the founders Kunal Bahl and Rohit Bansal took a 100 per cent pay cut in early 2017.

In its early years, Snapdeal with its marketplace model had created a moat for itself in a market where the inventory-led approach ruled. The benefit for e-commerce players in an inventory model was that they owned the inventory stocked in their own warehouses and shipped directly to customers. This gave them greater control on how a purchase was packaged and delivered to consumers—a customer-centric model made famous by Amazon.

In contrast, in the marketplace model, the technology platform alone was run by the online company. In turn, it would host multiple sellers or merchants on its platform who stocked and shipped products. This model, widely termed the TaoBao model, was made famous by the Chinese e-commerce giant.

In India, as regulatory constraints put paid to the inventory approach, bigger and better-funded rivals would also build large online marketplaces. Snapdeal in 2016 discovered that its once-robust competitive advantage was being steadily whittled down. From then on, it was a question of how successfully it could raise more cash at what valuation and with what consistency. And this was when Snapdeal began to fall back. Online retail by then was a heavy-hitters game in India.

Investors had to have a deep chest of capital to enter the field. This in itself reduced the number of funds or large corporations willing to wager a bet. Large players had already taken sides and they would either look to shore their bets further, not bet on a rival. Those looking to enter anew would want to do so on the cap table of the eventual winner.

One thing was becoming crystal clear: the first phase of internet retail in India was drawing to a close. Firms that had taken early positions such as Accel were coming to the end of their fund cycle. It was eight to ten years since their first bets in the sector, and they wanted to deliver returns to their investors or limited partners, as they are referred to in the industry.

As for strategic investors like Naspers, the goal was to cash in big returns from investments made in the industry leader. Naspers was already an investor in Flipkart. Son's investment firm at that point was also going through a top leadership churn with Arora, who had led the investment in Snapdeal in 2014, leaving the company. The Japanese investment giant increasingly trained its sights on gaining a stake in Flipkart.

Not to be outdone, the Alibaba-backed Paytm also made a play for the Bahl–Bansal-led company. It was keen to grow its e-commerce business. The respective investors—Alibaba in Paytm and Son in SoftBank—were old comrades-in-arms. There was a belief that there could be a deal. Additionally, Snapdeal's newly acquired payment arm, Freecharge, was seen as an attractive fit to the Paytm Wallet. More so in the era of a UPI-led transformation of digital payments that was already underway. This wave was being led by PhonePe, the fintech startup that had already been folded into Flipkart in early 2016.

Amid all these various pulls and pressures, Snapdeal became just a variable in a complicated and layered situation. The to and fro would go on for the better part of a year, beginning from the early negotiations in mid-2016. Sometime in March 2017, the issue turned serious. Paytm declared that it was no longer interested in taking on Snapdeal. The discussions would not progress for want of agreement on a suitable selling price.

By then, the question was not whether Snapdeal would be sold or not, but how much a buyer would be willing to pay. It had already raised close to $1.8 billion in capital by then and had some of the biggest names on its cap table, from SoftBank to Alibaba, as well as the American online marketplace eBay. The going rate for the company, however, had fallen to below $1 billion, with some even quoting a low of $800 million.

Once Paytm dropped out, the field was down to just one buyer: market leader Flipkart. In April 2017, industry researcher Red Seer put out a note arguing that if the India-focused portals Flipkart and Snapdeal were to withstand the might of Amazon's money and execution capability, they would do well to 'join forces'. It presented a couple of reasons that could tip the balance in favour of the Flipkart–Snapdeal combine, the biggest of them being a well-set supply chain. While Flipkart had strengths in the southern market, Snapdeal had built inroads into the northern hinterlands. The New Delhi company had also built deep brand partnerships across areas like retail given its legacy as a marketplace. Flipkart at that point had a base of some 100 million users that it could speedily expand by combining with Snapdeal. All this was the chatter building up around one of the most talked about deals in Indian internet at that time.

For the main protagonists, Bahl and Rohit Bansal, this would be a deeply uncertain period. They recall being 'impatient' for an answer, a closure to months of frenzied discussions. To them, a final decision, whichever way it was structured, was a far better outcome than all the uncertainty. It was doing no good to the founders or the company or its employees. And while the combined outcome was to grow value in the business, the specific goals of the investors and the founders were proving to be different. The whole saga was shaping up to be a coming-of-age moment for the thirty-something founders.

The pace of the negotiations quickened and the complexity deepened as the monsoon set in over the country. Around the third week of July, Flipkart made an offer for an estimated $900 million buyout structured as a share-swap deal. Later, this model involving a transaction between India-based Snapdeal and Singapore-registered Flipkart would be cited as one of the deal-breakers because of the tax implications. No less fractious were reports of differential payouts to those on the cap table.

Snapdeal, meanwhile, in a fight for survival, sold its payments arm Freecharge to Axis Bank in the final week of July. It would be a garage sale with a sale price of about $60 million, a near-sevenfold decrease from what the online marketplace had paid to acquire the startup in 2015, when it was heavy with cash from the SoftBank deal. That deal, the biggest M&A in Indian internet till then, lost much of its lustre in the ensuing months. The Freecharge model, built on discounts to customers using its platform for recharges, would be overtaken by the spectacular launch of UPI and the inter-bank payments system.

But for a depleted Snapdeal in 2017, the deal was important. It would deliver much-needed oxygen to a company gasping for survival and embolden the founders. In a dramatic move, on the final day of July, the news broke that Bahl–Bansal had decided to call off the buyout deal with Flipkart. Events got fuzzy from thereon. The founders declined to sign off on the agreement at the final moment, choosing instead to adopt the Snapdeal 2.0 model, one in which they let go of attendant businesses and focused only on building a lean marketplace model. The Freecharge divestment was already done; in the coming months logistics arm Vulcan Express would be sold.

The abrupt no-show by the founders triggered a flurry of speculation, insinuations and conjectures. However, the dramatis personae—the board, investors and founders—would adopt the Omerta Code with regard to the happenings at the crucial board meeting when the Bahl–Bansal duo refused to sign. Snapdeal downsized, and Bahl and Bansal returned to running a trimmed-down company. What could have been the biggest M&A in the Indian internet sector came to a halt. But in the broad arc of business, this would only mark a blip. The real game was beginning to intensify. This time, the prize was Flipkart itself.

SoftBank, which remained invested in Snapdeal, made a whole new bet. Literally within a week of the Snapdeal–Flipkart merger falling through, SoftBank made its biggest investment in the country. It ploughed in a staggering $2.5 billion into Flipkart, the investment coming from the Japanese firm's $100 billion Vision Fund. It was launched in October 2016, and was the largest-ever amount of capital pooled together for technology investments anywhere in the world. The sovereign wealth fund of Saudi Arabia, the Public Investment Fund, had contributed 45 per cent of the corpus while about 15 per cent came from its Emirati counterpart Mubadala Investment Company. Phone maker Apple too was a contributor to this one-of-its-kind fund.

Son himself is unique in the way that he approaches the business of investing. Two months after the Vision Fund was launched, he travelled to Delhi. In an interview with *The Economic Times* in December 2016, he said that he might 'overachieve' on his commitment made two years before to invest $10 billion in India over a decade.[5] He spoke at length about his plans for investments in India's solar sector, as well as his 'wish' to donate 1 million electric vehicles to drivers working for Ola, a SoftBank portfolio company.

The small-framed Korean-Japanese billionaire with a soft-spoken mien offers no visible clue that he is one of the world's most aggressive technology investors. In India, he would exhort founders to think big, think disruptive. Founders of his portfolio company were 'family guys' to him. They had his long-term support but if there were any 'other entrepreneurs' who impressed him he was always open to new opportunities.

Less than a week after the failed merger, Son's approach became clear. Flipkart's Bansals had clearly impressed him. In what the two co-founders termed a 'monumental deal', Son bought a fifth of the company they had founded exactly a decade ago.[6] His firm became one of the largest shareholders in Flipkart alongside South African conglomerate Naspers and China's Tencent which together also owned 20 per cent stake in the company.

The deal was a landmark development in the evolution of India's internet industry itself. It was a mix of direct funding to the company, termed as primary investment, and the purchase of shares from existing shareholders, described as secondary investment. This would provide a partial exit for Tiger Global, until then the biggest and most influential investor in Flipkart, and by extension, in the country's internet market itself. Others would cash out too, including the co-founders and the storied company's first backer, Accel Partners.

A decade into the journey of Indian internet enterprise, the big payouts had finally begun. In what was then still a sparse cohort of unicorns—startups valued at over $1 billion—SoftBank owned stakes in the biggest four: Flipkart, Paytm, Ola and InMobi.

The deal also marked the real start of the Indian e-commerce war. Bezos had already made his intentions plain—he wanted to be the king of Indian online retail and was willing to wager up to $5 billion for that. Son's largesse had taken Flipkart over that mark. It would have drawn down nearly $6 billion in risk capital since it was born as a small online seller of books. Sure, it had burnt cash aplenty on the way. But as it squared up for the final battle, India's largest e-commerce company had a staggering $4 billion of cash reserves. A tiny seed had blossomed into a giant canopy.

Inside the company's bustling workplaces spread across south-east Bengaluru, anticipation was building to fever pitch. For nearly a decade, Flipkart and a handful of other internet startups had done the hard work of tilling barren ground. They didn't have the luxury of beginning in a market with mature infrastructure. There was no logistics network to deliver parcels within a day across a country with 19,101 postal codes across some 720 districts. Only a fraction of Indians qualified for credit cards; even fewer would use them to pay online. The country did not even have a unified GST allowing for smooth transit of shipments across state borders. They had to build the highways and draw in the customers, and only then could they deepen the business of buying and selling. In the corner offices and in the hallways of the sprawling Flipkart office, the tension and fatigue would begin to show.

The company also went through several iterations at the top. The startup that had begun from a two-bedroom flat now had multiple arms: a payment arm, PhonePe; a logistics network,

Ekart; fashion portal Myntra–Jabong; and the mother ship, the e-commerce arm. It was now the Flipkart Group.

Since the start of 2017, the company, for the first time in its history, was being run by a non-founder CEO, Kalyan Krishnamurthy. The forty-four-year-old, a close aide of Tiger Global's Fixel, was no stranger to Flipkart. As early as 2013, he had come in as CFO at the still-young startup for a near-two-year stint. On his return in 2016, when Binny Bansal had taken over the CEO role from Sachin Bansal, Krishnamurthy took charge of product categories. His elevation to CEO marked a seminal change for the startup, with neither of its founders in charge of operations at the company.

Sachin remained executive chairman of the Flipkart Group and Binny took over a newly formed role as Group CEO. From the Bansals' perspective, an outsider was in charge of the company for the first time. It was a consequential shift. Not only had the fledgling startup grown into India's most valued tech startup, the contours of its ownership had changed. The Bansals were now small minority shareholders with their stake in low single digits. Big money comes at a cost and the Bansals had paid the price.

But there was still work to be done. For one, the capital moat that SoftBank had helped build was a tenuous one. It didn't change the fact that Amazon was investing from its balance sheet and as such had the deeper, stronger pockets. Another crucial factor for risk-capital-funded companies is that management attention has to be constantly focused on raising the next round of cash. At the early stages of a company's growth, this might be enjoyable and manageable, but as the stakes rise, capital accumulation becomes complicated, arduous and a distraction that the best entrepreneur-managers will do well without. But only a few have that choice. A startup founder sprints from one big-ticket fundraise to the next, much like a politician who trains his sights from one election to the next. And while a manager at Amazon can concentrate on the business knowing the money will be taken care of, a Flipkart founder had to strategize for both cash and operations.

That crucial difference had begun showing up in the Indian e-commerce industry in 2016 itself. As Flipkart went through its leadership churn, Amazon had been quietly building up its supply chain and warehouse networks. Moreover, in India, e-commerce companies still required cash to retain existing customers and attract newer ones. Which meant that the next round of funding would soon become important even for a company like Flipkart, not just for the business but also for the early investors. Tiger Global would have been less restive after divesting some stake to SoftBank, but by no means content.

There was no time to rest after the SoftBank cash fest. It was time to think of the next funding round. Even before the high-octane events of mid-2017, the Bansals had begun to think of long-term moves. Financial investors with cyclical investment flows were no longer sufficient for the quantum of money their business required. For stability to grow, Flipkart would need a strategic investor. Walmart, America's iconic retailer, had already made a few forays into India. But it was in the pre-internet era when it had partnered with telecom major Bharti Airtel. It retreated in the face of regulatory constraints. Meanwhile, in its home market, Amazon had emerged as the online leader. The Bentonville-headquartered corporation was testing the waters in India yet again, this time looking for more than just to gain a foothold in India. It now wanted to gain e-commerce expertise. It had begun 'engaging' in discussions with Flipkart for a possible investment. Amazon got to know of this and more. In September that year, Sachin Bansal met Jeff Bezos at a conference in the US. The American entrepreneur expressed an interest to go all out to acquire Flipkart. It was a bold thought. Walmart, meanwhile, would up the ante as well.

For Flipkart, this explosion of interest came at an opportune moment. The company was not profitable but it was growing rapidly and it required a cash infusion to maintain the pace. It clearly needed strategic capital. Walmart and Amazon both fit the bill. The period from September to December 2017 was a frenzied time at the company as talks intensified with both suitors.

As winter set in, the thinking amongst Flipkart stakeholders was that the Walmart deal had a better chance to fructify. They had an eye on the regulator as well. An Amazon–Flipkart deal, it was thought, would be stuck in the sights of the country's competition watchdog. Bezos would stay interested and even pony up the bigger deal. But finally, the chips settled in favour of Walmart. In May 2018, the American retailer paid a whopping $16 billion for a 77 per cent stake in Flipkart.[7]

The final denouement came with its share of drama. Sachin Bansal, who had stayed close to the discussions until the final stage, failed to secure the minority shareholder rights that he was seeking. He would sell his entire stake and leave with a $1 billion payout. Binny Bansal, who would not dilute all his holding, remained for a while longer.

A ten-year saga from start to finish had catapulted the Bansals into the ranks of the world's internet billionaires. Their story of grit, ambition and outsize vision had transformed Indian internet entrepreneurship. Those who came after them would dream bigger, execute better and build stronger.

10

Sassy Networks

In much of middle-class India, where a person's social worth is directly proportionate to his standing in the great arranged-marriage market, young entrepreneurs with no 'steady income' would often be found wanting. It took the 'unicorn mela' in the consumer internet space to turn that narrative on its head, what with tales of billionaire founders and their overnight fortunes littering the daily narrative. Suddenly, startup entrepreneurs became the new aspirational grooms in middle-class homes.

But such good fortune is limited only to founders of consumer internet companies, argue those who are not part of that magic circle. They are quick to narrate an apocryphal tale about what transpired when the founder of a business software startup met a prospective bride's father. The irate parent reportedly asked him, 'How dare you come for my daughter's hand! We are looking for at least an e-commerce founder, if not a hyperlocal founder, for an alliance.'

Tales such as these are guaranteed to draw the loudest guffaws at gatherings of founders running enterprise software or SaaS companies. Their businesses offer software-as-a-service, a model that allows a company to host a software application on its servers that users can access remotely by paying a subscription fee, often monthly.

One such grouping, 'Daru Pe Charcha', or DPC, with some two score members, is the go-to setting for rants, raves, learning, advice, mentoring, dealmaking—and the choicest jokes about industry peers. The tale of the spurned SaaS suitor is, in fact, a DPC spoof on how venture investors were once in thrall of e-commerce companies to the exclusion of all other ideas.

For years, these enterprise technology makers had watched from the sidelines while money and attention were lavished on the fast-growing consumer internet companies. With such businesses having already delivered blockbuster returns in other markets, investors deploying cash in India were looking for similar outcomes from local online commerce startups. The overlooked SaaS founders vented in private and brought the house down with their brand of startup humour at regular meetups. In the case of DPC, the unabashedly desi and brutally candid grouping is clear that it is not an exclusive club for the privileged and the successful. In fact, it is the reverse. This network, where felicity with either Hindi or Tamil is a prerequisite, expects 'pretence to be left at the door'.[1] Very soon, however, its gatherings would evolve into more than just fun and games. The group became the default helpline for SaaS entrepreneurs looking to make a breakthrough in the industry. It provided connections, counsel and handholding in an otherwise lonely entrepreneurial journey.

Just as the old-school tie and the right club membership could once script social and professional mobility within corporate India, it is groupings such as DPC and larger peer networks like SaaSBoomi that are providing professional ballast to new technology entrepreneurs. Much like what more formal groupings such as TiE and industry pioneer NASSCOM have previously done. In a Darwinian industry where there are more rivals and few friends, these networks play a critical role in providing safety nets. Sometimes, such groupings can be powerful enough to even break new ground. One such cohort that called itself the Black Shirts gained recognition for being the splinter group that carved out the software product conclave from within NASSCOM way back in 2009.

The motivations for these networks is better understood when viewed through the prism of how technology entrepreneurship first took off in India. While software exporters like TCS and Wipro were offshoots of traditional conglomerates, Infosys, with its middle-class flair, drove the democratization of entrepreneurial opportunity.

By the late 1990s, when internet entrepreneurship took seed in the country with the likes of Sanjeev Bikhchandani's Info Edge, Deep Kalra's MakeMyTrip and Sridhar Vembu's AdventNet (later Zoho), dreams of starting up had taken hold of legions of graduating engineers. Unsurprisingly, they hired their dorm mates, college mates and colleagues to launch new businesses. Several others with experience of having worked in the United States at consulting and financial firms backed more of their own ilk.

TiE too was an elite grouping, set up as a bridge between successful Silicon Valley entrepreneurs looking to further their success in their home country. There was definitely a touch of noblesse oblige about these groupings in the early days that was at odds with the iconoclastic nature of internet entrepreneurship itself. More so for aspiring founders who were not part of the IIT–IIM networks or among the US returnee cohorts. One such technology founder in Chennai, young entrepreneur Suresh Sambandam, set up a SaaS venture, OrangeScape, in 2004. The former analyst at Hewlett Packard was not new to computers but he was certainly new to business. He knew little about angel investors or venture capital and the only source of funding for a new business in his mind was by 'pledging personal property like jewellery or a home'.[2]

There was good reason for this. While the internet was there, there wasn't yet a vibrant ecosystem of bloggers and content writers who would democratize knowledge-sharing in the industry. That boom would coincide with the explosion of entrepreneurial activity in 2007–08. And in cities like Chennai that were off-centre from the vortex of action, professional networking would be even more difficult. Sambandam would interact with city-based groups like the Open Coffee Club until he discovered that NASSCOM was the go-to IT industry grouping. However, once he plugged into the network, he surmised that it was designed for the big boys of the industry, those leading India's storied software export boom. Emerging entrepreneurs were like small fish in a big pond. Soon, he had banded with like-minded founders. Among those he connected with was enterprising NASSCOM executive Avinash Raghava, who led its activities in the northern region. They joined forces and launched a community-driven forum called the NASSCOM Emerge Forum with some 2,000 actively engaged founders. It was also the time when communities for free software, open software forums and other such movements were taking off.

The internet was driving massive transformation. Software services were being sold online on a subscription basis and Indian SaaS entrepreneurs were asking why they shouldn't simply build products themselves. This was a tectonic shift. For people like Freshworks's Girish Mathrubootham, it all started with one dream: of making 'India a software product nation'.[3]

Soon, these entrepreneurs wanted an industry forum that reflected the ongoing changes. The trigger was simple. Software product enthusiasts were of the view that the NASSCOM structure suited IT services companies, prioritizing their needs to get things done, lobby with the government and so on. In addition, the voting rights were based on the quantum of subscription fee, which was in turn linked to a company's revenue. This privileged large companies over smaller startups.

Around the same time, one of the pivotal personalities in the development of software industry groupings, Sharad Sharma, would join NASSCOM. Once head of Yahoo's research centre in India, Sharma was widely regarded as a champion for Indian software products. He had soon rustled up a group of ten others who thought likewise and formed a pressure group. This marked the start of a pivotal time for the software product industry in India.

This group of ten called itself the Black Shirts. It was a splinter group within NASSCOM which met religiously every Saturday between 9 a.m. and 10 a.m. The members ran companies themselves but wouldn't miss Black Shirt meetings. With the experience of building the community forum for Emerge Out at NASSCOM, they had sufficient know-how to strike out independently.[4]

Together, they launched the first community-curated, volunteer-driven NASSCOM Product Conclave in 2009–10. The first conclave drew 300 people, the second had nearly 700, while the third was nearly double that, at 1,300 delegates. So much so that in 2013, the group wanted NASSCOM to create two divisions: one for the reigning biggies, the IT Services Division, and the second for the product division with its own budget.

Finally, thirty product companies decided to leave NASSCOM altogether and launch a new grouping. They called it iSPIRT: Indian Software Product Industry Round Table. For three years, 2013 to 2016, iSPIRT—one of the seminal groupings in the Indian technology landscape—tirelessly championed the cause of software products. Its volunteers created a new conference for software product-makers, SaaSx.[5]

Two successful editions down the line, the grouping grappled with an existential crisis of its own. From its beginnings as a lobby group for Indian software products, iSPIRT had evolved into a think tank focused on building India's public digital infrastructure, India Stack. The core group turned its focus to taking forward the country's vision to build a digital infrastructure framework born out of the Aadhaar ecosystem.[6]

For the SaaS champions, this evolution would again push them off-centre. They retreated into silent mode until, finally, in 2018, a die-hard group of SaaS champions led by the likes of Raghava, Sambandam and others regrouped to launch SaaSBoomi, a non-profit focused primarily on building the SaaS ecosystem in India.

By then, the technology product space itself had taken on a different shape. The e-commerce sector had its own communities—the problems they faced were very different from the problems that SaaS founders grappled with. Then there were separate groups talking about drones and embedded software and more. It was futile to club all these conversations under one umbrella. It made a lot more sense to combine all the business software makers together. And that's how SaaSBoomi was formed.

Specialization had come to industry groupings as well, and with good reason. These founders were clear that they didn't want the next industry unicorn after Freshworks to take nearly a decade to flower, as the Chennai major had done. Nor did they want the next lot to make the same mistakes. For the likes of Mathrubootham, the question was whether he could help accelerate the next wave of SaaS startups from India.

Communities and networks have fast grown to be the bedrock of the startup ecosystem, validating the depth and reach of the entrepreneurial upsurge. They are prized for sharing knowledge, providing access and building a culture of 'paying it forward'. This is a culture where those who get to the higher rungs of the ladder are almost duty-bound to provide a hand to those waiting below. Entrepreneurs starting out estimate that being part of such networks could be as good as getting a first-seed investment of $1 million.

This is what Arvind Parthiban would discover when he started out in 2015. He was famously a member of the Zoho gang, alumni of one of India's best-known SaaS companies and one of its oldest. In some ten years at Zoho, the computer-science engineer from Chennai's Anna University had climbed from a pre-sales engineer to leading the marketing for its customer delivery services. In early 2014, he was part of a bold gambit by the Sridhar Vembu–led company to offer one of its flagship products, an IT helpdesk software product, for free. The argument was that the revenue loss incurred from making a popular product free would be recouped by winning a larger share of the overall IT management market. It was a bold ploy designed to trip up not just incumbents but also newer entrants like another Chennai-based SaaS venture, Freshdesk. To broadcast the offer, Zoho pulled off an innovative marketing campaign.

At a crowded technology industry event in London, Parthiban and his team brought in a food truck offering fish and chips and mini burgers. Attendees were urged to walk up and eat for free to underline the point that 'there is indeed such a thing as a free lunch'. As marketing campaigns go, it was an unbridled success.

It grabbed attention, not least that of Freshworks co-founder Mathrubootham.

In time, when Parthiban was looking to found a startup, Mathrubootham put up the seed money alongside two investors from his company's board, Sequoia and Accel Partners. Parthiban's startup, Zarget, would build tech tools for e-commerce and other SaaS companies. They would help companies track when visitors were dropping off from their sites and what to improve in the check-out pages, among other tools. The startup clocked some half a million dollars in revenue in six months. But Parthiban noticed that there was little customer stickiness as Google had launched a competing product at the same time. He was left with two choices: bite the bullet and move to the large enterprise space or sell out to a larger SaaS company. This is where network effects would come into play. Mathrubootham, who was already on the board of Zarget, was aware of the situation. He acquired the venture, which had a ready base of customers that would prove useful to Freshworks. Parthiban worked there for a few years before the startup bug bit him yet again.

In the early years of the 2010s, the Indian startup space had seen a similar explosion of entrepreneurial action. At that time, founders would vie with each other to set up consumer internet ventures. At the end of that decade, as Flipkart's sale to Walmart marked the close of one era of consumer internet activity, there was a similar upsurge in starting up. But this time it would be the SaaS ventures and the likes of Parthiban riding the wave.

This was an evolution that had been nearly two decades in the making, with the pieces being put together unobtrusively in the background. In the early 2000s, as the world's technology giants began establishing back offices in Bengaluru, they were unwittingly creating a pool of cutting-edge technology talent that would seed India's startup boom. The back offices not only supplied refined talent for consumer internet ventures, they also spawned thousands of enterprise software companies. As early as 2004, US-based SaaS companies had set up back offices in India and hired an average of 200 people who would take on the entire engineering, marketing, sales and onboarding from India. This led to ventures that would, for example, build products for sellers on the eBay marketplace.

Mathrubootham, whose SaaS venture is now listed on NASDAQ, contends that it was Lee Fixel, the early backer of India's consumer internet ventures, who also lit the SaaS fire. The SaaS space became an accidental beneficiary of the consumer internet boom. It created a market for engineers and for products and services required to run large internet platforms. Growth would come at a blistering pace. At Chennai-based Freshdesk, revenue surged from \$1 million to \$5 million to \$15 million to \$34 million in a couple of years. All this while consumer internet startups were hogging the limelight—in terms of funding, in terms of valuations—even while having to pay to win customers. SaaS companies, on the other hand, were being discovered online by paying customers from across the world. For the likes of Mathrubootham, 'winning is the best deodorant'. And there was pride aplenty in what these upstart companies were able to pull off.

Take, for example, BrowserStack. Once feted for being a winner in the bootstrap category at *The Economic Times* Startup Awards, the Mumbai-based venture was valued at \$4 billion in 2022. Investors put in about \$200 million into the company, which has been profitable since six months of starting up in 2011. It is a business that does one thing, and evidently does it very well. A mobile- and web-testing platform, it offers developers tools to test the compatibility of their products. Like the best ideas, this too would take time to gain its full stature. Founders Ritesh Arora and Nakul Aggarwal were classmates at IIT Bombay. Even as students the two of them had toyed with the idea of starting up in 2003 and had tested out nearly twenty-five ideas, of which only 'three would achieve some sort of material scale'.[7]

Finally, around 2006, they hit upon a machine-learning tool they decided to pitch to investors. The computer-science graduates met some fifty investors and barely get a nod from any of them. For Arora, whose family was fully into business, the idea of doing anything apart from starting up was alien. But both Aggarwal and he were also clear that they wanted to do this on their own, without turning to family for funding. Instead, they would find jobs. Arora worked as a software developer at US firm LimeLabs, all the while testing out new business ideas of his own.

Some of the fundamental tenets of how to create and run a business he would later follow were learnt during this phase. More so when he became a 'follower' of 37 Signals. The American web software company's founders started out to build a web design company. Over time, as they gained more business, they struggled to stay on top of the many moving parts that go into a project. It was a common enough problem. But instead of looking elsewhere for a solution, they turned to building a solution themselves. In time, its popularity with clients and others made them turn from design to building web software. At one point, the billion-dollar-plus enterprise was run by just thirty people. It is a model that the Chicago-based venture has evangelized through books and blogs that Arora would pore over. His ideas of building a deep-technology business built on community software such as Ruby on Rails was also forged during this phase of discovery.

The young engineers were also keenly aware that whatever they built had to be at global scale. Location did not matter, but the global mindset was central to what Arora was planning. The final piece was also to be self-sustaining, and not having to turn to investors to back a cash-guzzling business.

Armed with these learnings, Arora and Aggarwal would start up anew in 2011. This time they had more than a robust plan in place. They had spent some time thinking about the problem they wanted to solve. To Arora this came down to what they as developers had themselves struggled with. They decided to build a tool that would allow developers 'compatibility testing' across various applications. They put the tool out online for testing and found nearly 10,000 free users.

To their surprise, they began receiving queries from developers asking if there was a paid version. Arora and Aggarwal were astonished. They added pricing and packaging, and to their utter amazement got ten paying customers one day. So precise and painful was the problem that developers faced of testing their software across multiple platforms seamlessly.

It was a sweet spot for the new business. Within three to four months of starting up with about a thousand paying customers, Arora and Aggarwal had found their niche. They have stayed true to it even ten years after starting up, as the company grew in size and raked in profits.[8] The journey, though, was not linear. Around 2015–16, there was a phase when it grew so fast that the young entrepreneurs struggled with managing scale. They were techies who had made a spectacular success of what they did, but they began to feel the need for outside counsel, and perhaps to reconsider the decision to remain bootstrapped. This was when the network effects of being a SaaS venture in India would become apparent.

Investors had always been drawn to the fairy-tale progress of the two computer-science graduates. Arora had been talking to partners at Accel in the US for a while. In India, he connected with Accel India partner Shekhar Kirani, who was already an investor in Freshworks. Kirani introduced Arora to Mathrubootham, to just shoot the breeze and trade thoughts on what it took to build scale in a business.

It would be the start of what has proven to be an enduring connection. The Mumbai entrepreneur and the experienced Chennai founder hit it off. Arora says the conversations were so helpful that when it was time to zero in on the investor he would sign up with, it was clear to him that Accel India was the best bet for BrowserStack.[9]

For Arora, that first investment was clearly not about the capital. His was anyway a thriving, profitable business. What the investment did was set a valuation benchmark for the company, one which subsequent investors would use to enter his cap table. This allowed him to create an ESOP pool for employees and reward them with wealth. In a market where money has emerged as the differentiator, even companies like BrowserStack can feel the competitive pressure. Without tools for wealth creation, employees would leave for fresher pastures. This, then, was the moment that Arora and Aggarwal had to bite the bullet, when they had to give up their closely held tenet of remaining a bootstrapped venture.

The question of whether to bootstrap or not is one that continues to catalyse endless debate in the enterprise software sector. Unlike other startup domains, in the SaaS space there is a long-standing example of a thriving bootstrapped business. Sridhar Vembu's Zoho, the oldest and most storied SaaS business in the country, has taken no outside capital in a journey that began in 1996. It is now an established unicorn that is an industry leader and profitable.

Those in the know argue that there's a clear trajectory until when a company can afford to remain bootstrapped. To begin with, SaaS companies can find it is easy to bootstrap as the business is a revenue- and profit-generating one. And if the company is in a niche segment with a wide enough moat—like BrowserStack—it can keep going as an independent entity. But when the competition heats up, many startups will feel the need for outside capital to hire fresh talent and spend on marketing in a bid to protect and expand their turf. This is if it wants to reach the magic goalpost of, say, $100 million in revenue.

If not, there's the real danger that a startup with promise will remain stuck at the $10 million to $20 million revenue range. For many, it can prove to be a Hobson's choice of picking from options that are not attractive. To grow the business, they will need to hire more leadership talent. To hire more and hire better, they will need more money than what company revenue alone can provide. Companies like Freshdesk raised venture capital and accelerated to outexecute competition, taking the bull by the horns.

A second model is to keep winning bigger and larger deal sizes. Here, the customer provides the cash flow to allow a venture to remain bootstrapped. This can be a delicate balance because the startup will also have to keep removing cash to create newer and newer products to stay ahead of the curve. Not everyone can do this. Except, say, a Zoho. Vembu's company keeps innovating at a scale that has allowed it to remain independent.

Startup founders realize late that while it is hard to clock the first $1 million in revenue, it is incredibly harder to move to $10 million and then to $100 million. Many fall by the wayside. The other factor driving greater adoption of the venture capital model is the need to generate wealth for founders and employees. If, say, a Freshworks is valued at $3.5 billion, a good chunk of that value is with its employees. And if the company continues to grow and the $3 billion-plus becomes $5 billion or $10 billion, it is money in the hands of employees that will change the lives of many. In a country like India, which is still looking to climb out of the low-middle-income trap, wealth creation for employees can be a virtue and not a vice. Greed can be good.

However, one SaaS company has sidestepped most of these existential challenges and quietly gone about building a user base of some 20 million users worldwide in a matter of eight years or so. It began as quietly as it has gone on.

In 2012, a young graduate from the Birla Institute of Technology in Goa started a small project to ease the problems he faced as a developer while working with APIs, the programming interface that allows computers to speak to each other. He had hunted around for solutions but there were none available. So he had to build it himself.

Abhinav Asthana had been working around computers since he was in high school. On a computer gifted by his father while they lived in a remote town in Uttar Pradesh, Asthana learnt to code. He got so good at it that he began designing websites and offered his skills online to clock his first earnings. By the time he got to engineering college, he had the startup bug. His first venture was a web-design startup which he would later morph into a second venture called Teliport.

None of these would find much purchase from investors, but not for want of trying on the part of the founder. The nerdy engineer made a conscious effort to learn about the world of venture capital and searched for ways to find backers for his company. At one industry event in Delhi in early 2012, he listened to LinkedIn founder Reid Hoffman speak, and also met founders from MMT and InMobi. He was enthused. But his efforts to get a venture investor's ear would bear no fruit.

Disheartened, he turned to his coding project. And there he would begin to find real purchase—the tool he had built to help developers was born out of an actual problem faced by him, one that a million more like him were experiencing as well. He would call it Postman. Sometime in 2013, Asthana reconnected with a colleague he had met while interning at Yahoo, Ankit Sobti. The idea for a developer tool had been seeded at that time. By then, Postman was also beginning to be known among the developer community. And in further validation for the young developers, Google featured it on the Chrome website. It was all the support Asthana and Sobti needed. They hunkered down in a rented house in a Bengaluru suburb and started coding in earnest. It was then still a project that had emerged out of pure passion. By 2014, it had notched up some half a million users—what Postman was doing was startlingly simple: giving developers a tool to build software faster.

Then a bunch of curious things happened pretty much all at once. Some of the world's biggest developers got in touch with the small group, pushing them for newer and newer tools. Startups and corporations began using it both at home and abroad. And suddenly, word about Postman spread like wildfire in technology circles. One day, a venture capital investor turned up at their doorstep; he had heard of them from his portfolio companies. Next thing they knew, Nexus Venture had offered them $1 million in seed money and said: take it, and go set up a company.

It was very much movie-style, a Silicon Valley modus operandi almost. For Asthana and his friends, the question was whether to accept the money or go it alone. In the end, they took the money for one reason: they had realized that what they had stumbled on was really big, and they wanted to do it right and grow it into a really big company. For that, they needed resources: money and know-how. So they signed on the dotted line and within the next eight months raised a total of $7 million and added on three more employees.

Things would move in a blur after that. As APIs proliferated, so did the network of developers using Postman tools. From a single tool, the company grew to become a platform of APIs. By 2021, it had over 10 million developers using the platform. It raised a new funding round of $225 million at a valuation of $5.6 billion. What had begun as a side project for a couple of nerdy engineers was the most valued venture-funded SaaS company. Asthana had by then moved to San Francisco to be closer to his customer base. And as the pandemic receded and it became business as usual, Postman grew to become a 400-employee company with over 15 million developers on the platform and half a million companies using its tools.

'It's been pretty crazy,' is all Asthana will say to surmise his spectacular journey.[10]

For India, this SaaS boom with its proliferating network of employees, founders, investors and users will begin to have a flywheel effect on economic growth. The IT services boom created an engineering class. Then came the back office, BPOs and so on that created employment for those other than engineers. It was then the turn of the consumer internet companies that have spawned the gig economy and created a new class of blue-collar workers. The SaaS boom that is taking wing in the 2020s will bring to the fore a new class of highly skilled workers and usher in a gigantic wave of economic expansion for the country.

Across every startup hot spot worldwide, there is one unique sector that grows bigger than the rest. In China, it was consumer internet. Investors who witnessed and gained from that phenomenal growth would attempt to recreate that scenario in India. But India's strength lies in building software, for the world's biggest corporations to the smallest of businesses. And while consumer internet companies have to burn money to win consumers, SaaS companies generate cash. This is the difference that could fundamentally change the trajectory of the country's economic growth in the coming years.

Part III:

2019–22

11

Desi Hustle

Every day, for about an hour or so, Nithin Kamath, the co-founder of India's largest retail brokerage firm, Zerodha, answers questions on Trading QnA, a community forum curated by his company. Everything related to trading and the stock market is discussed. One day, he was taken aback by one particular question from a user. It wasn't a query on trading; instead, the curious trader wanted to know why the 'CEO of a large business' was fielding questions on a community site. Stumped by the query, Kamath would take 'twenty–thirty minutes' to frame a reply.[1] The best he could come up with was that he had never set out to build a 'business'. He had begun by wanting to educate other traders about the pitfalls and challenges he had faced for nearly a decade. That his company grew to become the country's biggest trading platform was just the 'outcome'.

What Kamath terms as the 'outcome' reads as follows: profits of ₹2,094 crore on a revenue of ₹4,964 crore in the pandemic year of 2021–22. Zerodha is a debt-free company that has never raised a single rupee or dollar of external capital.

These numbers by themselves do not make Kamath the outlier among Indian technology founders. Rather, it is his commentary on the company's financials. He freely acknowledges that Zerodha gained handsomely from greater digital adoption during the COVID-19 pandemic. Going further, he adds that its revenue and profits may not continue to grow at the pace that it did in those extraordinary circumstances. It could even drop from the highs it attained during the pandemic. At a time when the only currency of note—for a startup—is unbridled growth, Kamath's candour is proving to be his biggest calling card.

So when he settles down to take questions on the trading forum, the forty-two-year-old entrepreneur is doing what he originally intended when he launched his company in 2010: make it a bit easier for a trader to navigate the world of equities. His brother, Nikhil, and he are the sons of a public-sector bank employee. They grew up in a south Bengaluru suburb amid other families from one of India's famed trading communities, the Marwaris. Nithin, seven years older, picked up stock trading with the guidance of one such neighbour. But he burnt his fingers with trades in the early years, which coincided with the dotcom meltdown of the 2000s. To recoup, he put in a stint at a BPO firm and later took on wealth and portfolio management for some clients. All the while, he kept trading.

His example set Nikhil on the stock market path too. In quick time, the younger sibling would emerge as the better trader, while Nithin turned to doing something that held them in good stead in the years ahead. He ran groups on Yahoo and Orkut—the now-defunct social network—sharing best practices, tips and guidance for traders. He was the community man. While his brother traded, he built the networks.

By 2007, they were trading on the NSE platform Net on Web (NOW), which was free for brokers. They both knew first-hand the troubles a trader faced in the market from high brokerage fees to the difficulty in reaching out to the right person at a brokerage firm. The brothers realized that there was an opportunity in building a no-fuss, clean trading platform for people like themselves. They had about ₹25 lakh in the bank after the initial deposit to the exchange, which they used to set up the business, by launching a platform with 'zero barriers to trading'. And thus was born Zerodha—the word is an amalgamation of zero + rodha, the Sanskrit word which means 'barrier'.

The Kamaths set a fixed price of ₹20 per trade that a day trader or options trader had to pay on their broking platform. But when they began it was a bad year for trading. Markets were down, there was little activity and it was difficult to get customers. But Nikhil managed to keep the business in clover with his bets in the first year of Zerodha's launch. By year two, the business took off. Kamath credits an article in *The Economic Times* in September 2011 on discount broking that mentioned the fledgling firm for the turnaround.[2] It piqued interest and the business began opening first a hundred, then 200, then 300 accounts in a month. Finally, growth began to quadruple.

That was when the brothers discovered the limitations they faced in building the technology framework for the business. Neither of them was a techie; in fact, both had dropped out of college. They realized they needed in-house technology to grow. Their office at the time was in the midst of suburban homes, some of which had morphed into quiet workplaces. Serendipitously, in a house opposite their office lived the co-founder of a technology startup that was looking to build a robot advisory platform for capital markets. One day, a group of techies from there walked across to Kamath's office, seeing the brokerage board hanging out front.

In that cohort, which included some IIM graduates, was young engineer Kailash Nadh, who had a PhD in artificial intelligence. The two groups would get talking, discover they liked each other and soon begin to hang out together. Meanwhile, the regulators wouldn't approve the robot solution that Nadh's startup was working on as it was seen to be way ahead of its time. Kamath, meanwhile, was in the market for a CTO. Things moved fast from thereon. Nadh agreed to join the brokerage firm as he could see that building technology for such a venture would be a greenfield opportunity. There was no talk of terms or money or business opportunity. Nadh decided to team up because each liked the other.

Kamath terms that as the tipping point for Zerodha, the fact that he now had an innovative technologist on the team. Someone who could think of the business from fresh eyes, not as a trader, not as a founder, but as a pure technology creator. Nadh would become Zerodha's brahmastra. He built Kite, which became the company's flagship trading platform, accessible first on the web and then as an app for Android followed by iOS. And all the while the company was still charging one flat rate of ₹20 per trade for everyone: day traders and retail investors.

For two years, it would run on this initial innovation, after which competitors entered the market, offering exactly the same thing as Zerodha. Kamath realized that his moat was not deep enough—innovating constantly was the only way to stay ahead. In 2015, he made one of his most impactful moves. Nadh and Kamath were on a flight to Kochi when they got talking about how they hadn't done anything new for a while. Just like that, Kamath asked why they shouldn't go zero-brokerage. Nadh laughed it off as yet another example of Kamath's yen for product announcements. But he was wrong—Kamath was dead serious. The way he saw it was simple. Zerodha was regarded as yet another platform for day traders. But with the launch of Kite it became much more—it was also a platform for retail investors. The ambition for his business was now very different. Why should my customer go to another bank or platform to invest, he asked Nadh on the plane that Friday. It took them thirty minutes of discussions to decide.

The next Monday, Kamath announced that Zerodha would charge no brokerage fees for retail investors. It was the start of a tsunami of growth for the company. It wasn't actually giving up any income because the bulk of revenue—75 per cent almost—came from day traders who would continue to pay a brokerage fee. With the promise of zero-brokerage, the company began to acquire millions of new retail customers without having to spend any money on marketing or advertising. So the CAC (cost of customer acquisition)—a term Kamath rues he had never heard of—would remain nil. At a time when e-commerce companies were raising billions to lure customers, Kamath's no-cost initiative was a game-changer. His bold move also coincided with the rise of a new class of Indians who turned to retail stock investing in 2016.

Kamath reckons that what really changed for his business was being able to use Aadhaar—the unique identification number—to verify incoming customers. The unique ID had by then enrolled nearly half the country's adult population. Zerodha had discovered that drawing retail investors to its easy-to-use investment product was of little use without a simple way to verify their identities. Till the introduction of Aadhaar-enabled biometric identity verification, the traditional know-your-customer or KYC method involved filling up nearly thirty to forty verification documents.

By September 2016, the twelve-digit number given as a unique identity to all residents of India had come into force as an Act of Parliament. It would allow businesses to verify customers using the Aadhaar-enabled eKYC system in real time. Simultaneously, there was an explosion of internet coverage via low-cost data on mobile phones—pioneered by Reliance Jio—which became publicly available on 5 September 2016.

This was not all. There was more disruption on the way. From early 2017 onward, India felt the impact of demonetization, when nearly 86 per cent of currency in the country was estimated to have been wiped out by the scrapping of ₹500 and ₹1,000 banknotes. Cheap data plans drove people's interest in turning towards online transactions.

In conjunction, these developments triggered a new era of internet enterprise built on innovation directed at the unique needs of Indians. It was no longer just about building the Amazon of India or the Uber of India or even the Alibaba of India. At Zerodha, 'growth would go bonkers'.[3]

There was also the correlation between the growth of the trading platform and the boom in public equity markets of the time. As long as the stock markets outperform other asset classes, users will have a need for platforms like Zerodha. And that year, the markets were indeed being kind to the desi brokerage firm.

The BSE Sensex ended 2017 with a gain of 29.58 per cent while the NSE Nifty rose 30.28 per cent. India was the third-best emerging market in the world that year after Argentina and Turkey, according to news wire Bloomberg. Smaller Indian stocks did even better—the BSE midcap index rose 48 per cent while the small cap surged 60 per cent.

To be sure, the stock market boom, demonetization driving online adoption as well as the uptick due to Aadhaar-enabled user signups were external catalysts. But winners don't only latch on to a rising wave. They do much more. Kamath and Nadh demonstrated this compellingly in the months ahead. They had quietly begun building a technology moat around the business very early on. The bootstrapped venture had set up a fund, Rainmatter, to start investing in young fintech startups. These would mostly be ventures building technology useful to the online trading platform.

They had long ago concluded that Zerodha alone would not be able to build all the apps that a full-fledged fintech investment platform would require. With this in mind, Nadh had built the in-house technology back end, Kite, as an open software platform where APIs could be used by others to build new innovations on top. It was the magic API model that even platforms like the government-backed Unified Payment Interface or UPI had adopted. Many indie developers began coming in and building extensions on Kite.

One of the best-known examples from this initiative would be Small Case. Even before Kite was formally launched, the startup launched by three IIT Kharagpur graduates in 2015 would approach Zerodha. They had looked at the API offerings under Kite and figured that they could build their demat investment platform on it. It became the first investment from the Rainmatter fund. Small Case would go on to build a sleek platform and raise capital from top-notch investors like Sequoia Capital and Blume Ventures. It proved to be the first and most potent validation of Zerodha's API model of opening up the platform and allowing other startups to come and build atop it.

Another fintech venture, Tijori, a data and research platform for investment professionals, connected with Zerodha executives in early 2019. To the surprise of its co-founder Siddharth Hegde, his team got to meet Kamath within a few days of the initial outreach and was 'starstruck' when the widely celebrated founder asked them what he could do to help. The young entrepreneurs asked for time to build their technology back end before returning to do business with Zerodha. As it turns out, Kamath gave them his time and more. Two years later, Zerodha would collaborate with Tijori. Zerodha users could now access financial data and analysis collated by the young startup for investment decisions .

As profits grew in the parent company, Rainmatter also expanded its horizons. It would invest in ideas from fintech to taxation tools and even a platform for e-signatures, which was critical for the financial industry. Nadh describes Kite Connect as Amazon Web Services (AWS) for the financial markets. AWS is the eponymous cloud platform built by the online retail giant. Used by millions of businesses worldwide, AWS is the primary income generator for the American e-commerce company.

Meanwhile, Zerodha's success was by no means going unnoticed in the hyper-competitive world of startup investing. Scores of VCs began making a beeline for the quiet office on a leafy street. One even flew Kamath halfway around the world in a private jet to meet the one person the fintech founder considers an idol: a celebrity basketball coach. It was a last-ditch effort to enter Zerodha's cap table—wooing a man with no visible needs or wants, a near-obsession with basketball was the only chink that eagle-eyed investors had spotted in his armour. So Kamath would fly out to meet his idol in person. On his return, he received a recorded video message from the coach asking him to take venture funding from the investor who had hosted the meeting.

'That's how cheesy it was,' is all Kamath will say about the episode. It only strengthened his belief that as soon as you say no to money, 'you become a lot more attractive'.[4] Incidents like this have made the forty-two-year-old even more determined to keep close to his roots. He shares a villa in a decidedly low-key suburb of India's technology capital with his parents, wife and six-year-old son, eschewing an address in far more luxurious enclaves where peers reside.

But he's no ostrich. He knows that investors are 'sharp and smart' and have business tricks he may be unaware of. So, he meets everyone. Literally, everyone. To boot, he has been offered it all, including a chance to take his company public via the special purpose acquisition company (SPAC) route that became famous as an exit option for investors in privately held technology firms during the go-go years of the pandemic.

As the demand for digital products and services peaked amid the fearsome spread of COVID-19 worldwide, investors floated a new idea. Technology startups looking to cash in on unprecedented demand for their shares could be acquired by an SPAC. These shell companies that were listed on a stock exchange would acquire privately held technology startups, allowing them to become listed entities without having to go through the pain of an IPO.

Kamath was given a standing offer to do an SPAC listing of $1 billion. When he demurred, there were other offers. A blank cheque allowing him to name Zerodha's valuation. Or having its valuation pegged at $5 billion without even a peep at its financials. Amid all the frenzy, Zerodha stayed true to the common-sense approach. It actually told users not to trade without thought during one of the biggest stock market booms the country had seen. Nudge, a feature on their trading platform, gently warns investors shaping up to make a risky trade to just not do it.

'Who can actually tell people not to trade—that itself gives us a moat as a business,' declares Nadh.[5] And this at a time when more and more founders have been drawn to a self-fulfilling prophecy that new-economy businesses are built by focusing on growth first, profits later. In a market where raising the most money at the highest valuation has turned into the de rigueur model for startup entrepreneurship in India, Kamath and Nadh's south Bengaluru insouciance comes as a breath of fresh air.

As does the remarkable iconoclasm of another technology entrepreneur who calls the remote Tamil Nadu town of Tenkasi home. He began in an era very different from the internet-led startup wave of today.

Indian technology entrepreneurship began with the labour arbitrage model that reigned from the 1980s right up until the

2000s. IT services companies sent engineers who were paid rupee-linked salaries to client locations worldwide, most often the US. These were software coders who provided services and were not building full products. Separately, the dotcom boom built on the 'eyeballs model'—or that of users first, profits later—provided the first glimpses of a new way of doing technology business.

The journey away from labour-cost arbitrage to a more product-based software industry was seeded around the dotcom era. It was largely tied to the subscription model where users could buy software products for specific needs, shrink-wrapped and paid for per use. This gave rise to the now-famous model of software-as-a-service or SaaS.

But in 1995, it was barely an idea when brothers Kumar Vembu and Sridhar Vembu were both working at Qualcomm in San Diego, California. One evening, they would get talking about wanting to start something in India. They had no concrete ideas, just shooting the breeze.

Kumar, the elder one, suddenly declared that he would return to India the next day and start up. A nonplussed Sridhar asked if he was serious, if he was sure. The next Monday, Kumar resigned, and on Tuesday night he was on a flight back home. He went back with two computers and started up in the Vembu family home in east Tambaram in Chennai, with an aim to build enterprise software products.

Back in California, Sridhar Vembu stayed on at Qualcomm for another six months or so before quitting and moving up north to Silicon Valley. He rented a cheap one-room apartment and started 'doing something' to support his brothers back home in Chennai, where third sibling Sekhar Vembu had also joined the business.

The Silicon Valley of the 1990s with its affordable housing was a magnet for others like Sridhar. He is rueful that people now forget how important those factors are for young people looking to start up. Sridhar had by then been in the US for a while, but his exposure to business was minimal. He had graduated from IIT Madras and taken the classic route to the US for a master's and then a PhD at Princeton. He was a mathematician and had little time for the technology startups that were taking off on the west coast.

To be sure, there were twists and turns in his journey before he turned entrepreneur. The reluctant researcher who claims all he could do was some mathematics would increasingly begin to feel that it was an ivory-tower occupation. He persevered to get his PhD and even applied for and was selected to a professor's post at an Australian university. But just short of his visa being cleared, Sridhar decided to turn the job down. He was unenthused by the prospect of an academic career and was unwilling to make a compromise. he recounts in hindsight. Interestingly enough, he points out that the company he went on to launch, Zoho, today runs a thriving business in Australia. Clearly, academia's loss has proven to be commerce's gain. Sridhar then travelled west to join Qualcomm in California.

In 1995, he again disrupted this career path, this time with a plan to help his brothers sell the software they were building in Chennai. He had realized the missteps he was taking. For instance, he had tried building hardware for a spell, which was way too capital-intensive a project for bootstrapped founders. And there he was, the man slated to be a billionaire one day, with no job, sitting in a low-cost flat and coding up 'something'.

Around that time, he met a senior from IIT Madras, Tony Thomas, who had independently started work on building APIs on the new computing language Java. Sridhar introduced Thomas to his brothers in Chennai, and they started working together.

Meanwhile, in his digs in the Valley, Sridhar had taken to contract software jobs to stay afloat. One day, Thomas turned up and over lunch asked Sridhar if he knew anyone who could join his company for a sales job. Sridhar volunteered, and joined Advent Network Management as vice president. This was in 1997. They had travelled to Las Vegas for an industry show where the company had put up a booth. To his surprise, Sridhar closed a deal and marked the launch of a career as IT salesman.

The two units of AdventNet would still run as independent companies, one in the US with Tony and Sridhar at the helm, managing sales, and one in India with Kumar Vembu leading product research and development.

That bootstrapped SaaS giant, which has constantly reinvented itself since its arrival on the scene in 1996, is now highly regarded by peers, fans and competitors. So much so that industry peer and one-time Zoho employee Girish Mathrubootham, founder of Freshworks, points out that 'constantly launching new products' is the reason for Zoho's longevity and growth.[6]

Back in the Valley, Sridhar Vembu put to work his newfound sales skills. In his first year, AdventNet clocked $350,000 in sales. By 1998, it crossed $1 million. By 1999, Thomas was pushing Sridhar to take charge of the company. He was already the primary salesperson. The mathematician who grew to be a reluctant researcher had found his metier in being an IT salesperson, much to his mother's amusement, he recounts. He thought he was making progress until he did a deal with a Valley-based customer of Indian origin. Sridhar closed the deal at $30,000 and shook hands with the customer, who paused to ask if he could give him some advice. Telling Sridhar he was 'an idiot', he went on to explain that he had undersold his software, which was worth at least thirty times the price the customer had paid. Sridhar had been told in no uncertain terms to hire a qualified sales person.

The company did that, and in a year revenue tripled. By 2000, it expanded to nearly $10 million and Sridhar became CEO. But the music would stop there. The dotcom bust and the telecom industry meltdown in the US followed by the disruption created by the terrorist attacks on the World Trade Center on 11 September 2001 put paid to the business.

Sridhar realized that a fresh beginning was required. The company would launch enterprise IT products under the brand name ManageEngine after the dotcom bust. In 2005, it would diversify by adding SaaS products under the brand name Zoho.com. Such a rebirth also made it necessary for the company to have a new name. By then, it had set up headquarters in Pleasanton, California. Seated in his office with colleague Raju Vegesna, Sridhar Vembu tooled around for a new name. He wanted it to be called SOHO.com as it focused on 'small office, home office'—their target customer base. But the domain name was taken, so the two prefixed a Z instead. As luck would have it, they found it available for a princely sum of $5,000. Sridhar, who describes himself as a 'cheapskate', didn't want to spend so much. But Vegesna, with admirable foresight, goaded the boss to make the purchase, threatening to do it himself if he didn't. A chastened Sridhar now admits that a domain name of that sort would be priced at millions of dollars today.

The product business was also proving to be a long-haul business. It required a long gestation period, with typically not much happening for three, four or five years, until a company could find its footing in the market. The scrappy startup would invest heavily in R&D.

During that time, Zoho built an impressive array of products, including its flagship product for customer service management called Zoho CRM. More importantly, the young business started pioneering new ways of running a company. Sridhar and his team looked away from the tried and tested model of hiring only IIT graduates, instead taking a bet on beginners from small towns. Around 2005, they set up Zoho University as an alternative to college education. The company would recruit students who had completed high school and train them to be engineers. To be sure, they would continue to hire college graduates, just not from the IITs.

In 2021, when the company was celebrating its silver jubilee, they discovered that a colleague, Abdul Ali, who had been with them for some thirteen or fourteen years, had actually joined them as an eighteen-year-old or so. The teenager from Assam had travelled to Chennai in search of a job and found one as a security guard at Zoho. Soon, an engineer at the company noticed that Ali was showing a lot of interest in computers. He took him under his wing and taught him the basics of website design. In time, Ali graduated to becoming what Sridhar describes as 'a good engineer'. It is stories such as these that have contributed to the Zoho legend, of an unconventional company that set the standard for India's billion-dollar-plus SaaS industry.

By 2009, AdventNet had transformed into Zoho Corporation. Kumar Vembu moved on to start his own venture, GoFrugal, as did Sekhar Vembu. Thomas too had moved to California to set up his own venture. Sridhar would now be the guiding force at the enterprise software maker, although all the earlier leaders would remain connected, some serving on the board or as advisers to the company. Of the six founders, Sridhar Vembu and Shailesh Kumar Davey continue to be at Zoho.

Sridhar's uncanny ability to keep his ear close to the ground has in many ways shaped the destiny of his company, which he partly inherited and mainly built on his own. In 2009, when he set it on a new direction, it would be based on the increasing trend worldwide of businesses turning to the internet for subscription software. It was the advent of the pay-as-you-use model for software tools ranging from email to business productivity tools, customer, vendor and partner management. Zoho offered the entire suite of such products that businesses could pay and use as required rather than buy a one-time licence.

In doing this, it placed itself head-on with industry giants from Microsoft Office to Google's suite of apps. In 2007, bigger rival Salesforce reportedly made a bid for an outright purchase of Zoho. In a much-publicized blogpost, Sridhar detailed the reason he had turned down the offer. He pointed to a cultural mismatch between the two companies and also spelt out his belief that Zoho had enough legs to run on its own.

Recounting the episode in 2022, Sridhar underlined the importance of that call to not merge with a larger rival. For India's SaaS story to take off, it needed an anchor company, and Zoho would go on to play that role. Today, Sridhar takes pride in the fact that there are nearly sixty-odd companies that have come off the Zoho ecosystem. The Indian SaaS industry is now poised for hockey-stick growth, where the momentum is all upward.

Sridhar is quick to point out that this would not have happened without the foundation laid over the past fifteen to twenty years.

The foundation had proven difficult to build. Once a colleague told him that his prospective in-laws would baulk at the fact that he worked for a tiny company in Chennai. Two decades on, the colleague's wife confirms to Sridhar that her parents now tell her she did a good thing in staying firm. To a gleeful Sridhar, this is more affirmation that in India the best reflection of what is hot and what is not is the great Indian marriage market. And Zoho is winning big out there.

He stayed on in the US—shuttling back and forth to India—as Zoho gained bulk and renown through the better part of two decades. Finally, in the summer of 2019, just before the pandemic upended lives worldwide, Sridhar relocated entirely to India and set up base in the town Tenkasi. For years, he had been building an alternative headquarters there, advocating remote work, working close to nature, and working out of small towns and close to native communities—long before the pandemic turned all of it into buzzwords and memes.

In the early years, when the business was about three to four years old, he had also looked at raising venture capital. As AdventNet hit about the $10 million mark in sales, VCs began expressing interest. Sridhar even got a term sheet from one such suitor. He scrutinized all the terms, and one would catch his attention in particular. It required his startup to deliver an exit or liquidity to the investor in seven years. Sridhar was taken aback, wondering why he was required to agree to such a clause. He consulted a lawyer who told him these were 'pretty much standard industry clauses'. That reply confirmed his stance.

He was not there to do 'business the standard way'. He declined the offer and went on to build the Zoho lore of an independent bootstrapped venture, one that in 2022 crossed the $1 billion mark in annual worldwide revenue. It sells its products in some 150 countries and employs over 15,000 people. Again, as with Zerodha's Kamath, it is what Sridhar would say about those revenue figures that sets him apart. In a nod to the tightening of economies worldwide in the aftermath of the pandemic, the CEO cautioned that revenue growth for his company would likely slow down.

If that sounds familiar, it is no surprise. With their candour, India's two best known and most widely celebrated bootstrap founders have more than just the first letters of their companies in common.

Sridhar believes in plain speaking, and to him, fear drives mistakes. It pushes companies to 'death by MBA', he declares.[7] Think about people who went to prison for India's independence. Nelson Mandela spent twenty-seven years in jail. So, what then is fear? What are business people afraid of, he demands to know. Is it fear of losing a lifestyle? Of becoming obscure? Instead, he exhorts startups to remain nimble, to keep building new products. Just as he does, sometimes even cracking code alongside his engineers at Tenkasi. To these mavericks, it is always the journey, never the destination.

Zerodha's Kamath is quick to point out that he is just going out there and speaking common sense. 'It's quite crazy how much love I get for that. I'm like, dude, what is wrong with this world,' asks the bemused entrepreneur.[8]

12

Indian Angels and More

For decades, Pidilite Industries, makers of synthetic adhesive Fevicol, had forged a 'mazboot jodi', an unbreakable bond, with its consumers. Carpenters, the primary consumer base for the adhesive brand, had traditionally worked on-site, crafting furniture and woodwork. In its early years, the company had pulled off a marketing coup by approaching them directly. It had coaxed them to shift from using the animal-based glue sold in hardware stores and timber marts to the range of easy-to-use synthetic adhesives that it manufactured. That fast relationship would be bolstered in popular imagination by one of the country's most iconic advertisement campaigns. There appeared to be little to fear from change.[1]

But cracks can form in the most solid of bonds, as twenty-six-year-old family scion Sanket Parekh would discover. It was 2008 and Parekh had moved back from the US to join the family business, managing sales for Fevicol in one territory. He soon realized that signals on the ground were discomfiting. Increasingly, furniture-making and woodwork was moving off-site, and along with it the decision-making on what products would be used in the trade. A once-firm 'jodi' with the carpenter appeared to be fraying. Parekh rang the alarm bell at the company headquarters, warning that the brand which had been a cash cow for fifty years or more might not remain so forever.[2]

As it turns out, the sixty-year-old brand continues to thrive. But Parekh's alacrity and search for new answers has proven to be useful in other ways. Among other things, it spurred the creation of a corporate venture arm at the consumer retail company, helping it participate in India's booming technology startup wave. Parekh's quest to be future-ready would lead him to setting up his own fund in the US. Back in India, Pidilite turned to backing local venture funds. In 2021, it participated in the $118 million fundraiser by Fireside Ventures, a consumer-focused venture fund set up by industry veteran Kanwaljit Singh.[3]

By no means was Pidilite the only Indian company to back the genial venture manager. In five years, Singh has raised an impressive ₹3,000 crore across three funds that invest in startups building consumer brands. And in 2022, even as global venture capital pulled back from India in the aftermath of the COVID-19 pandemic, Singh raised his third and largest fund to date of ₹1,830 crore. What's more, 90 per cent of the corpus in that fund would be domestic rupee capital from the likes of India's biggest consumer companies such as Emami and ITC Ltd, family offices including that of technology billionaire Azim Premji, as well as from the Self-Reliant India Fund.

This composition of limited partners in Singh's third and largest fund to date offers a stark contrast to the LPs who would have backed his first foray as a fund manager way back in 2006. At that time, Singh, along with co-founders like Aashish Gupta, would have pitched to some of the world's most storied university endowments, multi-family offices and global pension funds to raise money for their debut fund Helion Venture Partners. It was the time of the gold rush, when the formation of a number of India-focused venture funds would herald the start of internet entrepreneurship in the country. In the following years, Helion would go on to back some of the biggest names in the startup space, including grocery e-tailer BigBasket, MakeMyTrip and realty portal Housing.com, among others.

Even as technology startups grabbed all the attention and money, Singh, turbaned and softspoken, would keep his inner fire burning for the consumer bets that always got his interest. With good reason. His first job out of college was in Hindustan Lever way back in 1987. An engineer-MBA, he spent a decade working on HLL brands, including the iconic tea Lipton, leading sales across most of Punjab in the early years.

In the late 1990s, as technology marketing took wing in the country, Singh moved to Intel. It was a good time to make that switch. The Pentium chip, designed especially for home computers, marked the start of the era of personal computing. The American chip-maker was looking for people with experience in consumer product sales to lead the charge.

Singh would begin to hawk silicon chips, and do so well that colleagues took note. One such former colleague who quit to launch the venture practice for private equity major Carlyle roped in Singh to join him. Again, timing would be on the side of the marketing whiz. Singh spent about five years there learning the ropes of venture capital investing. So much so that by 2005 when the idea of Helion Venture Partners took shape he would be a perfect fit with experience in consumer and technology marketing, capped with venture investing all rolled into one.

As internet entrepreneurship gained pace in the 2010s, fuelled by the aggression of Tiger Global's Lee Fixel and investment firms grown rich on exits from Chinese internet ventures, Singh found that he often had to park his interest in consumer brands in the background. Helion Venture would take on a more aggressive technology investment mode.

He persevered, though, and led bets on beauty salon chain YLG and restaurant chain Mast Kalandar, among others. He was a marketer at heart and one with an instinctive understanding of the Indian consumer. Some of his best bets even while at Helion would bear this trademark. For instance, in 2010, he spotted promising intern Neeraj Kakkar, who had spent a summer working at the venture fund.

Singh would encourage him to branch out on his own and launch an India-focused consumer brand. Kakkar's company, Hector Beverages, created one of the country's best-loved consumer brands, Paperboat, zingy, flavoured soft drinks with a strong ethnic taste. When Helion, with its outsize focus on technology investing, demurred from backing Kakkar's startup, Singh made a personal investment. It was one of several he would make in the next few years as he grew more convinced of the potential to create new brands for an emerging Indian consumer who was unafraid to spend on quality products with a strong local flavour. Investing from his family office, he picked small stakes of 1–3 per cent with ticket sizes of ₹25 lakh to ₹50 lakh.

By 2015, Singh knew he was on to something big. He approached Indian business groups in the consumer space, such as Marico's Mariwalas, Wipro's Premjis as well as Sanjiv Goenka and Sunil Munjal. They backed his idea of a domestic fund focused on investing in direct-to-consumer startups. His first fund with a corpus of ₹340 crore allowed him to pick about 10 per cent equity for cheques of ₹3.5 crore to ₹7 crore. He picked two outsize winners in this fund—wearables maker boAt and organic baby care product company Mamaearth.

He would return nearly 70 per cent to investors within four years from this first fund. Emboldened by the strong performance, the second time round, Singh raised over ₹860 crore. Cheque sizes would now go up to $2 million. Finally, with his third fund of ₹1,830 crore raised in October 2022, a staggering 90 per cent of the corpus would come from domestic rupee investors. It was a thumping validation of the thesis that Singh has pushed from the start of his personal investing career—Indian money for Indian startups.[4]

With his intuitive grasp of the Indian consumer's pulse points, Singh points also to the near-coincidental rise, in the period after 2015, of India's digital infrastructure. This ranged from telecom networks to payment options built on UPI and banking regulations supporting digital payment innovation.

It was in such a scenario in 2017 that Singh was badgered on his LinkedIn account by a couple of little-known entrepreneurs. They told him they were building a brand of wearables custom-made for India. He invested about ₹6 crore in the company called Imagine Marketing, founded by Sameer Mehta and Aman Gupta. The two had teamed up to distribute audio equipment for the Indian market from the House of Marley after the country manager of the American brand introduced them to each other.

If starting up is all about serendipity, the story of boAt and its founders contains an abundance of the stuff. It was the time of the cheap data rollout, inspired by Reliance Jio, which was putting a smartphone in the hands of millions. Mehta and Gupta realized that the next buy for the average consumer would be headphones for listening to music. The image they sketched for their wearables was that of a person sailing on blue waters with headphones in his ears, nodding to music. It was an image as close to nirvana as possible. The two founders decided their brand—boAt—would deliver just that to the Indian consumer. Within three years of the launch, sales would catapult to ₹100 crore and then rocket to over ₹2,000 crore amid the pandemic blues in 2021–22.

There are a bunch of factors that make this venture founded by the Gujarati–Bania duo stand out from the clutter. First, it has turned in a profit before tax since the second year of operations, without fail. 'EBITDA positive' is how Mehta describes it. Second, its claim to manufacture products for specific Indian needs is genuine. So much so that when cricketer Hardik Pandya told them their wearables weren't sports-ready, they built a set of headphones that cannot be dislodged even in the rough and tumble of active sport. Third, within a couple of years of inception, the founders made way for a professional CEO, setting a standard that very few in the Indian startup scenario can either connect with or emulate.[5]

As for Singh, his thesis born out of conviction was now being backed by hard performance on the ground. Indian money for startups now has the potential to swell into hundreds of thousands of crores, he asserts.[6]

He is not alone. This conviction is echoed strongly by yet another VC, Sudhir Sethi. The founder of Chiratae Ventures, named for the elusive leopard that stalks Karnataka's jungles, has a career arc that shares several parallels with that of Singh. For starters, both are engineers who went on to get a postgraduate degree from the Faculty of Management, School of Management in Delhi. And while Singh would find his footing in consumer product sales, Sethi would gravitate towards technology early on, building a successful career first at HCL and then Wipro.

In 1998, Sethi was among the very first Indian managers to make the switch to venture capital investing. He joined the India franchise of the Silicon Valley fund Walden International. It was the time of the dotcom boom and then the bust. This provided Sethi with a ringside view of the inherent volatility of risk capital investing. By 2006, as the unprecedented capital flows towards India gained pace, he had branched out on his own. He led the IDG India Venture Fund, now known as Chiratae Ventures, through which some of his most consequential investments would come to be routed, including fashion portal Myntra, baby products retailer FirstCry, eyewear brand Lenskart and more in tandem with partner T.C.M. Sundaram. In the coming decade, Sethi would emerge as one of Indian venture's most outspoken and dynamic investors.

By 2015, as the waves of global risk capital once pooling, then retreating and reforming would become commonplace, Sethi began articulating the concept of rupee capital for Indian startups. He had begun pitching to hundreds of family offices, local business groups and even traditional 'ittar makers' as he criss-crossed the country indefatigably. He was asking Indians to back the great Indian entrepreneurship wave.

It was a good time to do this. The first wave of internet entrepreneurship had delivered some exits by then. TaxiforSure had been sold to Ola, Myntra to Flipkart and Freecharge to Snapdeal. These were only the biggest ones. Small deals had also gained pace, including the sale of small productivity toolmaker Little Eye Labs to Facebook for about $10 million. Missed call marketing platform Zipdial was bought by Twitter for a deal estimated at $30 million to $40 million.

Such wealth creation would be among the most impactful developments in the wave of internet entrepreneurship that has washed over urban India in the past decade. Infosys co-founder Kris Gopalakrishnan, counted among India's most active angel investors, points to the disproportionate impact of this sector on the imagination of twenty-first-century Indians. India might boast of some hundred unicorns and 80,000 startups countrywide by the start of the 2020s, but the ripple effect of the wealth these ventures have generated for the few, not the many, would stoke a spirit of adventure in the larger population itself.

Starting up was becoming real for everyday Indians as well as Indian business owners. Risk-taking would become acceptable for middle-class Indians, who until then ranked among the most conservative of people worldwide, with a well-known penchant for saving. With the educated Indian from a middle-class salaried home now able and willing to risk starting up on his own, traditionally wealthy Indians began to smell the opportunity in backing such enterprise.

There was a reason why cities like Bengaluru and Delhi would take the lead in technology enterprise in these years. Bengaluru had a base of professionals who had cashed in on the ESOP pool from IT services companies, as well as a large population of pensioners. Unsurprisingly, the city would emerge as one of the earliest centres for angel capital for startups. Young, enterprising engineers wanting to start up could be certain of tapping into networks of family, friends and relatives who weren't averse to putting some money out to help a youngster on the way. Meanwhile, the two factors required for a vibrant startup culture—inbound immigration of skilled workers and deep networks of educational institutions—were available in plenty in the national capital region of Delhi. The two cities would emerge as the focal points for the great Indian startup saga.

Sethi and Sundaram, a former colleague from Wipro, would narrate this inspiring tale of starting up to hundreds of wealthy Indians who would flock to listen. Gradually, they would loosen their purses too. IDG Ventures raised nearly 50 per cent of its fund corpus from rupee capital from 2015 onward.

Sethi wears his desi heart on his sleeve. In 2017, he rebranded his venture capital firm as Chiratae Ventures to reflect the Indian ethos it was rooted in. A passionate wildlife photographer and collector of antique locks, Sethi has also published collections of his photographic work. To rename his firm for the shy cats that haunt the jungles of his home state was an obvious choice. The firm, which lists Tata Group supremo Ratan Tata and Infosys's Gopalakrishnan as advisers, manages assets of over $1.1 billion. It has invested in over 125 companies and exited from forty-five of them.[7]

There were external triggers at work too that led to the entry of a sizeable amount of rupee capital into the startup sector from 2015 onward. In 2012–13, the so-called taper tantrums or the imminent threat of an interest rate overhaul by the US Federal Reserve, had put the brakes on global capital flow, primarily from the West. Sure, there was a flood of hedge fund money that came in from investors who had earned outsize returns from bets placed in China's internet economy. But this capital from the likes of SoftBank and the Hong Kong–based hedge funds like Dragoneer, Falcon Edge and Steadview Capital would compete to pick up massive stakes in Indian internet leaders. They poured big money into the big e-commerce players.

For the rest, capital wasn't so easy to come by. More so as the waning years of a central government enmeshed in 'policy paralysis' ahead of ensuing elections had brought business sentiment to a standstill. Indian fund managers, finding no purchase from overseas investors, had increasingly begun to turn inward and look for alternatives. The idea of rupee capital for Indian startups gained greater currency in this period—a trend that the likes of Singh and Sethi were among the first to spot and capitalize on.

At the same time, wider acceptance for online transactions had taken root in the urban Indian milieu. The likes of Flipkart, Myntra and others had done an exceptional job at keeping consumer trust, 'While some e-commerce founders, like the Bansals of Flipkart, were winning on the stress-test parameter better than peers, the e-commerce industry as a whole was winning the 'trust test' with consumers. What was more, there was a growing realization that India would not be another China. 'You have to think about what India means for India,' argues Fireside's Singh.[8]

Some investors had begun doing that even amid the din and noise of Tiger Global's extraordinary punts on Flipkart. As early as 2010, in fact. For Sanjay Nath and Karthik Reddy, it would begin fittingly enough on a note of happenstance. Early that year, the two young Indian engineers who were both in the US would meet up and shoot the breeze at a Starbucks café when they spotted an arresting tableau. Walking past their window was a posse of crisp-suited businessmen in animated conversation. One person in the group was easily recognizable to the duo who had been swapping tales of the startup wave building up back home. Nath recalls that it was 'amazing to see Deep Kalra walk past that window with his group of investment bankers ahead of his startup's upcoming IPO'.[9]

Reddy was an engineer who had gained double management degrees—from IIM Bangalore and Wharton School in the US. Nath, a BITS Pilani graduate with a management degree from the Anderson School of Management at UCLA, had by then proven to be a smart angel investor. A member of the Mumbai Angels network, he was among the early ones to take a bet on mobile advertisement technology firm InMobi. As they watched Kalra's MakeMyTrip debut in spectacular fashion on NASDAQ during the summer of 2010, Reddy and Nath were inspired to wade into India's buzzing startup sector.

By 2011, they had raised a modest fund of $25 million and become among the first investors to tap only Indians to raise that first corpus of risk capital. Memorably, that first fund which saw small investments in a batch of some three-score startups included two big names—TaxiforSure and ZipDial. That these two would be among the big-ticket buyouts from India's internet sector at that time proved to be talismanic for the young fund. It was such a strong shot in the arm for the young venture investors who would go on to raise a bigger fund of about $65 million by 2015. And again, 40 per cent of this corpus would be raised from rupee investors.[10]

Others such as Orios Venture Partner's Rehan Yar Khan would ride this crest of rupee capital as well. Khan, a Columbia

Business School graduate, had made a name for bankrolling nearly 70 per cent of the early angel round at Ola when literally no one from his angel network would even consider backing such an idea. So successful were his angel investment forays that by 2015 Khan decided to raise his own venture fund of over ₹300 crore. He would raise the capital entirely from his own network of high net worth individuals and Indian rupee capital investors.

Today, there is a certain sensibility or positivity around India and Indianness, which is acknowledged. Far different from the sentiment of the early 2000s when it was best known for its promise as a countermagnet to China. The question now is why we can't build billion-dollar brands in global markets, which come from India, with authentic Indian offerings, Indian value systems and Indian capabilities. So far, India doesn't have that kind of global presence in the form of brands, whether they are technology brands or in software.

But in the consumer space, the country has a very natural advantage that is becoming more apparent by the day. All the supporting pieces—infrastructure, market, talent and capital—fall into place, the great stories that India has to tell, from yoga to Ayurveda, Indian fabric and cinema, are all starting to gain global recognition. Countrywide, there is an effort to promote 'Indian' as the nation's firepower to take on the world. So be it the push for make-in-India or the local-for-global initiative, whether it's putting a lot of money into startup funding or supporting the fifth building block of infrastructure—which is early regulatory and government support for manufacturing—it's all happening.

'Ab takh jo dekha, woh bus trailer thi, picture abhi baaki hai.'[11]

13

Daughters of Bharat

A severe bout of jaundice would keep Kirti Jangra out of school for nearly four months in class eleven. When it was time to return, she just did not want to make the trip back to Kota, the northern Indian town where many children dreaming of an entrance into the country's elite engineering colleges spend their teenage years. Once there, they are schooled to single-mindedly cram in order to crack one of the world's most arduous entrance exams, the IIT-JEE.

Jangra had already spent a couple of years in the dusty Rajasthan town and lived through the pain and dislocation of being wrenched from her family. Travelling from Hissar, her hometown in the neighbouring state of Haryana, the fifteen-year-old sobbed inconsolably along the way, until her father delivered an ultimatum. If she wanted to stay home, she was welcome to return. But if she wanted to make something of herself she needed an education. Staying home was therefore not an option. Jangra's father was a government employee and living in one of the country's most patriarchal societies. Yet he and his wife wanted different for their daughter. He told the teenager that sobbing was also not an option. It is a lesson Jangra has never forgotten. She returned dry-eyed to her coaching classes at Kota. In time she gained admission to IIT Delhi.

As would another young girl from the northern hinterlands. Born to a farming family, Neetu Yadav would be the first girl from her village in Rajasthan to get a college degree. Her father is a dairy farmer. Her mother has never been to school The couple sent their daughter to Kota too. The only girl in her entire batch, she too would make it to IIT Delhi. On admission day, her brother accompanied her as she signed up for the biggest adventure of her life. Among the first people the siblings met on the college campus was Jangra. Yadav's brother heaved a sigh of relief, telling his sister, 'Bas ek friend toh mila.'[1]

His words proved prophetic. Small-towners both, the girls were allotted the same hostel room and forged a friendship that extended beyond their formative years. They were two out of a group of just eighty young women in their batch, and were acutely aware of the privilege of their situation. They promised each other that once they graduated they would start up together.

But first, there was work to do. While Yadav signed up at Pratilipi, an online self-publishing portal in Bengaluru, Jangra worked at Japanese financial services major Nomura, and followed that up with a two-year stint at publishing major Penguin. Yadav, meanwhile, was absorbing the innovative culture at her workplace. Internal hackathons would give her a platform to experiment and learn. In one such competition where they were asked to build a service or product for the next 500 billion internet users, Yadav teamed up with four co-workers. They built an app to trade livestock, an idea that snagged a prize and provided the kernel of an idea for a real-life startup. They used the prize money of about a couple of lakh, in addition to pre-seed funding from senior colleagues and others, to launch Animall in 2019. The startup, which provided a platform for peer-to-peer trading of cattle, counts dairy farmers as its primary customers.

Yadav remembered her promise to start up with her college mate, Jangra. She was enthused by the scope and idea of transforming the dairy industry, and knew well that it was a sector Jangra was intimately aware of due to her family's ties with the business. She called up her old friend. Jangra needed little persuasion—this was an idea that resonated with her. It was her nani, dadi, parents, uncles and aunts who were the next 500 billion internet users. Building services and products to make their livelihoods better was a no-brainer. She quit her job and signed up with Yadav and her team in January 2020.[2]

The premise of the business was simple: they were aiming to usher in the next White Revolution. The last one, Jangra holds, was led by Amul's legendary founder Dr Verghese Kurien. Since then, little has happened from the farmers' perspective. Innovation has mostly been focused on the farm-to-consumer end of the business, while inputs required for the farmer and livestock to thrive have received lesser attention from entrepreneurs.

Jangra and Yadav found that cattle productivity in India is about one-sixth of that in the US. They also discovered that the problems were common to both buyers and sellers of cattle. A platform to connect both parties directly evidently provided a great entry point into the business. They would take pictures of cattle for sale and upload them—people would laugh and say, 'Batao gaayi bhains kabhi online bhik sakti hai?'

Things moved in a blur from thereon. As the app grew at a rapid pace, with nearly a million downloads by mid-2020, investors saw the scope of the business and lined up to back the young team. Within just over eighteen months of starting up, the young venture raised over six rounds of funding. In July 2021, Animall received nearly ₹100 crore in a round that valued the company at about $80 million (about ₹580 crore at that time).

There was good reason for some of the biggest investors to step in to back the gritty ambition of Yadav and Jangra. Staying close to their home states, Animall would focus on markets across Haryana and Rajasthan as well as in Uttar Pradesh. The cattle-trading business is all about liquid cash, no deferred payments. The two girls, daughters from dairy-farming families, had not lost sight of what a 'cash cow' meant, degrees from IIT Delhi notwithstanding. By 2021, the Animall app had clocked nearly 10 million downloads.

And then, the impact of the COVID-19 lockdown began to kick in. The government banned transport of animals as it did not come under essentials. Animall had to scale down operations. But they began noticing an interesting trend. Rising digital adoption during the pandemic, which has buoyed technology spending worldwide, began to manifest itself in the small villages. Just like others of their ilk, Animall's customers, who were primarily rural agrarian folk, began to use their phones for more than just entertainment. They were looking for the utility features on their smartphones that could help boost livelihoods.

As the pandemic rolled on, these users began to push Animall for a wider range of services, from veterinary consulting to livestock insurance. Brand recognition continued to grow despite lesser focus on the primary business of trading livestock, so much so that in mid-2021 when the startup hired a local decorator to set up their new office in Jaipur, he asked them, 'Kis cheez ka office hai?' Jangra and team explained that it was a small app, 'Gaayi bechnewaala app, Animall.' And pat came the reply, 'Haan, isse toh maine apna pashu becha hai.'

Bharat had indubitably arrived on the digital stage. Bringing with it mitti ki mehak, the scent of untrammelled earth, of people, their ways and habits that have remained unchanged for decades. These people were now reaching out to a new world where terabytes, giga bytes, pixels and download speeds dominated the conversation. And the likes of Yadav and Jangra were acutely aware of the need to build for this cohort of users.

When Flipkart's Bansals and the ones who came in their wake began building internet businesses in India, they were addressing the first 100 million users. These were people who were urban, affluent and global natives. It was little surprise therefore that internet entrepreneurs aimed to build the Amazon of India, the Uber of India or the Instacart of India for such users. Alongside, they would burn cash to acquire customers, who had to be taught how to shop online, how to pay online, and how to buy and even return and exchange goods online. It took tens of billions of dollars to build this logistical infrastructure. What Flipkart, Swiggy and Delhivery had done was also build the railroads for internet commerce in India.

As Jangra and her ilk entered the stage, they were entering a maturing industry. The digital highways were in place. They could turn their attention to the next 500 billion users. The

Animall team had also honed in on one of the timeless truths of entrepreneurship. If a founder addresses the pain a customer is experiencing, the likelihood of success is far higher; rather than trying to impose a service or a product that users have to test, experiment and then finally pay for.

As the pandemic eased, startups faced a funding winter that took hold of the sector in mid-2022. Yadav and Jangra hunkered down and looked to cut their losses. They also turned to building a community of dairy farmers who could interact with each other on the app and have their trade questions answered by others in the field. Deepening the use of technology to assess cattle online, they looked to build tools in-house to improve the efficiency of the online platform. They had broken through generations of social conditioning to get to where they now stood. But for the IIT graduates unafraid to get dirt under their fingernails, the challenges were only beginning to magnify.

As they had for another twenty-four-year-old some years back. Kitty Agarwal, who is a partner at Info Edge Ventures, counts the serendipity of being mentored by industry veteran Sanjeev Bikhchandani as one of the major drivers of her career. 'It takes a lot of leaps to finally land up in a place that you feel is where you wanted to be, especially for women,' says the young VC.[3] Born into a Marwari business family in Kolkata, Agarwal says her choice of undergraduate and postgraduate courses were all determined by the fact that some day she would either join the family business or marry someone whose business she would work for. Breaking these moulds and the enabling social conditioning that fosters them proved to be her biggest hurdles.

Social conditioning also plays a role in women being more risk-averse compared to male peers. For instance, Agarwal was the first in three generations of her family to step away and work outside the family business. Breaking out of the cocoon proved to be seminal in more ways than one.

But it took years of swimming against the tide to get there. Her family allowed her to travel to Bengaluru for an undergraduate degree in business management because she had an aunt in the city, the only such relative outside of Kolkata. Soon after, she had to make them agree to her plan to sign up at IIM Ahmedabad. In her second year there, Agarwal was drawn by the startup bug and decided to learn the ropes at a joint venture between the Future Group and the National Innovation Foundation. A few months into the job, she realized that the project was moving slower than she wanted it to. Determined to break new ground, she returned to Kolkata and thought through what she wanted to do next. She was toying with the idea of launching her own edtech startup when she received a call from a former teacher. Sunil Handa, professor of entrepreneurship at IIM Ahmedabad, asked her to speak to a friend of his, Sanjiv Bikhchandani, the founder of hiring portal Naukri.com. Handa had given him Agarwal's CV and in turn asked the young graduate to meet Bikhchandani.

Absolutely fortuitous, is how Agarwal recounts that development. She was hired at the first meeting and with no clear plan as to what her job was. She shadowed Bikhchandani in the initial years as he segued into investing after having stepped down from a full-time role as CEO of Info Edge in 2010. He was cutting deals in startups such as Zomato and PolicyBazaar at that time. Agarwal was literally learning on the job and doing it at a rapid pace.

Within a couple of years, Zomato would emerge as a sort of racing horse in the Info Edge stable—it got the attention of the big bosses, while Agarwal got more leeway to work directly with another portfolio company, insurance portal PolicyBazaar. Info Edge had first invested in 2008 and seven years later, in 2015, it sold part of its early holding to facilitate the entry of other investors. But Agarwal, doing the sums, realized they had a winning deal in the insurance retailer. She backed her data, number-crunching and, most of all, what she terms as her 'instinct' to persuade Bikhchandani to re-enter the company in 2017.

The then twenty-nine-year-old investor got the approval of her bosses to increase their investment in what has now gone on to become a winning bet. When PolicyBazaar listed on public bourses in November 2021, Info Edge's 13.3 per cent stake was worth ₹7,193 crore.[4] It was luck that it panned out, says Agarwal. But PolicyBazaar founder Yashish Dahiya credits Agarwal with 'amazing insight', far beyond her years almost.

And that's where the importance of women founders, investors and managers comes to the fore. In a quote in the 360 Blog by SalesForce, Tracy Allison Altman, founder and executive director at the Museum of AI, says, 'Mature decision-making requires defining a repeatable process. The process should bring in meaningful data and also the intangible, anecdotal, and qualitative information influencing a decision. It's not really gut instinct; it's a highly sophisticated cognitive exercise that should not be underestimated.'[5]

In essence, Agarwal's experience illustrates the rare case of a woman investor who gained both backing and a clean slate to build a professional profile that is quite rare in an industry dominated by men. One where the case of the missing woman VC is now almost popular folklore. In fact, this is hardly an India-specific issue—that venture capital has a diversity problem is a global truth. While in America, the world's largest startup ecosystem, VCs are likely to be white, male and hold a degree from Harvard or Stanford, in India, they're mostly men with degrees from IIT or IIM.

Even globally, the gender balance in alternative assets continues to be uneven, with the proportion of working women in the industry increasing only to 21.3 per cent from 20.9 per cent a year earlier.[6] This proportion drops substantially at senior levels, where just 12.9 per cent of jobs are held by women, according to Preqin, a financial data information provider for alternative assets in a report released in March 2023. This despite 21.8 per cent of VC employees being women, the highest across such classes.

To be sure, research points to women being better money managers—a study by Kauffman Fellows showed that more women investors means more women-led companies funded, and the investment paying off. Privately held tech companies headed by women 'are more capital-efficient, achieve 35 per cent higher return on investment, and when venture-backed, bring in 12 per cent higher revenue than male-owned tech companies', according to research presented at a 2013 Women 2.0 conference. In fact, microlending initiatives such as Bangladesh's famed Grameen Bank are based on the premise that women are more effective at managing money and pulling their families out of poverty.

Take the case of Agarwal. She was given a larger hand in a low-risk investment in the portfolio after a handsome partial exit from PolicyBazaar had already been registered by Info Edge. However, the returns delivered by her bold gamble to re-enter the company bears out the Kauffman study's contention. 'What was supposed to be a learning experience in a low-risk portfolio investment—because we had taken our exit and I was left to be more hands-on—just over time graduated to becoming a big portion of our market cap, or our overall exposure,' Agarwal says.

Equally, research shows that women tend to invest more in women than men do. In fact, VC firms with women partners will invest in startups with a woman on the executive team at a rate that is nearly thrice that of venture firms with only male partners (34 per cent vs 13 per cent), and they are nearly four times as likely to invest in companies with women CEOs (58 per cent vs 15 per cent).[7]

These weren't thoughts that Vani Kola was entertaining in 2005. The India-born technology founder had just sold her startup in the US and wasn't sure what she would do next. She had been away from India for nearly twenty-two years by then. Leaving the country to join a graduate course in the US at age twenty-one, she would not return for the next five years. That was how challenging her early days were. She wrote home religiously though, every Sunday, and wondered how her parents were, if they were happy. Meanwhile, she went on to build the American dream, a robust career and handsome returns in the two decades she was there. By November 2005, she could afford to turn her thoughts and attention back to the country of her birth.

She was an outsider by then, spending the first few months after her return travelling the country and heading into villages. At one village panchayat in Andhra Pradesh, she was shown a computer that villagers could access and use to seek information on things like availability of railway tickets, for instance. Next, Kola headed to Delhi and experienced first-hand the emergence of the mall culture in a place like Gurugram, and the rise of organized retail. It was all so alien to the newly returned techie, very different from the India she had left behind.

Customer service expectations were rising, but they weren't being met. On a random taxi ride, Kola got talking to the driver, who told her he was taking his family for a holiday. She asked him where to, expecting him to say Manali or some other hill station. But the answer turned out to be Bangkok. To Kola, this was so different from the India she had left. As the daughter of a government employee who took his family on a holiday once a year on leave travel encashment, Kola had never been on a plane or stayed even once in a hotel until she left for the US. 'When we went somewhere we'd look for a relative; we stayed in somebody's house, we never stayed in a hotel,' she recalls.

It was apparent to her that technology could be harnessed to meet the aspirations of this new Indian consumer. The big takeaway for her was also the democratization of access that the mall culture had ushered in. In an older India, the retailer, the shopkeeper, would provide services commensurate with the 'social status' of the buyer. In the new malls of aspirational India, a millionaire or a house help could receive the same service at a Big Bazaar or a Star Bazaar.

It was a consumer market and Kola decided to raise a fund and segue into it. She launched IndoUS Venture Partners with a fund corpus of about $190 million. Among her early bets were companies like pharma retailer MedPlus, which would go on to successfully make a public listing in 2022, and Via, a travel portal that was sold to EBIX.

Meanwhile, Kola, back in India, was also trying to be a 'supermom' and had planned a Harry Potter–themed birthday for her daughter's tenth birthday. She ordered a stack of party merchandise from a small startup called Myntra which was focused on personalized gifting. It was a last-minute order, and the night before the party she had badgered them to deliver. Finally, at 11 p.m., the head of customer service landed up at her doorstep with all the items she had ordered. Intrigued, she reached out and asked for a meeting with CEO Mukesh Bansal. She had the advantage—she was already a customer who had been wowed by his startup's service while Bansal had no clue she was a VC. She went on to make that first bet in the young startup, an investment that would return many times the money and also give her a stake in the country's biggest e-commerce company, Flipkart, when Myntra was bought by Flipkart in 2014.

Kola had stumbled upon a surefire method of due diligence. In the years ahead, she tested out the customer service of scores of startups before investing. There are many that have never received capital from her due to faulty customer service, she now recounts. She would make some of the seminal bets that have catapulted her to the upper ranks of the venture capital league table in India. Such as a famous cold mail that she received from unknown founder Kunal Bahl that would lead to her early investment in online marketplace Snapdeal. All the while she kept her hunger for fresh ideas constant, emerging as one of the very first investors to back young gaming startup Dream11 much before others in the industry picked up on the opportunity.

In 2010, Kola decided to rebrand her fund to reflect the new ethos of aspirational India—she renamed it Kalaari. Although she had raised her fund with capital from global LPs, she began to think about how to build deeper connections into India.

She realized that in a new India raising capital from Indian LPs would become important in the future. Nearly half her fund corpus would come from domestic investors by 2020. But none would be as important as a conversation that she started with the leaders of the Reliance Group. For over a year, she would keep the conversation going with Mukesh Ambani and Manoj Modi. She would be inspired by their commitment to Indian entrepreneurship and would develop a deep respect for their long-term thinking. She would ask them to become an LP in her fund. Finally, the country's most valued company took a stake as a limited partner in Kola's fund in January 2021, making it the first fund in which the oil-to-retail conglomerate had taken such a role. It was a seminal development that has brought the arc of Kola's journey from a returning techie to one of the country's most highly regarded VCs, and an outspoken voice for greater participation for women in the Indian startup sector.

And that has come not a day too soon. In May 2022, when the Indian startup ecosystem clocked a major milestone by recording its hundredth unicorn with neobanking startup Open breaching the $1 billion mark in valuation, many raised a red flag about the gender imbalance in the world's third-largest startup ecosystem. Only 15 per cent of Indian unicorns have at least one female founder, the news portal reported.[8] A pronounced gender imbalance that has for long been a feature of the rapidly growing industry. No different, observers will aver, to the prevailing state of women's participation in the formal workforce countrywide. Though women in India represent 48 per cent of the population, they contribute only around 17 per cent of GDP compared to 40 per cent in China. Between 2010 and 2020, the number of working women in India dropped from 26 per cent to 19 per cent, according to data from the World Bank,[9] which estimates that it declined further during the pandemic as infections surged and jobs were lost due to the lockdown.

This at a time when research points out that boosting women's participation in the workforce can expand India's GDP by close to a third by 2050. It is against this backdrop that the remarkable rise of Falguni Nayar's Nykaa, an omni-channel retailer of beauty products, must be measured. Nayar was the first female founder of an Indian unicorn to float her company's shares on the bourses. The Nykaa IPO was subscribed 81.78 times on the last day of the initial share sale that closed on 1 November 2021.[10]

Ten days later, the shares posted a strong debut on the exchanges, trading at a premium of over 82 per cent at ₹2,054 per share on the NSE as compared to its IPO issue price of ₹1,125 apiece. Its market capitalization crossed ₹1 lakh crore in early deals. The stock closed over 10 per cent higher at ₹2,208 per share on its first day on the BSE. What's more, unlike most startups, it had also achieved profitability, posting a consolidated net profit of ₹61 crore for the year ended 31 March 2021 (FY21) as compared to a loss of ₹16.3 crore in FY20.

Founded in 2012 by former investment banker Nayar, the company's portfolio includes beauty, personnel care and fashion products as well as its own manufactured brand products under two business verticals: Nykaa and Nykaa Fashion. By the time it hit the stock markets at the end of 2021, the company had cumulative downloads of 55.8 million across all mobile applications.

On the day of Nykaa's public market debut, a panel of women founders and investors took to the stage in Bengaluru to discuss the challenges besetting women entrepreneurship and the action needed to overcome them. In a nod to that day's highlight, Vineeta Singh, CEO of Sugar Cosmetics, argued that more than providing skills and training programmes, what women needed to see was more women succeeding and their success being celebrated. Societal change, having and celebrating role models and easier access to capital are some of the key factors required to make it easier for more women to take to entrepreneurship. Take the case of Nayar, a successful banker who grew up watching her father, a businessman, run a bearings company. A mercantile background and a career in banking are no surefire steps to an entrepreneurial career, but they did help vault Nayar into the highest echelons.

If it's the old boys' network, the IIM college-dorm and IIT hostel-room milieus that dominate the world of male entrepreneurship, for women it's more family networks and support structures that deliver a safety net for those looking to start up. As it did for Portea Healthcare's Meena Ganesh, a serial entrepreneur whose first venture, Customer Asset, came as far back as the 1990s, in the company of her entrepreneur-investor husband, K. Ganesh. It isn't a lack in skill or capability that holds women back, but a lack of opportunity and confidence, which needs to be addressed.[11]

The increase in conversations around women in leadership have helped mitigate some of the biases in the ecosystem but unconscious biases still exist. In the past decade, the number of women-owned enterprises have increased from 14 per cent to 20 per cent, and these businesses have the potential to create over 150 million jobs by 2030. No greater reason can exist for the Jangras, Yadavs, Agarwals and Kolas of this country to be celebrated, loudly and equivocally.

14

The Digital Age

In February 2021, doctors and virologists began noticing an alarming uptick in COVID-19 infections in Amravati, a dusty city in northern Maharashtra. Unlike the previous year, when symptoms would subside in about a fortnight, this time illnesses were raging on for nearly a month. Only frontline workers were being vaccinated in India at that time, with shots for even senior citizens still a month away.

Holed out in Goa, his operational headquarters, Sahil Barua was subsumed in work. He was exploring a public listing for his ten-year-old logistics company Delhivery. An unprecedented inflow of risk capital was raising the profile of technology ventures countrywide—for many entrepreneurs and investors this was a now-or-never moment to register the bumper exits they dreamt of. That was when a family diktat came Barua's way to desist from travel and guard against a coming explosion of the infection. It was a tough ask for the young entrepreneur. He was talking to bankers and gauging reactions from investors to a draft prospectus. All this even as business on the ground was expanding furiously in response to the pandemic-induced demand for online deliveries. It was not a time to be grounded.

Externally, India was battling the virus. But within the ambit of the country's technology startups, 2021 was shaping up as a seminal year. Some forty-two companies breached the $1 billion mark in valuation that year to be termed unicorns. They would gain from a record inflow of over $36 billion of venture and private equity capital for privately held companies into the country, the highest ever in a single year that the startup sector has recorded till date.[1] There was more than a touch of the surreal in the events of those days.

In April 2021, a deadly wave of the Delta strain of the COVID-19 virus would spread across the country, unleashing fear and havoc. Technology ventures, meanwhile, grew at a massive clip amid the rising demand for digitization and online services. The lockdown drove people indoors, stoking demand for home deliveries of everything from food to medicines and other essentials. Delhivery, which had seen its losses recede in the preceding months, clocked a major milestone. On 18 April, the company delivered its billionth order: a shipment of medicines from e-pharmacist Netmeds. Barua recalls there was a collective pause as the company dashboard lit up with news of the billionth order. His colleagues and he got on to a hurriedly arranged conference call as they stopped for a moment to digest the development. They would recall the time they had started up in 2011 with the aim to deliver maybe 500 orders a day. And here they were, a decade later, with a billion orders completed. They asked, 'How many households have we delivered to, what kind of goods have we delivered, what is the value of goods we've carried over this time?'

These are important questions in the journey of a company. But they were being framed in the backdrop of a pandemic that was taking lives. It was not business as usual. They were in the midst of life-and-death situations. And there were decisions to be made. Preparing the company for an IPO was an eventuality they had factored in, but in the preceding six months, across the global startup sector, a new trend had emerged. Private companies were taking what was being described as the SPAC route, wherein a special purpose acquisition company was created to raise money through an IPO to buy another existing company, often a startup.[2] Loosely termed 'blank-cheque companies', SPACs were not a new phenomenon. What was spectacular was the currency they would gain in US markets during the pandemic. In 2020, 247 SPACs were created, a number which ballooned to 613 in 2021.[3] In comparison, there had been just fifty-nine SPACs in the market in 2019. Predictably enough, by 2022, US regulators toughened norms for SPACs so much that over a hundred SPAC deals would be terminated. It was a brief flare but one that would spur the interest of even Indian entrepreneurs, more so as it came in a year when at least a dozen Indian startups filed a draft prospectus to list their companies on bourses both local and global.

For Barua, the decision to disregard this route was an easy one to make. His business had turned profitable for the nine months preceding May 2021. With real infrastructure on the ground—warehouses and trucks moving freight—it was also easier to explain to traders and retail investors unlike other pure-play digital businesses. The logistics company decided to take the IPO route in India, but the question of timing remained. Amid the ravages of COVID-19, Barua and his team finally decided to stay their hand and take the company public in 2022. Meanwhile, food-delivery app Zomato jumped the queue and listed in what would be a spectacular opening in July 2021.[4] For Barua, who had drawn inspiration from Zomato co-founder Goyal's early venture FoodieBay, the Indian listing by the Gurugram-based company was a matter of import.

Such eventful happenings did not go unnoticed. The leaders of Indian business, who had circled the startup sector for years, finally revealed their hand in 2021. That summer, the Tata Group waded into the thick of the action. As May drew to a close and the ferocity of the Delta wave abated, it announced the purchase of a controlling stake in e-grocer BigBasket.[5] That deal, the Tata Group's first big buy in the e-commerce space, would have received clearance from India's competition watchdog the previous month. It now pitted one of India's oldest conglomerates in direct rivalry with the online businesses of overseas giants like Walmart's Flipkart and Bezos-led Amazon.

For Indian startups, this was the deal that marked a coming of age. In 2011, when Krishnan Ganesh, the venture-investor who first seeded the idea of online grocery purchase, was looking for follow-on funding for BigBasket, there weren't many takers. At a panel discussion hosted by a financial daily in the summer of 2011, Ganesh asked co-panellist Raja Kumar, the head of private equity firm Ascent Capital, why his firm was not interested in backing startups. Not content with the query, Ganesh pressed his case in spectacular fashion. Weeks after the meet-up at the discussion forum, Ganesh would serendipitously be seated next to Kumar on a flight. He took the opportunity to pitch his idea in more detail. Kumar, with little choice at hand, ended up perusing the business deck for BigBasket. In time, he went on to take a bet on the business. It would be among the first few deals where a pure-play private-equity firm took a chance on a raw, digital startup.

In the coming decade, the e-grocer would grow and clock $1.1 billion in gross sales as the pandemic spread in 2020–21. In the course of its journey it attracted buyout interest from Amazon, and received capital from the other global e-commerce giant, China's Alibaba. In fact, the Tata-led buyout which would see BigBasket valued at $2 billion also marked the exit of Alibaba from the company.[6]

For the Chinese e-commerce behemoth, this was only the first exit from the Indian startup sector. Starting in May 2021, when it sold its stake in BigBasket, the company steadily sold all its holdings in Indian startups one after the other. In February 2023, it sold its holding in fintech major Paytm, which it had acquired to much fanfare following the blockbuster listing of the Chinese e-commerce major on US bourses in 2014. In November 2022, it had sold its stake in Zomato. It marked the end of a high-profile chapter in its Indian startup journey that had begun with much pomp in the mid-2010s, seeking no doubt to replicate in India what it had attained in its home market. In tandem with SoftBank's Masayoshi Son, Alibaba founder Jack Ma had wagered on Indian startups and gained an almost cult-like following among desi founders.

Meanwhile, for India's most storied conglomerate, the Tata Group, the tryst with startups was only just taking off. For the Mumbai-headquartered group, the BigBasket acquisition was only the beginning. In the weeks ahead it went on to acquire e-pharmacy company 1mg and also buy a controlling stake in health and fitness startup Curefit. That investment in the venture set up by Myntra founder Mukesh Bansal would cement the salt-to-software conglomerate's aggression in the digital sector. Bansal would—for a two-year stint—lead its forays into the internet space as the group gathered all its digital properties under one superapp that it titled Tata Neu. In August 2023 Titan Industries, a Tata Group company, would ascribe a whopping ₹17,000 crore valuation for the online jeweller CaratLane while buying out its founder's stake. The landmark deal, which provided a bumper exit to CaratLane founder Mithun Sacheti, would underline the deepening interest of India's largest corporations in buying out technology startups. A trend which had begun to take wing amid the pandemic.

As India grappled with economic and societal disruption triggered by the spread of COVID-19, the technology sector would grow exponentially. As learning, working, entertainment and more moved online, it would draw investments in billions of dollars. In 2020, the then-richest Indian, Mukesh Ambani, snagged mega investments from some of the world's largest corporations such as Google and Facebook for his newly minted digital arm, Jio. The telecom provider with low-cost data services had drawn millions of Indians into the embrace of internet connectedness.

The valuation of internet startups was also soaring. The deluge of investments was not limited to giants like Reliance Jio. It was flowing even to the likes of doorstep-delivery stalwart Dunzo. The six-year-old Google-backed startup received $200 million from Reliance Retail in 2022 for a 25.8 per cent stake.

Buoyed by demand for digital services amid the pandemic, global investors poured about $12.1 billion of venture capital into Indian startups by July 2021, more than the total of $11.1 billion invested in all of 2020.[7] This flood of capital would have gained from the quantitative easing by America's central bank in response to the pandemic. The monetary policy, which is used by central banks to increase domestic money supply and spur economic activity, would lead to an unprecedented flood of global risk capital through 2020 and 2021. Much of this would find its way to Indian startups, mirroring a similar response by the US Federal Reserve to the subprime mortgage crisis in 2008 when the meltdown of financial services provider Lehman Brothers had led to a global economic downturn. The quantitative easing of that era had also stoked global risk capital flow, just as it would in 2021.

The global money glut helped propel the Indian startup ecosystem into the world's third-largest unicorn hub. In 2021 it clocked a total of ninety such ventures compared to the US with 487. China, with about 301, stayed ahead of the UK, which had thirty-nine. Capital flows into India were also drawn by the lure of the market that boasted of 600 million broadband users, with some 500 million users active on the internet daily, consuming 70–80 gigabytes per user per month. For perspective, even as late as 2015, there were zero broadband users in the country when some 100 million internet users were online.

Broadband connectivity is regarded as crucial to improving online transaction experience with fewer connection drops and greater bandwidth allowing for more sophisticated content downloads and user interfaces. Moreover, broadband users are typically drawn from cohorts with greater purchasing power.

It was no surprise, therefore, that the hyper startup activity in the country during the pandemic would draw the attention of the giants of Indian business, from the Tatas to the Reliance Group, among others. Until then, starting up in India had been the domain of the professional classes. Capital to back these fledgling ventures typically came from overseas in the two decades since technology-led entrepreneurship expanded in India.

The first flush of success enjoyed by the likes of Flipkart's Bansals and others drew rupee capital into the sector. It would take the explosion of money and demand for digital services and products amid the pandemic to attract India's mega corporations into the arena. Reliance had already begun to take strategic bets in the startup sector, all with the aim of bolstering the reach of its two new-age businesses: Reliance Retail and Reliance Jio. As early as 2018, it had picked up a majority stake in edtech startup Embibe. Later, it bought similar holdings in retail technology venture Fynd, on-demand delivery platform Grab, artificial intelligence startup Haptik and small-business technology provider Now Floats. In August 2020, it ploughed in ₹630 crore to buy e-pharma portal Netmeds.

That deal, which came close on the heels of Amazon testing pharma deliveries in key markets like Bengaluru, was a clear indication of the extent of ambition within India's most valued conglomerate to also gain leadership in the country's online market, and the extent it was ready to go to fulfil it. In close succession, it then bought out online furniture portal Urban Ladder, apparel startup Zivame and online grocer Milkbasket. In all, in a span of some three years, Reliance bought out some three dozen companies, primarily tech-based startups. The intent for the Ambanis may have been to create a strong ecosystem as they dove deeper into the retail and telecom businesses. For Indian startups, however, this was a clear sign of the emergence of a domestic M&A market, which is critical in the maturing of any startup ecosystem. It was something that had been sorely lacking in the Indian technology entrepreneurial system until then.

For investors ploughing in money, Indian startups had offered promise but lesser hard cash in return. In contrast, a vibrant buyout market for startups in markets like the US has done much to deepen that country's entrepreneurial culture. Consider the M&A market for tech startups in the US during the decade 2009–19. Google, the most aggressive of them all, would have bought some 182 startups, Microsoft some 89 companies, IBM some 87 companies, while Apple, the world's most valuable corporation, snapped up 81 companies.[8]

Tata and Reliance stepping up to the plate in the pandemic years has done much to drive hopes of a similar market for startup buyouts developing in India as well. Startups themselves would display aggression. Edtech company Byju's acquired three-decade-old brick-and-mortar coaching company Aakash Tutorials for a whopping $950 million in January 2021.

It would be no exaggeration to note that India's technology sector experienced a blitzkrieg of growth during the pandemic years. Providers of business software and software services were on a decadal upsurge too. As global businesses raced to transform their operations for a digital future, Indian IT veterans gained as well. The IT services industry expanded by 26 per cent to reach $227 billion in revenue by the time the pandemic eased in early 2022.

Little surprise, therefore, that subscription business software sales too peaked during this period. SaaS companies, including the best-known ones such as Zoho and Freshdesk, as well as Icertis and newer entrants like Postman, Zenoti, ChargeBee and others, would all post exponential growth. So much so that an early investor in these firms declared that very soon half-a-million-dollar salaries would become the norm for mid-managers in an Indian SaaS company.

The financial upside was becoming evident even then. Buoyed by the rush of capital from investors, Indian startups delivered record buybacks of ESOPs in 2021. A report by data researcher Zinnov and industry lobby NASSCOM found that nearly $400 million worth of ESOPs were bought back by Indian startups that year. Some 10,000 startup employees are believed to have benefited from this largesse. It was a gold rush. And for founders who needed to deliver returns to investors, this was the opportune moment. No less than eight startups floated public listings in 2021.

Interestingly, gaming company Nazara Technologies would be first off the block in March 2021. It became the country's first publicly traded gaming company. Its listing-day premium of 80.74 per cent delivered a bonanza to iconic stock market trader Rakesh Jhunjhunwala, whose stake in the company was worth ₹656 crore at listing.[9] The over-two-decade-old company was making the most of the surge in mobile gaming during the large-scale lockdowns induced by the pandemic, when cloistered Indians took to digital services, including gaming, in exponential numbers.

Just weeks later, Indian bourses gave a rousing welcome to food-delivery and restaurant aggregator Zomato. Deepinder Goyal snagged a $9 billion valuation for his decade-old company, one of India's earliest internet startups. It popped on listing day, as trading lore goes, ending on a first-day high of ₹138, an 81 per cent increase over the issue price. Once the euphoria settled down, Goyal said that he listed in India as it would allow his customers to own a part of the company—a sentiment that carries currency in the startup industry, where there were few opportunities for retail consumers to benefit from the considerable amount of wealth that the internet industry had generated in the decade.

As India celebrated the festival of lights, Deepavali, the country's bourses would be set alight too. In quick succession following Zomato's blockbuster listing came an IPO from online cosmetics retailer Nykaa. It would rise as much as 89 per cent over the issue price on its debut and close with a market capitalization of $13 billion. Its founder, Falguni Nayar, with a net worth of $6.5 billion, joined the ranks of India's wealthiest women, marking many firsts for the internet industry and indeed for women at work.

Nayar, who had put in a near-two-decade stint to become one of India's most successful women bankers, had turned to entrepreneurship in her fifties. The wife of private-equity investor Sanjay Nayar, she would turn heads when she got into the weeds of starting up, beginning at an office in the gritty Mumbai suburb of Sakinaka. A startup founder who visited her at the tiny digs where Nayar and her daughter Advaita were working from remembers thinking the IIM Ahmedabad graduate and investment banker didn't have to do this. But she did. Not only would she start up the copybook way but she would also bring her startup to the culmination most founders dream of: a public listing. And that in just over seven years of starting up. She emerged as a role model for a generation of women entrepreneurs. She rode the internet wave to emerge as one of only two self-made women billionaires in the country, the other being storied biotech entrepreneur Kiran Mazumdar Shaw.

Yashish Dahiya's PolicyBazaar, a ten-year-old financial services platform, was next up at the listing bell. It was backed by Sanjeev Bikhchandani, one of the country's earliest internet entrepreneurs to list his company, Info Edge, way back in 2006. Dahiya had built India's largest insurance aggregator that would list at a 17 per cent premium. An endurance athlete who once completed an ironman triathlon in 11 hours and 39 minutes, he had come away wanting to improve that timing. An entrepreneur for the long term, Dahiya was among the first to cite the importance of fitness for startup entrepreneurs, something that another founder whom he regards highly, Zerodha's Kamath, is backing at his firm. These are the entrepreneurs who breathe life into the adage that endurance pays. They helm companies that last for years, they roll with the punches and pull off wins against the odds.

Something that Paytm's Vijay Shekhar Sharma has shown in the years since his company's landmark listing in November 2021. Coming weeks after more nimble peers had lit up the bourses, the digital services company posted a lacklustre opening. Dubbed as the biggest initial share sale in Indian corporate history, it would be subscribed 1.89 times. It listed at a discount of 9 per cent from its issue price of ₹2,150 per share.

Retail investors, it appeared, had had a surfeit of internet startups coming to market with the mantra of growth first, profits later. Paytm's opening actually marked a turning point in the surreal euphoria that had accompanied internet business all through the pandemic. They had risen on the back of the demand for digital services, accumulated capital, employees and customers. But not many were actually doing what businesses do, and must do—that is, turn a steady, healthy and consistent profit.

Meanwhile, emboldened by the listing gains, Zomato took a bet to broaden its footprint. It turned into an investor and put in $100 million into grocery-delivery startup Grofers just weeks after its public listing. A year later, in a strong signal of its ambition to dominate the instant-delivery market, it bought out the startup, which by then had been renamed Blinkit, in a $568 million deal. Zomato was not alone in its well-directed aggression towards a market segment gaining from massive demand for doorstep delivery during the pandemic. Its main rival, Swiggy, also kick-started a competing service, Instamart. Reliance Retail waded into the market, as did the Tata Group's newly acquired play, BigBasket.

Amid all this activity by the giants, a minnow took birth in Mumbai, with its focus firmly on getting grocery and essentials in express time to users grounded by the lockdown. It wasn't just a minnow in the instant-delivery market, Zepto was a business founded by people who were minnows in age—to be precise, all of nineteen years old. Cooped up at home in Mumbai during the pandemic, Aadit Palicha and Kaivalya Vohra struggled to get groceries in the first lockdown in April 2020. They watched their neighbours go through the same difficulties. The only thought they had was that there had to be a better way to do this. So they began solving the problem for fifty to seventy-five of their immediate neighbours, then for the next 500 users, and so on. They began by manually delivering groceries themselves for orders placed on WhatsApp, and then over time on a 'crappy app' which they built themselves.

You could say they had some practise at using technology. The two had met at age seven at an Indian school in Dubai, where their parents were based. They had stuck together to become fast friends. When the pandemic struck, the two had signed up for undergraduate courses in computer science at Stanford University. Forced to hunker down in Mumbai during the lockdown, they took to delivering groceries at a fast and furious pace for neighbours. They would first call their business Kirana Kart. By the summer of 2021, eight months after their first delivery, the two teenagers realized they were on to something.

By then, people who had more than an interest in grocery delivery had begun to take note of them. One of whom was the Mumbai-based VC Suvir Sujan, who was an early investor in online marketplace Snapdeal and co-founder of Baazee. He knew a thing or two about online delivery at scale. What's more, he knew a lot about spotting entrepreneurs via customer references. His fund Nexus Venture Partners had done that famously with SaaS startup Postman. Now, with friends and neighbours all extolling a superfast grocery-delivery service in his city, Sujan took note. He spoke to them over the summer and by mid-2021—as the pandemic raged while risk capital flooded into India—Nexus led a $9 million round in the startup.

In the coming months, as the startup, which by then was focusing on deliveries in a micro-market in the tony Mumbai suburb of Bandra, was close to snagging 10,000 orders a day. They were now official, with angel and institutional investors on board. They needed a new name, and drew Sujan into the hunt. He came up with an idea. Since it was a business focused on delivering at speed, why not call it Zepto, the shortest unit of time in physics.

As the brand and the business caught the imagination of users, Palicha and Vohra got down to brass tacks. They needed a team, and they needed it fast. They scoured LinkedIn résumé, spoke to recruiters and started looking for experience and track records. Sure, they had investors such as Sujan helping them along, but in the space of six to eight weeks the teenagers had hired a senior leadership team.

After the first year of testing their premise, the two took the massive decision to drop out of Stanford. Unsurprisingly, they were nervous, as were their parents, but the duo decided it was their once-in-a-lifetime opportunity to do something big. They were also in a mature market by then. For sure, the pandemic was driving greater digitization, but the railroads for internet commerce had been laid. More specifically, instant grocery delivery, a space that had been tested as early as 2002–03 by Fabmall, had gained maturity with the likes of Zomato, Swiggy,

BigBasket and Blinkit now in the fray. For Palicha and Vohra, therefore, execution was where they had to differ. It was their only wriggle room.

Palicha lists their sole focus on just superfast grocery delivery as their competitive advantage. In a market where rivals were also delivering groceries, Zepto's infrastructure was built with laser focus on a single outcome: contactless delivery in ten minutes. This gave the startup speed and agility, and investors would take note. In the first year of operations, it raised a phenomenal $360 million. The startup was built to be profitable at unit level and gained investor traction for that reason as well, more so as sentiment turned against cash-guzzling internet businesses as the pandemic tapered down in late 2021.

By then, Vohra and Palicha had emerged as the country's youngest rupee billionaires. And while their closest rivals had built businesses where they had to discount to attract customers, the Zepto team was competing on quality of service. It was a sea change. And it came not a moment too soon. In the first month of 2022, stock market gyrations eroded billions of dollars of investor wealth. India's posterchild startup stock Zomato saw its valuation drop from a lifetime high of about $17 billion to about $9 billion.

The startup sector, though, posted a decadal high—snagging fresh investments of about $3.4 billion across some 130 deals. But it was the final flare of a dying light. As the pandemic waned and central banks, including the US Federal Reserve, began rolling back their liquidity-inducing monetary policies, widely referred to as taper tantrums, this triggered a sharp reduction in the quantum of risk capital available to startups as tightening monetary policy worldwide constricted global economies in 2022. In India, it gave rise to the great funding winter for Indian startups that would set in by mid-2022. Cash grew staggeringly scarce, and startups began layoffs in the thousands. Many would down shutters. Only those with the deepest stash of capital would survive.

Stanford students Vohra and Palicha had started up amid the upheaval. They had dropped out of college to ride the entrepreneurial opportunity in one of the world's most dynamic places to star tup. Two decades before them, another person from Stanford, Binford, had made the journey to India to start up too. While the Indians were teenagers, Binford was a retired professor in his sixties. What united them, however, was their affinity to the siren call of entrepreneurship, and in a country where growth was the one constant.

India, meanwhile, was changing. Binford had come in search of technological prowess. While the Zepto founders were chasing consumers in one of the world's largest internet markets. What's more, they were startup natives. One was chasing skill, the other two were chasing scale. In the coming decade, when entrepreneurs return to starting up, they will do as natives, just as the Zepto founders did. In a time when both skill and scale will combine to deliver change like never before.

15

Big Dreams and Doubting Thomases

In the space of one week at the end of August 2023 when India stretched to reach the moon and saw a young champion come within a heartbeat of being crowned the king of 64 squares, celebratory was the only mood that desis—local and global—would agree to.

Pragyan, the rover, would enthral the country with tantalizing sights and shadowy glimpses of the south side of the moon, unseen until India's Vikram lander touched down during that historic week. Space travel, seeded by the public sector, has been steadily attracting private enterprise. The Indian Space Research Organisation's ecosystem of vendors built over the past fifty-four years was estimated to number up to four hundred by the time India's third and most successful tryst with the moon, Chandrayaan-3, came to pass.

Amid all the extra-terrestrial excitement came news also of the near triumph of a remarkable 18-year-old Indian chess grandmaster. Rameshbabu Praggnanandha, or Pragg as he is popularly known, came close to besting the reigning world champion. His exploits served to underline the rise and rise of Indian prowess in chess. With a total of 83 grandmasters and some 33,000 rated players, India's chess ecosystem is proving to be a tale of skill and perseverance and, intriguingly enough, concomitant with the explosion of online gaming across the country.

So much so that in reply to a question on what his most painful miss in an otherwise stellar career in venture investing would be, one of India's most successful VCs admits there are times when he 'dreams of Dream11'.

The fantasy gaming company set up in 2008 by Harsh Jain and Bhavit Sheth has bided its time before exploding into the limelight nearly a decade later, when cheap data and affordable smartphones transformed the market for digital services and products. It was the era of Jio that ushered in the third phase of internet entrepreneurship in India. As cheap internet connectivity brought millions more into the fold of the digital economy, it spurred demand for education, entertainment and more on smartphones. The pandemic would only serve to deepen the pace of this digital adoption.

Dream11 would emerge among the gainers. It ended FY22 with operational revenues of around ₹3,840 crore, and—more to the point—₹143 crore in net profit.

By 2022, Dream11 had raised capital of $1.62 billion. Investors would make a beeline to the company that Jain describes as a sports technology venture 'by Indians, for Indians, in India'. By early 2023, as the spike in digital adoption—induced by the pandemic—began to taper off, the startup would see its user base reduce. And as the year drew to a close, the online gaming sector would face stiff regulatory pressure and be slapped with retrospective tax running into the thousands of crores.

For sure, the big moment for online gaming came from being able to snag the interest of Indians from beyond the metros. Even as the dust settled on demonetization in November 2016, India's overall economic growth would sputter but it would open the doors for digitization of financial services, particularly online payments.

The convenience online transactions could offer enticed urban Indians as much as it would the next 500 million internet users. From the novelty of paying for nariyal pani using Paytm's QR code to moving online for entertainment and education, Indians were beginning to do it all. And this was even before the pandemic hit in 2020.

A research report by India's largest public-sector bank, State Bank of India, estimated the size of the country's informal economy in 2017–18 at about 52.4 per cent of formal GDP. By 2020–21, it would shrink drastically to 15–20 per cent[1] as rising digitization stoked by the pandemic drew more citizens into transacting with the formal online economy.

The building blocks for this near-revolutionary transformation were also laid by the low-cost internet access that became available countrywide. This was led in large part by the aggressive discounting that telecom provider Reliance Jio offered as it raced to sign up a million users in late 2016. This data revolution had triggered the creation of new categories and in some cases the revitalization of categories.

In 2019, innovation would come from the venture firm Sequoia Capital, now known as PeakXV in India and Southeast Asia. The blue-chip Silicon Valley fund best known for being the backer of the world's most valuable company, Apple, as well as other technology icons like Google, launched a programme to mentor and back very-early-stage startups in India through an initiative called Surge. For a period of sixteen weeks, cohorts of some two dozen startups that would also receive seed funding of up to $3 million were given one-on-one mentoring as well as support from a community of star founders and the Surge community of alumni.

What's more, the funding would be granted at the start of the programme to allow founders to focus on execution without worrying where the next million will come from. That distinction is vital to how Surge has been designed, according to Shailendra Singh, the firm's chief across India and Southeast Asia.

To anchor the initiative, Sequoia picked Rajan Anandan. A former Google executive, Anandan was best known as one of the most prolific angel investors in the country who had backed over two hundred startups by the time he signed up with Sequoia. When he came to head Surge in 2019, India was maturing as an internet market. Nearly 250 million people were paying online, and the country had over 600 million broadband internet users.

What's more, companies could ship products to any zip code within two or three days. All this in a country with a per capita income of $2,000.

Anandan, a Sri Lankan Tamil, had grown up during the three-decade-long civil war in Sri Lanka. Following graduate school in the US, Anandan put in nearly eleven years at consulting firm McKinsey. His intuitive understanding of what it takes to build a technology-based startup came from varied experience he had gathered from working at some of the world's biggest tech corporations and building one of the most diverse angel investment portfolios. He had started early, making his first investment as an angel in an Indian startup way back in 2006, much before it had become fashionable to do so.

Meanwhile, in his day job, he worked with some of the world's biggest technology corporations, from being executive assistant to Michael Dell, working at Microsoft and finally leading the South and Southeast Asia business at Google. His stint at the search giant coincided with the buildout of locally built technologies, including payment service Tez, which would morph into the now-ubiquitous Google Pay. Anandan had seen first-hand the vim and vigour of business in the trenches and also the innovation at the grassroots level. He was well aware also of the strength of products and services built in India that could be adapted to global markets. Something Google Pay had demonstrated clearly.

He came to Sequoia at a time when India's startup sector was expanding at a healthy trot. In 2019, the country attracted $14 billion in venture capital. From zero unicorns in 2010, there would be a score and ten more at the close of 2020. When the Bansals and the Goyals had begun, India had fewer than 10 million connected internet users who could transact online—there were at least 250 million such users by the end of the decade.

At the start of the decade, with no cheap data, no cheap smartphones, no logistics or delivery networks, the early movers had been forced to burn cash to lure customers and also build the digital infrastructure. It was just money in and literally no money out. No surprises, therefore, that it was only those with the stomach for such risk who could ride this tumultuous phase of the great Indian internet wave. It was a phase when it took a cash burn in the billions for Flipkart to snag a valuation of $22 billion, when it was bought by Walmart in 2018.

In contrast, for later entrants into the e-commerce game, like eyewear portal Lenskart or online fashion retailer Nykaa, the view altered considerably. Most importantly, the quality of founders looking to start up had changed exponentially. Introducing the fifth cohort of Surge in 2021, the fund posted a video of Anandan grooving to the James Brown single 'I Feel Good'. The startups logging into Surge ranged from those looking to bring a spike in agricultural yields to those building battery-swapping technology, and even one offering small, sachet-size, self-improvement tips to women who could make micro payments to access such content.

Anandan was among those to have seen this coming. As early as 2015, he had held that India would have twenty unicorns by 2020. The actual number turned out to be forty. And his bet that by 2025 there would be 100 unicorns too was bested, the number reaching 102 by the end of 2022. To be sure, Surge was a response to the argument that once the underlying infrastructure—internet connectivity, digital payments, capital flow and skilled entrepreneurs—was built out, starting up in India would become endemic.

It is a model that has played out true to form—in India in the post-Jio era of 2017. On New Year's Eve in 2021, food-delivery company Swiggy's Sriharsha Majety tweeted: 'On Swiggy's first NYE in 2014 as a three-month-old food-delivery platform, we did one order for every three minutes. How times have changed. Love India's hunger for more!' On that day, Swiggy crossed 2 million orders, while rival Zomato said it had done the same during the day.

This tectonic change in consumer preferences has played no mean part in the upsurge of consumer internet businesses, catapulting the country's startup sector into third place in the ranking of the world's largest such ecosystems. The building blocks for the fast growing internet businesses—data, mobile telephony, digital identity—literally exploded in the years since 2007, with mobile subscribers doubling every three years, snagging 100 million–200 million users a year as it raced to the billion mark. In addition, the consumption wave was building among millennial Indians who joined the workforce in droves in the mid-2010s. If the first half of the decade was about introducing and even perhaps snaring customers to an online platform, the second half was about offering those already online more choices while speaking directly to millions of Indians who could now be termed 'digital natives'—by then, those born in the 1990s were joining the workforce while the savvy new set of Gen Z-ers were defining online mores and behaviour.

It was this cohort of first-time internet users, digital-savvy customers, millennials and Gen Z-ers that a new set of Indian internet startups were looking to woo. Take, for instance, the journey of Byju's, which began as an offline coaching class for MBA aspirants from non-metros primarily in southern India. The venture focused on K–12 coaching and received a Series A investment of $9 million. In the next two years, it got further funding of $25 million, led by Sequoia Capital, as it expanded offerings to include tablet-based learning for competitive exams. But the big money for Byju's came after the launch of its app and its transfer to the smartphone-based economy in 2015 with the eponymously labelled Byju's Learning App.

In the next year, the startup hooked big-name investors including Sofina and the Chan Zuckerberg Initiative catapulting it to global attention. By 2017, it had started on its now seminal acquisition moves. By 2020, when Byju's snapped up Aakash Learning, a test-prep institution, for $1 billion, it set up consumer internet startups as the new dealmakers of corporate India, a coming-of-age that in actual terms was built on the foundation of the smartphone revolution of the mid-2010s.

However, the sugar high to digital businesses delivered by the pandemic waned with a rude jolt for Byju's. The startup, once valued at a staggering $22 billion—the highest-ever for an Indian startup barring Flipkart—saw its worth marked down to almost $8 billion in the summer of 2023.[2] It was rocked by a series of downturns. The inordinate delay in filing audited results for the pandemic years was only the tip of the iceberg. Legal wrangling with its debtors marked a rude awakening, bursting the bubble of hype that surrounded Indian startups.[3]

Investors, founders and startup boards soon came to agree that one couldn't expend money to accelerate. 'I don't think money accelerates,' declares a venture backer who believes the same outcomes could have been had with 'probably half the capital', a premise that several in the industry would come to appreciate in the years post-demonetization in particular. The deluge of capital did recur in the pandemic, with record billions invested in 2021, but before that the value of prudence had gained currency across large swathes of the ecosystem. Awareness of the importance of unit economics pretty much defines the startup industry's reigning mood in the months after cash literally dried up in late 2022, giving rise to the term funding winter.

Elsewhere, investors were beginning to ask very different questions. Can this company make money? How soon can it make money? How much capital will it take to make money? It is in this backdrop that one has to evaluate the rise of online businesses of the post-2017 era that have chosen to prioritize positive-unit economics while also chasing growth and size.

Indian founders were also learning from the experience of the likes of Uber in the US, which famously hunkered down after a massive valuation correction. With no visibility to profitability, the company sold off allied verticals like Uber Eats piecemeal in various markets. In India, it was Zomato that acquired Uber's food-delivery business. Rid of flab, the San Francisco startup focused on unit economics and showed the world that it too could turn a profit.

But the story was never going to be linear. While frugality did come back into fashion, investors were also coming around to the view that profitability could be farther out than initially estimated. There were reasons for this sobering of expectations. India's GDP, which had consistently expanded in the first half of the decade (barring a 3.26 per cent contraction in 2011), peaked in the year 2015 when it grew 8 per cent, further expanding to 8.26 per cent in 2016, the highest for the decade. However, the slide began in 2017, when it contracted by 1.46 per cent, worsening to a decline of 2.49 per cent in 2019. The severity of the pandemic saw it shrink by 12.01 per cent in 2020.[4]

Venture capital investors argue that this trajectory of economic growth (in the 2010s) has put paid to that oft-repeated shibboleth about twenty-first-century India, that it is a market of ever-expanding consumption. 'That's a myth,' declares an investor bitten by the expectations woven around such myth-making. Once consumer internet startups had finished selling to the top 10 per cent of the population, it didn't take long to gather that for the rest it was still roti, kapda, makaan and a mobile (a modification of a 1970s tagline that denotes the bare necessities of life: food, clothing, housing).

Consumers lacking purchasing power and being armed with a mobile phone would mostly use it to watch videos with free data but simply not have the money to shop or purchase anything else online. Entrepreneurs soon realized that whatever they had on offer—whether it was Bitcoin or Ethereum, fantasy sports or dal chawal—didn't matter. Finally, it's cash flow and margins that count.

Anyone checking in on the health of the Indian startup ecosystem in 2022 will aver that it is indeed in rude good health. But it's quite clear that this has come at the expense of blood, sweat and toil over nearly two decades. During that time, too much capital has gone in and not enough has come out, admit even the most diehard of believers. What global investors want is public companies where everyone who has wagered cash see a way to pull out multiples of what they've put in—perhaps through a steady stream of IPOs and M&As.

In 2021, Indian startups finally began to deliver on that promise, as no less than eleven technology startups listed on public markets in India and abroad. Among those debuting on a global bourse was Freshworks, the SaaS company that has come to typify the promise and power of the Indian software sector.

As a patchy monsoon took hold over the Indian subcontinent in June 2023, Sequoia Capital, among the earliest to have put down dibs on the Indian startup story, announced that it was splitting from its Indian franchise, as also from its Chinese one. The news raised as many questions as answers. Its Indian and Southeast Asian franchise was renamed PeakXV, channelling the aspiration of Mount Everest. Did its Indian fund managers decide to strike a bold new path based on the unique needs of the fund's portfolio companies in one of the world's fastest-growing large economies? Shailendra Singh, a veteran venture investor who has led the firm in India and the Southeast Asia geography for well over a decade, asserts it is so. The firm has approximately $2.5 billion of what it terms as 'dry powder' to invest in startups in this region. The IIT Kanpur graduate who earned a management degree at Harvard Business School is convinced that his firm's rebranding cannot have come at a more opportune moment. India, he argues, is poised to be a 'net exporter of innovation'.

In a world being upended by climate change as well as the promise and peril of AI, starting up—whether in India or anywhere else—will never be the same again.

In a world searching for miracles, however, there will still be those who will go long on India, and go long on Indians.

NOTES

INTRODUCTION

1 www.startupindia.gov.in
2 https://www.mospi.gov.in/publication/women-men-india-2022
3 https://www.mckinsey.com/~/media/mckinsey/industries/public%20and%20social%20sector/our%20insight/outperformers%20high%20growth%20emerging%20economies%20and%20the%20companies%20that%20propel%20them/mgi-outperformers-full-report-sep-2018.pdf
4 https://www.worldbank.org/en/news/press-release/2023/04/04/indian-economy-continues-to-show-resilience-amid-global-uncertainties
5 https://pib.gov.in/Pressreleaseshare.aspx?PRID=169318
6 https://www.mckinsey.com/~/media/mckinsey/featured%20insights/india/indias%20turning%20point%20an%20economic%20agenda%20to%20spur%20growth%20and%20jobs/mgi-indias-turning-point-report-august-2020-vfinal.pdf

CHAPTER 1 THE GOLD RUSH

1 https://www.fool.com/investing/stock-market/basics/crashes/
2 https://money.cnn.com/2001/09/21/markets/markets_newyork/
3 https://www.livemint.com/Money/URhUQFjAqK7t90gJ55mk7N/SVB-to-focus-on-venture-lending-in-India.html
4 https://www.hindustantimes.com/india/india-s-it-ites-grew-31-in-2005-06/story-ekuPbM1ZocyANsT4JpA3EL.html; and https://epwrf.in/Upload/Mer/Mer10807005.Pdf

5 https://timesofindia.indiatimes.com/business/india-business/india-becomes-trillion-dollar-economy/articleshow/1962343.cms
6 https://prsindia.org/theprsblog/more-privatisation-on-the-cards?page=29&per-page=1
7 In interview with the author for this book.
8 In interview with the author for this book.
9 In interview with the author for this book.
10 In interview with the author for this book.
11 In interview with the author for this book.
12 RBI report August 2008.

CHAPTER 2 THE INDIAN E-COMMERCE MELA

1 https://www.deccanherald.com/business/stage-set-walmart-flipkart-deal-announcement-expected-today-669092.html
2 Sachin Bansal and Binny Bansal were both briefly employed at the back offices of Amazon Web Services in Bengaluru during 2006–2007 before they teamed up to launch Flipkart. They were hired at AWS by Jeyandran Venugopalan who would a decade later join the Flipkart Group as Chief Technology Officer.
3 https://www.sec.gov/Archives/edgar/data/1288776/000119312506206884/dex991.htm
4 https://www.business-standard.com/article/companies/seedfund-set-for-30-mn-second-fund-108070901041_1.html; https://www.siliconindia.com/shownews/seedfund-raises-30-mn-fund-nid-43558-cid-100.html; and https://www.bloomberg.com/news/articles/2007-09-04/googles-new-role-venture-capitalistbusinessweek-business-news-stock-market-and-financial-advice#xj4y7vzkg
5 In interview with author for this book.
6 In interview with author for this book.
7 In interview with author for this book.
8 In interview with author for this book.
9 In interview with author for this book.
10 In interview with author for this book.
11 In interview with author for this book.
12 In interview with author for this book.
13 https://www.financialexpress.com/life/technology/the-flipkart-story-a-timeline-of-funding-from-2007-to-2017/595740/

CHAPTER 3 THE SWELL OF ENTERPRISE

1 https://en.wikipedia.org/wiki/AngelList
2 https://community.nasscom.in/index.php/event/nasscom-technology-leadership-forum-2023;https://ispirt.in/; and https://saasboomi.com/
3 An investor who was present at that party, in interview with author for this book.
4 https://www.reuters.com/article/idINIndia-45607120100122
5 https://economictimes.indiatimes.com/small-biz/startups/inmobi-decoded-how-bangalore-based-firm-is-taking-on-google-and-facebook/articleshow/31567127.cms?from=mdr

CHAPTER 4 EXITS, AHOY!

1 In interview with author for this book.
2 https://economictimes.indiatimes.com/opinion/interviews/makemytrip-makes-a-dream-debut-on-nasdaq/articleshow/6302185.cms?from=mdr
3 https://economictimes.indiatimes.com/news/economy/policy/india-seeks-to-amend-retrospective-tax-law-fm-introduces-bill-in-ls/articleshow/85074291.cms
4 https://www.undp.org/india/271–million-fewer-poor-people-india#:~:text=In per cent20India per cent2C per cent20the per cent20first per cent20country,over per cent20the per cent2010 per cent2Dyear per cent20period.
5 https://www.statista.com/statistics/1121448/fed-balance-sheet-timeline/
6 https://www.orfonline.org/expert-speak/43208–the-rupee-slide-comparing-august-2018–to-august-2013–slump/

CHAPTER 5 THE GIG ECONOMY

1 https://tele.net.in/eventful-two-decades-the-peaks-and-troughs-in-indias-telecom-journey/
2 The GST journey began in the year 2000 when a committee was set up to draft law. It took 17 years from then for the law to evolve. In 2017, the GST Bill was passed in the Lok Sabha and Rajya Sabha. On 1 July 2017, the GST law came into force. Also see https://gstcouncil.gov.in/brief-history-gst

3 https://www.business-standard.com/article/management/zomato-wants-to-be-the-google-of-food-114090801209_1.html
4 https://blog.zomato.com/witaj-polska; https://yourstory.com/2014/11/zomato-raises-60-million; https://blog.zomato.com/welcoming-lunchtime-and-obedovat; https://www.zomato.com/blog/a-look-back-at-2014; https://blog.zomato.com/shifting-focus-to-what-matters-and-what-works; https://blog.zomato.com/lessons-from-2015
5 https://techcrunch.com/2016/05/09/zomato-demicorn/?guccounter=1&guce_referrer=aHR0cHM6Ly93d3cuZ29vZ2xlLmNvbS8&guce_referrer_sig=AQAAAJ1hgNDeZ8N0Y0DEDY5ufkggGH5-K3aDj47rnvSlzxn--SMqx9Otv1MXEffsLS8u06u32gHcml9bSalFQKNe50uA6u7LSztdfg7gmdVq57A0ED6eHL2QeFsRuUcTaiPfplFVa9rU2-31FVlIzQCDQxzx9K7XtQUjFWpJK5gjlt60q
6 https://podcasts.apple.com/in/podcast/insights-3-swiggy-taking-the-road-less-traveled/id1364412685?i=1000408810409
7 https://www.indiatvnews.com/business/india/ibibogroup-acquires-redbus-in-at-estimated-130-mn-6164.html
8 https://www.seedtoscale.com/podcast/learning-from-a-failure-the-making-of-swiggy-part-1-of-2
9 https://podcasts.apple.com/in/podcast/insights-12–digging-deeper-into-fundraising-abhiraj/id1364412685?i=1000417970950
10 https://www.seedtoscale.com/podcast/untold-seed-stories-first-500-days-of-urban-company
11 https://www.urbancompany.com/blog/urbanclap-is-now-urban-company/

CHAPTER 6 THE BIG-MONEY GAME

1 https://retail.economictimes.indiatimes.com/news/e-commerce/e-tailing/amazon-plans-portal-for-wholesale-merchants-in-india-first-country-outside-the-us/42322412
2 https://www.reuters.com/article/fashion-e-tailer-myntra-raises-50–millio-idINDEEA1604E20140207
3 https://economictimes.indiatimes.com/tech/internet/flipkart-acquires-myntra-gears-up-to-take-on-amazon/articleshow/35472670.cms?from=mdr

4 https://economictimes.indiatimes.com/industry/services/retail/amazon-in-talks-to-acquire-jabong-move-a-counter-to-flipkarts-myntra-buy/articleshow/44765139.cms?from=mdr
5 https://timesofindia.indiatimes.com/deals/-ma/myntra-acquires-jabong-for-70mn/articleshow/53394760.cms
6 https://www.ft.com/content/ff8c565c-1976-11e4-9745-00144feabdc0
7 https://economictimes.indiatimes.com/industry/services/retail/with-1-billion-in-a-year-team-india-is-just-fabulous-amazon-ceo-jeff-bezos/articleshow/43756389.cms
8 In interview with author for this book.
9 https://www.reuters.com/article/alibaba-ipo-board-idINL4N0QK3Q120140827
10 Investors /founders in interviews with author for this book.
11 In interview with author for this book.
12 In interview with author for this book.
13 https://economictimes.indiatimes.com/small-biz/startups/ola-buys-taxiforsure-for-rs-1237-crore-in-a-cash-and-stock-deal/articleshow/46436464.cms?from=mdr

CHAPTER 7 RAILROADS FOR COMMERCE

1 https://economictimes.indiatimes.com/nilekani-to-head-unique-database-authority-gets-cabinet-rank/articleshow/4702838.cms?from=mdr
2 Nilekani and Varma in interviews with author for this book.
3 https://economictimes.indiatimes.com/news/politics-and-nation/600–million-adhaar-card-by-2014–says-uidai-chairman-nandan-nilekani/articleshow/19691888.cms?from=mdr
4 https://www.internethalloffame.org/vint-cerf/; https://www.britannica.com/biography/Vinton-Cerf; https://www.discovermagazine.com/technology/the-father-of-the-internet-would-rather-you-call-him-vint
5 https://blume.vc/reports/understanding-india-the-indus-valley-annual-report-2022
6 https://www.bis.org/publ/bppdf/bispap106.pdf
7 https://government.economictimes.indiatimes.com/news/digital-india/indias-cloud-storage-app-digilocker-crosses-100–million-users/90320375; https://blog.digilocker.

gov.in/15–crore-and-counting-digilocker-leads-the-charge-in-indias-digital-revo'ution/

8 https://main.sci.gov.in/supremecourt/2012/35071/35071_2012_Judgement_26–Sep-2018.pdf

9 https://economictimes.indiatimes.com/news/economy/policy/reliance-jio-crosses-50–million-subscribers-in-83–days/articleshow/55670041.cms?from=mdr

10 https://carnegieendowment.org/files/Data_Democracy%2016th%20Aug%20Presenting.pdf

CHAPTER 8 THE FINTECH BOOM

1 PhonePe journey with Sameer Nigam: https://audioboom.com/posts/7896180-the-phonepe-journey-with-sameer-nigam

2 https://www.reuters.com/article/idINIndia-59932620111017

3 https://www.livemint.com/Companies/DbMTb2tDKuZoTfEa203XBL/Flipkart-acquires-UPIbased-payments-startup-PhonePe.html; https://stories.flipkart.com/tag/cash-on-delivery/; https://economictimes.indiatimes.com/small-biz/startups/flipkart-took-off-because-it-brought-in-cash-on-delivery-nandan-nilekani/articleshow/53533483.cms

4 'Young Turks from 2006: Vijay Shekhar Sharma'. https://www.youtube.com/watch?v=lTpoPqsLxoY

5 https://penguin.co.in/tips-on-impressing-a-vc-from-the-moonshot-game/

CHAPTER 9 THE ERA OF RECKONING

1 Aditi Shrivastava (1 July 2015). 'Housing.com CEO Rahul Yadav Fired'. *Times of India*. ET Bureau. Accessed 2 July 2015.

2 In interview with author for this book.

3 https://economictimes.indiatimes.com/small-biz/startups/startup-valuations-far-ahead-of-reality-warns-softbank-president-nikesh-arora/articleshow/48416926.cms

4 https://www.reuters.com/article/us-softbank-snapdeal-idINKBN0IH06R20141028; https://www.businesstoday.in/latest/corporate/story/softbank-writes-down-india-investment-by-usd-560-mn-67741-2016-11-08

5 https://energy.economictimes.indiatimes.com/news/renewable/india-will-get-at-least-100-bn-investment-from-softbank-masayoshi-son/55804115
6 https://www.businesstoday.in/latest/corporate/story/softbank-vision-fund-invests-usd-25-billion-in-flipkart-becomes-biggest-shareholder-84329-2017-08-10
7 https://corporate.walmart.com/news/2018/05/09/walmart-to-invest-in-flipkart-group-indias-innovative-ecommerce-company

CHAPTER 10 SASSY NETWORKS

1 A SaaS founder in interview with author for this book.
2 In interview with author for this book.
3 In interview with author for this book.
4 https://www.financialexpress.com/archive/nasscom-product-forum-sees-huge-potential/241242/; Avinash Raghava, Director- EMERGE-Products Forum at NASSCOM at Product Conclave-2010; https://www.youtube.com/watch?v=NWh-9y8DqRI
5 https://pn.ispirt.in/how-we-built-ispirt-from-scratch-with-nothing-except-a-lot-of-spirit-ispirtturns4/
6 https://the-ken.com/story/platform-ambitions-story-ispirt-lost-true-north/
7 In interview with author for this book.
8 https://entrackr.com/2023/01/browserstack-indias-profit-grows-57-in-fy22-revenue-crosses-rs-400-cr/
9 https://www.seedtoscale.com/people/ritesh-arora
10 https://yourstory.com/2020/07/postman-ceo-abhinav-asthana-untold-story

CHAPTER 11 THE DESI HUSTLE

1 In interview with author for this book.
2 https://economictimes.indiatimes.com/news/emerging-businesses/startups/why-venture-capitalists-are-flocking-zerodha-today/articleshow/msid-42578742,curpg-2.cms?from=mdr
3 Kamath in interview with author for this book.

4 In interview with author for this book.
5 In interview with author for this book.
6 In interview with author for this book.
7 In interview with author for this book.
8 In interview with author for this book.

CHAPTER 12 INDIAN ANGELS AND MORE

1 https://www.socialsamosa.com/2021/04/brand-saga-fevicol-advertising-journey/
2 https://brandequity.economictimes.indiatimes.com/news/advertising/pidilites-fevicol-returns-with-its-mazboot-jodh/70918628
3 https://globalventuring.com/corporate/fireside-ventures-finalises-118m-second-fund/; https://www.financialexpress.com/business/sme-fireside-ventures-closes-second-early-stage-startup-fund-at-rs-863-cr-with-backing-from-sidbis-ffs-itc-premji-invest-others-2174832/
4 https://globalventuring.com/corporate/fireside-ventures-finalises-118m-second-fund/
5 https://entrackr.com/2022/01/boat-revenue-crosses-rs-1500–cr-in-fy21–spent-only-rs-14–cr-on-salaries/; https://entrackr.com/2023/01/boat-posts-rs-2873–cr-revenue-in-fy22–profit-dips-20/
6 https://www.forbesindia.com/article/take-one-big-story-of-the-day/meet-the-accidental-venture-capitalist-fuelling-indias-d2c-boom/75209/1
7 'Visionary Encounter Fireside Talk Series by Sudhir Sethi in conversation with Kris Gopalakrishnan'. https://www.youtube.com/watch?v=13QSgsd83sg
8 https://economictimes.indiatimes.com/prime/consumer/with-mamaearth-and-boat-have-fireside-ventures-and-kanwaljit-singh-cracked-the-consumer-code/primearticleshow/96919618.cms
9 In interview with author for this book.
10 https://blume.vc/news/topic:fundraise
11 Rajan Anandan, Peak XV partner, in interview with author for this book.

CHAPTER 13 DAUGHTERS OF BHARAT

1 https://www.forbesindia.com/article/30–under-30–2022/neetu-yadav-and-kirti-jangra-bringing-the-digital-revolution-to-250–bn-cattle-market-industry/73473/1
2 She Builds | Animall | #SequoiaSpark | Partner Content-https://www.youtube.com/watch?v=4ZOO3uex1xA
3 In interview with author for the book.
4 https://economictimes.indiatimes.com/tech/startups/info-edge-softbank-among-biggest-winners-as-policybazaar-lists/articleshow/87721532.cms?from=mdr
5 https://www.salesforce.com/blog/business-leaders-data-versus-instinct/
6 Women in Alternatives 2023: Foreword Preqin https://www.preqin.com › insights › research › reports 08-Mar-2023 — The proportion of women working in the alternatives industry improved marginally to 21.3% from 20.9% the previous year.
7 https://www.kauffmanfellows.org/journal/the-rising-tide-a-learning-by-investing-initiative-to-bridge-the-gender-gap
8 https://inc42.com/buzz/only-15-indian-unicorns-have-women-founders-bridging-gender-divide-still-a-work-in-progress/
9 https://economictimes.indiatimes.com/news/india/trillions-at-stake-in-india-as-women-disappear-from-workforce/articleshow/91951655.cms
10 https://timesofindia.indiatimes.com/business/markets/ipo/nykaa-ipo-subscribed-81–78–times-on-final-day/articleshow/87470579.cms
11 https://www.reuters.com/world/india/indias-female-labour-participation-rate-falls-161–pandemic-hits-jobs-2021–08–03/

CHAPTER 14 THE DIGITAL AGE

1 https://economictimes.indiatimes.com/tech/startups/indian-startups-bag-record-36-billion-funds-in-2021/articleshow/88464088.cms?from=mdr
2 https://www.investopedia.com/terms/s/spac.asp
3 https://www.nasdaq.com/articles/a-record-pace-for-spacs-in-2021

4 https://economictimes.indiatimes.com/markets/stocks/news/zomato-delivers-a-full-spread-on-listing-day/articleshow/84695358.cms
5 https://economictimes.indiatimes.com/tech/startups/tata-says-acquired-a-majority-stake-in-online-grocery-bigbasket/articleshow/83029366.cms?from=mdr
6 https://www.livemint.com/news/the-gradual-exit-of-alibaba-from-india-timeline-11676026136245.html
7 https://inc42.com/reports/indian-tech-startup-funding-report-2021/
8 https://startupanz.com/infographic-which-companies-are-acquiring-the-most/
9 https://economictimes.indiatimes.com/markets/ipos/fpos/nazara-tech-stumbles-after-initial-listing-gain-locked-at-20-lower-circuit/articleshow/81755011.cms?from=mdr

CHAPTER 15 BIG DREAMS AND DOUBTING THOMASES

1 https://indianexpress.com/article/cities/mumbai/informal-sector-economy-grwth-sbi-report-7601151/
2 https://economictimes.indiatimes.com/tech/technology/blackrock-cuts-byjus-valuation-by-over-60–to-8–2–billion/articleshow/100627551.cms?from=mdr
3 https://economictimes.indiatimes.com/tech/technology/byjus-lenders-says-its-lawsuit-is-meritless-an-effort-to-avoid-obligations/articleshow/100866133.cms?from=mdr
4 https://www.macrotrends.net/countries/IND/india/gdp-gross-domestic-product; and https://www.forbesindia.com/article/explainers/gdp-india/85337/1

ADDITIONAL READING

https://www.bain.com/insights/how-india-shops-online-2022–report/

https://www.businesstoday.in/magazine/cover-story/story/cash-on-delivery-impact-on-e-commerce-companies-customers-134631–2014–01–29

https://timesofindia.indiatimes.com/business/india-business/90–of-rural-indias-e-comm-orders-paid-in-cash-study/articleshow/88244840.cms

https://economictimes.indiatimes.com/tech/internet/flipkart-set-to-receive-ed-notice-on-fema-breach-of-rs-1400–crore/articleshow/34393783.cms?from=mdr

https://economictimes.indiatimes.com/industry/services/retail/flipkart-reduces-dependence-on-ws-retail-aims-to-more-than-triple-third-party-sellers-by-year-end/articleshow/47240755.cms?from=mdr

https://www.statista.com/statistics/792047/india-e-commerce-market-size/

https://www.cnbc.com/2014/09/18/alibaba-prices-shares-at-68–a-share-dj.html

https://www.reuters.com/article/idUS14155456220140922

https://www.joincolossus.com/episodes/86607830/nilekani-inspiring-the-next-generation?tab=transcript

https://cdn.cseindia.org/userfiles/Shagun-dbt.pdf

https://static.pib.gov.in/WriteReadData/specificdocs/documents/2022/jan/doc2022153101.pdf

https://economictimes.indiatimes.com/news/economy/policy/13–central-schemes-under-dbt-for-direct-cash-transfer-rajeev-shukla/articleshow/21977959.cms?from=mdr

https://uidai.gov.in/en/about-uidai/unique-identification-authority-of-india.html

https://www.indiabudget.gov.in/budget2011–2012/es2010–11/echap-01.pdf

https://www.worldbank.org/en/country/india/overview

https://www.statista.com/statistics/942795/india-financial-institution-account-ownership-rate/#:~:text=In per cent202017 per cent2C per cent20about per cent2080 per cent20percent,only per cent2035 per cent20percent per cent20in per cent202011.

https://factly.in/rbi-report-indias-financial-inclusion-index-is-53–9–by-the-end-of-march-2021/

https://pib.gov.in/PressReleasePage.aspx?PRID=1856116

https://stateofaadhaar.in/

https://www.npci.org.in/

https://ispirt.in/

https://tigerfeathers.substack.com/p/the-internet-country

Stacking up the Benefits: Lessons from India's Digital Journey, WP/23/78, March 2023

https://www.matrixpartners.in/matrixmoments/the-phonepe-journey-with-sameer-nigam

https://www.reuters.com/article/idINIndia-59932620111017

https://stories.flipkart.com/flipkart-innovation-timeline/

https://stories.flipkart.com/tag/cash-on-delivery/

https://economictimes.indiatimes.com/small-biz/startups/flipkart-took-off-because-it-brought-in-cash-on-delivery-nandan-nilekani/articleshow/53533483.cms

https://www.pwc.in/industries/financial-services/fintech/dp/the-changing-landscape-of-indias-credit-industry.html

https://www.livemint.com/Money/JjiJ1MstQRcjwU2fubyMTO/Credit-card-spends-total-19–trillion-in-FY15.html

https://www.livemint.com/Companies/DbMTb2tDKuZoTfEa203XBL/Flipkart-acquires-UPIbased-payments-startup-PhonePe.html

https://timesofindia.indiatimes.com/business/india-business/government-plans-phase-2–of-digital-payment-push-from-january/articleshow/61549496.cms

Pai, Vivek (25 November 2014). 'Housing.com launches interactive home booking platform Slice View'. Medianama.com. Retrieved 8 September2015.

Griffin, Peter (20 February 2015). '30 Under 30'. Forbes India. Retrieved 8 September 2015.

'Housing.com CEO Rahul Yadav gives away all his ₹200 cr worth shares to 2,251 employees'. Financialexpress.com. 15 May 2015. Retrieved 8 September 2015.

https://economictimes.indiatimes.com/small-biz/startups/in-startup-valuations-signs-of-irrational-exuberance/articleshow/46710049.cms

https://economictimes.indiatimes.com/small-biz/startups/the-startup-winter-separating-winners-from-the-losers/articleshow/49762255.cms

https://economictimes.indiatimes.com/small-biz/entrepreneurship/an-uneasy-alliance-the-meeting-ground-between-investors-and-entrepreneurs-shrinking-at-alarming-rate/articleshow/47821724.cms

https://www.livemint.com/Industry/L3FaecLqkboxHeoG5d8dxJ/Online-retail-industry-grows-23–to-178–billion-report.html

https://blume.vc/reports/understanding-india-the-indus-valley-annual-report-2022

https://blume.vc/reports/indus-valley-annual-report-2023

https://economictimes.indiatimes.com/small-biz/startups/india-will-get-at-least-100–billion-investment-from-softbank-masayoshi-son/articleshow/55803071.cms

https://economictimes.indiatimes.com/tech/ites/has-nasscom-lost-its-way/articleshow/68314569.cms

https://economictimes.indiatimes.com/small-biz/startups/big-30–software-startups-see-valuations-climb-26–ispirt/articleshow/50859462.cms?from=mdr

https://economictimes.indiatimes.com/tech/startups/non-tech-business-keeps-counters-ringing-at-saas-firm-postman/articleshow/97958269.cms?from=mdr

https://twitter.com/Nithinodha/status/1463413084253474816 https://www.thehindubusinessline.com/blchangemakers/the-billionaire-brokers/article65865885.ece

https://economictimes.indiatimes.com/news/podcasts/et-startup-school/startup-school-understanding-secrets-of-bootstrapping-with-zerodha-founder/podcast/97156173.cms?from=mdr

https://www.zoho.com/blog/general/25–years-of-zoho.html

https://www.macrotrends.net/countries/IND/india/gdp-gross-domestic-product

https://www.forbesindia.com/article/explainers/gdp-india/85337/1

INDEX

ABOUT THE AUTHOR

In a career spanning three decades (and counting) as a business journalist, Archana Rai has extensively reported on India's startup and technology sector. From tracking investments made by India's earliest venture fund, the Technology Development & Investment Corporation of India (TDICI), to the big-ticket deals of Internet-era heavyweights, she has enjoyed a ringside view of the twists and turns, the highs and lows of technology entrepreneurship during its most consequential years. And as for Starting Up in India—the best, she's certain, is yet to come!